Western Europe's Global Reach

Pergamon Titles of Related Interest

De Rougemont   THE STATE OF THE UNION OF EUROPE
Feld   COMPARATIVE REGIONAL SYSTEMS: West and East Europe,
   North America, The Middle East and Developing Countries
Grieves   TRANSNATIONALISM IN WORLD POLITICS AND
   BUSINESS
Ra'anan   ETHNIC RESURGENCE IN MODERN DEMOCRATIC
   STATES: A Multidisciplinary Approach to Human Resources and
   Conflict

Related Journals*

ACCOUNTING ORGANIZATIONS AND SOCIETY
EVALUATION AND PROGRAM PLANNING
HISTORY OF EUROPEAN IDEAS
INTERNATIONAL JOURNAL OF INTERCULTURAL RELATIONS
LONG RANGE PLANNING
WORLD DEVELOPMENT

*Free specimen copies available upon request.

PERGAMON POLICY STUDIES ON INTERNATIONAL POLITICS

Western Europe's Global Reach
Regional Cooperation and Worldwide Aspirations

Edited by
Werner J. Feld

Pergamon Press

NEW YORK • OXFORD • TORONTO • SYDNEY • PARIS • FRANKFURT

Pergamon Press Offices:

U.S.A.   Pergamon Press Inc., Maxwell House, Fairview Park, Elmsford, New York 10523, U.S.A.

U.K.   Pergamon Press Ltd., Headington Hill Hall, Oxford OX3 0BW, England

CANADA   Pergamon of Canada, Ltd., Suite 104, 150 Consumers Road, Willowdale, Ontario M2J 1P9, Canada

AUSTRALIA   Pergamon Press (Aust.) Pty. Ltd., P.O. Box 544, Potts Point, NSW 2011, Australia

FRANCE   Pergamon Press SARL, 24 rue des Ecoles, 75240 Paris, Cedex 05, France

FEDERAL REPUBLIC OF GERMANY   Pergamon Press GmbH, Hammerweg 6, Postfach 1305, 6242 Kronberg/Taunus, Federal Republic of Germany

Library of Congress Cataloging in Publication Data

Conference of Europeanists, Washington, D.C., 1979.
   Western Europe's global reach.

   (Pergamon policy studies on international politics)
   "Sponsored by the Council on European Studies."
   Bibliography: p.
   Includes index.
   1. European Economic Community countries—Foreign
economic relations—Congresses. 2. European Economic
Community countries—Foreign relations—Congresses.
I. Feld, Werner J. II. Council for European Studies.
III. Title. IV. Series.
HF1532.93 1980.C65 1979   337.4   80-14543
ISBN 0-08-025130-7

Printed in the United States of America

Contents

List of Tables

List of Figures

Preface

Werner J. Feld

This volume is based on papers presented during the First Conference of Europeanists organized by the Council for European Studies in Washington, D.C. in the spring of 1979. The papers were delivered at two panels, chaired by me, which dealt with Western Europe's role in the world and focused in particular on the European Community and its member states. Revised to varying degrees and updated, the papers have become chapters of this book. In addition, four essays are included as chapters that have been specifically written for this volume or are major revisions of earlier works. These essays are chapters 6, 9, 10 and 12.

Although I have attempted to cover most major aspects and issues of Western Europe's external relations in the economic, political, and strategic sectors, there remain a few gaps. For example, the relations with South America, Southeast Asia, the Middle East and the Third World in general were touched upon only peripherally. Yet the European Community and its member states are reaching out to these regions, as well as to all other areas of the world, with increasing intensity. The recent cooperation agreement with ASEAN and the current negotiations for such an agreement with the Andean Common Market and the Persian Gulf states are evidence of this global reach.

This is the place to thank the contributors for their fine products and for their willingness to make repeated revisions of their manuscripts. I also would like to express my deep gratitude to Mrs. Janet Davis and Mrs. Glenda Wingard for typing and retyping parts of the manuscripts. My sincere thanks also go to the copy editor for a very thoughtful performance of her task, made especially difficult since five of the chapters were originally written in German. The index was prepared by Termsak Chalermpalanupap, to whom I would like to express my thanks for a job well done. In addition, I am grateful to Angela Clark for her assistance and excellent cooperation in putting this book together. Finally, my thanks go to my wife for her patience with still another book.

1
Introduction
Werner J. Feld

GROWING POWER AND EXTERNAL RELATIONS

During the 1970s, an increasingly frequent sentiment expressed in Western Europe was the need to "speak with one voice" in international affairs. By acting in such a manner, it was felt that greater influences could be exerted on shaping the course of international relations than if individual countries were to pursue foreign policy objectives on their own. The countries particularly attracted to the possibility of common external action were the members of the European Community. In a technical sense, there is not one, but three European Communities – the European Coal and Steel Community (ECSC), created by the Treaty of Paris in 1951 and entered into force in 1952; and the European Economic Community (EEC) and European Atomic Energy Community (Euratom) that were set up by the Treaties of Rome in 1957 and became operational in 1958. However, for convenient shorthand, it is appropriate to refer to only the European Community (EC), which has become common usage and is the terminology which is followed throughout this book, unless the particular focus is on a specific aspect of one of the three Communities.

The original signatories of the three treaties – France, the Federal Republic of Germany, Italy, Belgium, the Netherlands, and Luxembourg – were joined in 1973 by the United Kingdom, Ireland, and Denmark. In 1980, Greece became the tenth member state; Spain and Portugal are now negotiating for accession in the early 1980s.

By the end of the 1970s, the combined economic power of the Nine and Greece (the latest EC member) had reached an awesome level. With a population of 268 million in 1978, their gross domestic product (GDP) exceeded $1,970 trillion; their share of exports worldwide was 54 percent, and of imports, 53 percent. This compares with a U.S. population of 217 million, a slightly higher GDP of $2,095 trillion, and a much lower share of world imports of 20 percent.(1) This economic

1

strength of the EC is a significant source of political power in international politics and enhances the potential of the Community member states for the successful pursuit of their foreign policy goals, especially if unified action is taken.

POSSIBILITIES OF COMMON POLICYMAKING

The constituent treaties of the three Communities, in particular the EEC Treaty, provide some legal bases for common external policies. The EEC Treaty stipulates the formulation of common commercial policies toward third countries, and offers the member states the unusual foreign policy instrument of "association," which has been successfully employed on many occasions – in particular, to affiliate most African Third World countries with the EC.(2) Other factors promoting uniform external policies are the Common External Tariff, which was introduced as part of the customs union established by the EEC and can only be altered through Community action; and the Common Agricultural Policy (CAP) of the EEC, which compels a measure of uniformity for the external agricultural trade of the Ten. We should note that although these and other legal bases exist for common foreign policies, this has not always been tantamount to their conscientious application. Indeed, on many occasions, the EC member governments have been reluctant or, in fact, have refused to comply with the treaty provisions for common policies when, according to their perceptions, this would have been harmful to the attainment of particular national objectives.

The formulation and, to a lesser degree, the implementation of specific EC policies are entrusted to a substantial number of civil servants of the European Community. Most of these "Eurocrats" are assigned to Directorate-General (DG) 1 of the EC Commission, but they cannot act with full autonomy. The member governments keep close tabs on the European Community activities in external affairs through (a) directives by the EC Council of Ministers, representing mainly national interests; (b) liaison committees composed of national officials (e.g., the "Committee 113," named for Article 113 of the EEC Treaty which authorizes its establishment); and (c) the Committee of Permanent Representatives (CPR or COREPER). The CPR, which is headed by the ambassadors of the member states, prepares the agenda for the Council of Ministers sessions and has become very influential in all EC decision-making processes.(3)

During the past decade, the member states made increasing use of a policy coordinating mechanism which operated outside the legal framework of the Community. Under this mechanism, frequently referred to as European Political Cooperation or simply as Political Cooperation (PC), the EC officials of DG 1 play only a very limited role. Coordination is carried out through periodic meetings of the foreign ministers who now convene at least six times a year. The spadework for these meetings is handled by the political directors of the foreign ministries of the member states who, with their staffs, constitute the Political Committee. This body meets every month for a two-day session, or more often when issues warrant. In addition, there are over 100 working group meetings a year and an intensive direct telex interchange is maintained between the foreign ministries of the EC member states.

The major task of the foreign ministers at their periodic sessions is consideration of important foreign policy questions. The member governments can suggest for consideration any issue pertaining to general foreign policy problems or to such matters as monetary affairs, energy, or security. Whenever the work of the foreign ministers or of the Political Committee impinges on the competence and activities of the European Community, the Commission is requested to submit its own position on the matter under consideration and is invited to send a representative to the meeting.

The foreign policy coordination activities of the Political Committee are implemented by periodic sessions of staff members in the embassies of the ten, located in different capitals of the world. Such meetings had already taken place prior to the creation of this committee, when European Community affairs affecting third countries needed to be discussed and coordinated; but their scope has now been expanded.(4)

In chapter 2, Wolfgang Wessels provides a thoughtful insight into the mechanism of Political Cooperation and assesses its implications for the future of the Community and its member states. In particular, he examines the impact that PC may have as a vehicle for further political integration of the Community members and as a force for expanded influence of Western Europe in world affairs.

EXPANSION OF FOREIGN POLICY INTERESTS

Since the EC makes up the bulk of the population and GDP in Western Europe, it is appropriate to consider its foreign policy interests as being broadly representative of the whole region. Without doubt, these interests expanded during the 1970s and have benefited from the creation of various international arrangements and networks in that decade. Most members of the European Free Trade Association (EFTA) which did not or could not join the EC in 1973 concluded free trade agreements with the Community (except in the area of agriculture). The implementation of these agreements by 1978 resulted in a very large unified market for nonagricultural products from which all of Western Europe profited. At the same time, imports of competing goods from outsiders into this new free trade area became more difficult, and the economic power of the region received additional strength.

Another extension of power on the part of the Community and its member states has been the pursuit of a systematic policy under which preferential trade agreements were concluded with all countries (except Libya) that rim the Mediterranean, the refound mare nostrum. These agreements permit duty free entry of industrial products from the Mediterranean countries into the EC, with a variety of concessions made to the Community countries on the part of the former. The rationale of the Mediterranean policy has been the existence of historical relationships, the responsibility to extend to the countries of the area a helping hand, and the need to develop a spirit of solidarity. It is obvious that the extensive network of economic and political relationships established through this policy is likely to enhance the promotion of Western European interests. Between 1960 and 1970, EC trade with the area almost tripled, and it continued to grow during the 1970s.(5) This trend represents a hefty share of total EC exports and imports, including, of course, large amounts of oil.

The extensive network of EC economic and political relations with the Mediterranean countries, especially those in North Africa, may well further the attainment of Western European policy goals to ensure optimal petroleum-supply security and to influence price development and balance-of-payments patterns. In addition, individual EC countries seek to bolster links with the oil producers and to gain balance-of-payments benefits through sales of major capital goods and military hardware.

Against this background of the Community's Mediterranean policy, it may be useful to comment briefly on the Euro-Arab Dialogue, launched in 1975. This dialogue brings together EC officials, representatives of the EC member states, and Arab League officials. Its professed purpose is cooperation in the areas of industrialization, basic infrastructure, agricultural and rural development, financial cooperation, trade, science, technology, culture, labor, and social questions. Several working groups study these areas of cooperation, identify worthwhile projects, and make proposals for action to a General Committee.

It seems that concrete results of the dialogue have been meager as far as European hopes to obtain firm commitments regarding long-term oil supplies are concerned. Nevertheless, the new network of contacts established by the dialogue may be helpful in extracting some minor benefits and concessions from Arab oil producers and, under certain circumstances, may be useful as a damage control mechanism. In the meantime, the dialogue meetings and study groups are planned to continue into the 1980s.

With the accession of Greece and the future EC membership of Spain and Portugal, the influence of the EC and its members in the Mediterranean may well be bolstered. Four full EC members – France, Italy, Greece, and Spain – will then cover most of the Mediterranean northern coast and, as a consequence, the Community will have strengthened its sphere of economic and political interests in the area. However, as Christian Deubner demonstrates in chapter 3, the new memberships will also generate political and economic problems that might be difficult to solve. These problems involve political and economic adaptation of the prospective members to the existing political modes of the Community members and the powerful economies of the central EC states, conflicts of interests and structural differences between the "Big Four" EC countries (West Germany, France, Great Britain, and Italy), and the possible impact of the enlargement by three countries (which are in various stages of development) on EC policies toward the Third World.

With respect to the Community's policies toward the Third World countries, an important source of strength is the Convention of Lomē, which is examined in detail in chapter 4 by Michael B. Dolan. This Convention, which was renegotiated successfully in 1979 for a second five-year term, reaches beyond Africa into the Caribbean and the Western Pacific. The more than fifty Third World countries participating in the Convention, therefore, are often referred to as the ACP states. (They are mostly the former French and British colonies in Africa south of the Sahara and north of South Africa as well as in the Caribbean and the Western Pacific.) Despite recurring complaints of various kinds by these countries, the Convention is perceived as satisfying many needs and demands. Perhaps the most significant aspect of this relationship between Western Europe and the ACP states is the plethora of contacts established which may help in the achievement of West European foreign policy objectives in multilateral forums such as the United Nations and its agencies, or in other multilateral or even bilateral negotiations. More specifically, the Convention provides the EC member states with a high assurance of critical raw materials, especially in the mineral field.

FOREIGN RELATIONS IN FLUX

While the EC relations with the EFTA countries, the Mediterranean, and the ACP countries have become relatively stabilized, relationships with the communist states are not as yet settled and suffer from tensions stemming from differences in economic and political systems, as well as ideologies. Problems and uncertainties also exist in the relations with some Third World regions, such as South America and South East Asia, because some of the countries in these regions would like to have preferential arrangements with the EC similar to the Lomē Convention.

In the early years of the Community, the Soviet leadership refused to recognize it as an organization bent on economic and, perhaps, political integration through the establishment of a customs union and a common market. Nevertheless, the Soviet Union sought to expand its trade with individual EC countries. In later years, the EC was acknowledged as an "objective reality," but it remained condemned as a manifestation of imperialist rivalry. So far, the Soviet Union has not established formal diplomatic relations with the Community, although more than 100 countries (including Yugoslavia and the People's Republic of China) have set up diplomatic missions to the EC in Brussels. Robert M. Cutler analyzes the Soviet view in chapter 5, and explains how Western European integration is approached from a Soviet perspective and in Soviet policy. In his analysis, Cutler traces Soviet policies toward the EC from the 1950s and discusses the implications for the Soviet domestic power struggle.

The Council for Mutual Economic Aid (CMEA), better known as COMECON, includes the USSR and the East European communist countries. Despite the Soviet Union's dominant force in this group, COMECON's Secretary General approached the EC toward the end of the 1970s with a view to reaching some kind of a trade agreement. Evidently, the magnetic power of a unified market with more than 250 billion people and potential customers proved to be persuasive. Max Baumer and Hanns-Dieter Jacobsen explore in chapter 6 the reasons for COMECON's interest in the EC, as well as the Community's initial reluctance to involve itself in talks with the communists. They also speculate on the implications for Europe and the world if a trade agreement were to be concluded across the Iron Curtain between Western and Eastern Europe.

Whatever the outcome of the talks between the EC and COMECON may be, the phenomenon of Eurocommunism may have a bearing on this relationship. Indeed, the future evolution of this new ideology (or deception) may have a significant impact on every aspect of East-West relations, including NATO and the Warsaw Pact forces. Chapter 7, authored by Steven J. Baker, examines this issue area and projects possible future events including the international implications of communist participation in the Italian government.

In contrast to the Soviet Union's policy of nonrecognition of the Community, it is interesting to note the positive attitude of the People's Republic of China. That country opened a diplomatic mission in Brussels in 1975 and negotiated a trade agreement with the EC. Gavin Boyd, in chapter 8, provides a perceptive insight not only into the reasons for this new and apparently eagerly sought economic relationship, but also into its future international economic and political implications including East-West relations in general.

While, thus, it is clear that motion, activity, and some accomplishments characterize the Community's relationships with communist countries, South American and Asian needs and demands have been considered and talks have been held, but fully accommodating action on the part of the EC has only been forthcoming so far with ASEAN (the Association of South East Asian Nations). This may have been due to low economic and political priority and the perceived need to protect the Lomé affiliates. As far as South America is concerned, this attitude may change when Spain and Portugal become EC members, as the cultural and political ties between these countries and the South American region are strong. The two countries may become the advocates for South American demands in the councils of the Community. At the same time, the economic and political influence in South America of the EC and of all its member states may rise markedly, aided most likely by latent, yet pervasive, anti-Yankee attitudes in that region.

In South East Asia, ASEAN has concluded an advantageous economic cooperation agreement with the Community which may well become a model for future treaties with other Third World countries or groups of countries.(6) An important motivation of both organizations for such an agreement may have been the extensive economic influence of Japan in South East Asia. The EC does not want to see its exports to that region diminished, and ASEAN may welcome alternative increasing markets for its expanding production of industrialized products as well as for its raw materials.

THE AMERICAN CONNECTION

One of the most important aspects of the Western European relationship with the United States has been trade. This trade is of particular significance for the latter; for example, in 1977, 27 percent of U.S. exports went to Western Europe and 23 percent of American imports came from that region. On the other hand, Western European exports to the United States amounted to only six percent of total exports, and U.S. shipments of goods to Western Europe were 7.5 percent of total imports in that year.(7) The bulk of this trade is carried out by the EC. Since the inception of the Community, the United States has enjoyed a trade surplus with the exception of 1972, although at times this surplus was very slim. The U.S. government has been especially concerned that the Community's CAP would damage American agricultural exports to the EC, but these fears, by and large, have proved to be groundless. Over the years, there have been significant asymmetries in the trade relations between the Community and the United States, but as the very careful analysis by Hanns-Dieter Jacobsen in Chapter 9 shows, many of the advantages which the United States enjoyed in its trade relations with the EC have disappeared and the relationship has become more symmetrical.

Another economic problem with global implications for the 1980s is the wide swing of national currencies with respect to each other and their recurring devaluations and revaluations. This has been a problem which has not only affected intra-EC trade and the economic and political stability of the member states, but it has also had varying effects on third countries. Indeed, the U.S. dollar has been responsible for some of the more severe currency fluctuations. To reduce these fluctuations to a minimum within the Community, in 1979 the EC launched the European Monetary System (EMS), in which all member states except Great Britain now participate. If the EMS is successful, it is likely to have a number of short-range and long-term consequences for the currencies of non-EC countries and, perhaps foremost, for the international position of the U.S. dollar. In chapter 10, Robert R. Russell examines the EMS and its prospects for the future; he also assesses the effects of this new system which has aroused mixed feelings within and outside the U.S. government.

We now proceed to the security arrangements which Western Europe has with the United States. Without doubt, the security umbrella created through NATO (consisting of U.S. strategic nuclear weapons and the general cooperative effort by most NATO allies in conventional weapons) has been an essential factor in the extraordinary achievement Western Europe has attained in the economic sphere. In other words, the buildup of Western Europe's economic and corresponding political power most likely would not have been possible without the cooperative defense arrangements across the Atlantic. Of course, the United States benefited from the joint defense effort as much as Western Europe did.

Looking at the bottom line at the end of the 1970s, both trans-atlantic partners can be satisfied with NATO's accomplishments, considering the many frictions that arose as the result of misunderstandings, occasional American high-handedness regarding its obligation to consult with other NATO members, and the intrusion of nationalistic motivations in the procurement of weapons and equipment. During the last part of the decade, a greater degree of harmony in NATO operations among the allies was attained, and the commitment to NATO procedures and obligations is being taken quite seriously. Nevertheless, problems are apt to arise, especially in crisis situations, concerning the sincerity of actions by individual allies. Questions are often raised whether rhetoric is being substituted for actions promised. Very recent examples are the hostage crisis in Iran and the Soviet invasion of Afghanistan. While the Iranian problem is technically outside the NATO framework, American authorities hoped that U.S. economic sanctions against Iran, such as the freeze of that country's assets, would be complemented by similar actions in Western Europe. But initially support for the United States, except for concurrent votes in the U.N. Security Council, was mainly verbal. This is not really surprising because, while there was much sympathy for the United States, many Europeans did not consider it their problem. However, as domestic political pressure on President Carter mounted when the release of the hostages was delayed again and again, a number of common diplomatic actions and some initial economic measures were taken by the EC member states to help the United States in its efforts to free the hostages.(8) In late April of 1980 the foreign ministers of the EC countries meeting in Luxembourg decided to reduce their embassy staffs in Teheran, but did not fully break diplomatic relations as the United States had done earlier in the month. Nor did they follow the American lead of imposing economic sanctions on Iran with the minor exception of not buying Iranian oil above a certain price. However, stiffer sanctions were threatened if no "decisive progress" would be made within a specified time period to release the hostages. Some observers in the United States considered the outcome of the Luxembourg meeting somewhat disappointing because the EC countries did not immediately adopt the American position.(9)

The Western European reaction to the situation in Afghanistan initially seemed to be different. NATO was convened, and the European governments were stirring into action bolstered by an aroused public. But how far the Europeans will follow the U.S. lead in the boycott of the Olympic games in Moscow, halting or reducing agricultural and high technology sales and, perhaps, cutting down the long-term credits usually granted to the Soviet Union for its purchases remains to be seen and appears increasingly doubtful.(10) Although the European Parliament voted in support of the Olympic games boycott,(11) it appears that only a limited number of West Europeans are inclined to go along with the U.S. initiative.

The events in Afghanistan showed that the Community clearly is involved in this major military crisis, but the disparities in economic interests among the EC member states prevented the adoption of uniform measures and the pursuit of a united policy in this crisis. Nor does it seem that PC has successfully operated in this respect, although, during the February 18, 1980 meeting of the foreign ministers of the member states, agreement was reached to work toward a non-aligned status of Afghanistan guaranteed inter alia by the EC members if Soviet forces were withdrawn from that country.(12) However, the Soviet Union rejected the idea of Afghanistan's non-aligned status.

The problem of reconciling interests and measures of the West in the face of the Soviet invasion was aptly characterized in an editorial in Europe which stated:

> ... one would think that the accusing finger pointed at the invaders is accompanied by... understanding and tolerance, whilst the hand being openly extended to the ally is hesitating and unsure, as though defiance might rob the gesture of some of its sincerity.(13)

It seems fair to say that if the Atlantic Alliance members want to persuade the Soviet Union to adopt a more moderate conduct, they have to show solidarity and unity. Indeed, the conduct of Soviet policy in Afghanistan may well have been based on the anticipation of West European behavior as it has actually evolved in the wake of the Soviet adventure. Hence, a comprehensive and effective European-American crisis management is essential to deal with problems such as Afghanistan. In chapter 11, Reinhardt Rummel carefully examines the issue of crisis management, a mechanism which may be needed not only in military but also in economic and political crises, and which may involve an astutely-drawn division of labor between the transatlantic partners.

Finally, as Western Europe's economic and political power has grown, the view has been expressed again and again that, in the procurement of NATO weapons, European arms producers should receive a larger "share of the pie." When NATO was established, U.S. arms, planes, and other equipment were, indeed, dominant; but, as time went by, European manufacturers often working in cooperative ventures across national boundaries, were able to offer excellent products. In this connection, a number of questions have arisen. Should only the larger EC countries be drawn into such cooperative ventures? Should the Community framework be used to serve as a coordinating mechanism for European joint arms production? Should there be a transatlantic "two-way street" concept of arms and equipment procurement for NATO; and, if it is feasible and acceptable, how should it be organized? Again, we are faced with a division of labor problem which is examined and analyzed in chapter 12, by Eugene Mesaros.

SUMMARY

The chapters in this book will demonstrate that the foreign policy concerns and objectives of Western Europe in general, and of the Community and its members in particular, exceed the boundaries of the region and have become truly global. However, these concerns and objectives are primarily in the economic and, to a lesser degree, the political spheres; military-strategic goals remain, in general, confined to Europe and other areas covered by the NATO Treaty, although French and Belgian military actions have taken place in Africa. Within this foreign policy scope, there is no doubt that Western Europe has the economic and financial resources and the necessary political skills to act successfully. This has been shown by past performance, and has been recognized by the world community. In other words, as a unit, Western Europe is a world power, albeit a "civilian" power; and the Community and its members play a central role in its behavior. However, for "superpower" status, it lacks the necessary strategic arsenal.

What does this mean for the United States? Obviously, conformity with or consent to American foreign policy designs cannot be taken for granted. If U.S. and European or EC interests are congenial, cooperation can be expected; otherwise, competitive conditions might evolve or conflictual situations may emerge. In the economic sector, various levels of competition can be expected while, in the political sphere, cooperation may prevail more often than not. How effective this cooperation might be in terms of the attainment of U.S. foreign policy objectives is difficult to judge at this stage; but, clearly, it is better for the United States to have a powerful and influential collaborator than a weak one. Of course, this presupposes that Western Europe, or at least the Community countries, will act in a unified fashion. Here again, only the future will allow a firm judgment. There has been speculation in the political science literature that the pressure of external forces and the need to deal effectively with these forces through diplomatic means or international treaties would enhance the progress of political integration in regional organizations such as the Community.(14) But there is no persuasive evidence, up to now, that such a hypothesis can be confirmed. So far, the strong desire to "speak with one voice" in Western Europe has not produced a massive transfer of foreign policy competences from the foreign ministries of the member states to the Commission of the European Community.

Finally, from a general perspective on Western Europe's external relations and policies three common concerns of most contributors can be distinguished:

1. the conflict between the unifying and the disruptive forces which seems to constitute a basic internal problem of the European Community in evolving its international relations;

2. changes occurring in the international division of labor, in the economic and monetary fields, and the different ways they affect EC member states and external partners; and

3. changing international structure of power and of international security arrangements as well as conflicts over Western Europe's relative position.

NOTES

(1) The OECD Observer, no. 97 (March 1979), pp. 19-26.

(2) For details of the association policies used during the past, see Werner J. Feld, The European Community and the World (Port Washington, NY: Alfred Publishers, 1976), pp. 103-60.

(3) For details see Ibid., pp. 19-42.

(4) See Ralf Dahrendorf, "Possibilities and Limits of a European Communities Foreign Policy," The World Today (April 1971), p. 161.

(5) See OECD, Statistics of Foreign Trade (April 1979), pp. 42-43.

(6) Brazil and the Persian Gulf states are likely candidates for such agreements.

(7) Statistics on Foreign Trade, pp. 40-41, 48-49.

(8) See The Times (London), April 1, 1980.

(9) The Times-Picayune (New Orleans) April 23, 24, 26, 1980.

(10) See also Philip Revzin, "European Reaction to Events in Afghanistan," The Wall Street Journal (January 4, 1980), p. 6.

(11) See Agence Internationale d'Information pour la Presse, Europe, February 16, 1980.

(12) Europe, February 20, 1980.

(13) Europe, February 13, 1980.

(14) See Philippe C. Schmitter, Autonomy or Dependence as Regional Integration Outcomes: Central America (Berkeley, CA: Institute of International Studies, University of California, 1972), pp. 7-8.

2 New Forms of Foreign Policy Formulation in Western Europe*
Wolfgang Wessels

Since the beginning of the 1970s, Western Europe has made quite an impressive show on the international scene. From the Conference on Security and Cooperation in Europe (CSCE) over the Convention of Lomē and the Conference on International Economic Cooperation (CIEC) to the General Assembly of the UN and the Euro-Arab Dialogue, the European Community or the "Ten" has presented a uniform approach, speaking with "one voice" and acting as a unit. While this list of accomplishments looks indeed formidable, the real nature of how Western Europe formulates common policies remains somewhat unclear.

● Do the new forms of formulating foreign policies lead to a new coherent actor in international relations, or is it only a mechanism for coordinated national policies − merely an additional foreign policy instrument for nation-states?(1) Is there a European "foreign policy" defined by: "the existence of purposeful actors, a minimal unity of goals on substantive matters and a working agreement on procedures?"(2)
● Is this new actor a global power,(3) "becoming a real force in international relations";(4) or is it just a method(5) rendering substance only in uncontroversial and insignificant sectors of "low politics";(6)
● Does this actor have only "regional responsibilities or is his orientation worldwide?"(7)
● Do these new forms of foreign policymaking further the integration process by establishing new institutional capacities, by socializing additional national actors into the European System, and by mobilizing them for a common goal?

*This chapter draws on the author's contribution to Reinhardt Rummel and Wolfgang Wessels, eds., Die Europaische Politische Zusammenarbeit, Institut fur Europaische Politik (Bonn: Europa Union Verlag, 1978).

- Does this evolution indicate that <u>external federators</u> are the driving forces of European integration? Are these new forms a central characteristic of the "Second Europe," which is superior to the "First Europe"?(8) Or is the new actor, in fact, a step backward in history to a "Metternich style of diplomacy"? Are these new forms, thus, a further sign of the vain endeavor of the obsolete nation-state to find short-lived solutions to the dilemma between the objective necessity for a European federation on the one hand and its stubborn resistance to give up national sovereignty on the other?(9)

FROM THE 1960s TO THE 1970s – ECONOMIC GIANT AND POLITICAL DWARF?

Since their launching, the European Communities have been forced to define their role on the international scene. In the 1960s, a passive, attentive role was predominant; only some "external relations" were established: the Kennedy Round, association agreements with Greece and Turkey, and with former, especially French, colonies. Already these limited but substantial policies were more than just "natural spillovers" from the customs union. They were politically motivated and had strong foreign policy aims.(10)

In the 1970s, the framework in which the Community and the member states had to operate changed profoundly, and the challenges increased. In the international system, established postwar "orders," which needed few political inputs for their normal functioning, were replaced by a constant political management on a high level. This pattern is to be found in crucial economic sectors (monetary system, trade, energy, raw materials) as well as in political and security sectors (dissolving the polarized bipolar world). On their way to find a proper role, the Community governments had to cope with two phenomena for which they had to look for appropriate institutional and political instruments: the multilateralization of the international political and economic management and the strategy of linkage, by which the United States (e.g., the Year of Europe), the USSR (e.g., CSCE), and the Arab world confronted the Europeans with intersectoral packages.

In the Community itself, the first enlargement from six to nine (accession of Great Britain, Denmark, and Ireland), as well as the ambitious goals for the "Economic and Monetary Union" and "European Union" implied, also, a reappraisal of the international role. With Great Britain as a member and with new concepts the Community could no longer withdraw from larger international responsibilities.

On the nation-state level, the Federal Republic of Germany looked for more international influence within some form of common European framework. With the Ostpolitik of the Brandt government and with membership in the United Nations, major restrictions of the postwar period were lifted. At the same time, two former world powers, Great Britain and France, faced the question of how to have a global influence without being a global power.(11)

The reaction to these challenges led to an extensive increase of "foreign policy outputs"(12) and to a marked proliferation of institutional structures. The Communities, starting from the legal framework of the treaties, developed highly refined mechanisms to achieve internal consensus(13) and to become a coherent actor.(14) Besides the extended and refined Community instruments and procedures, a "second leg" became the new form of foreign policymaking – Political Cooperation (PC) among the foreign offices of the member states. The subsequent parts of this chapter will analyze the nature, the capacity, and the integrational dynamics of the new procedure.

POLITICAL COOPERATION – SOME FACTS

Political Cooperation (PC) was created to deal with international problems confronting the EC. According to the diplomatic agreements (The Luxembourg and Copenhagen Reports of 1970 and 1973) on which the working procedure of Political Cooperation is based, the aims of the new common endeavor are:

- to ensure a better mutual understanding on the great international problems;
- to strengthen their solidarity by promoting the harmonization of their views, the coordination of their positions, and, where it appears possible and desirable, to engage in common actions.(15)

Although the goals and the structures of the PC appear at first modest, the extent and intensity of the activities justify a closer analysis on the academic as well as on the political levels:

- Every week, an average of some 100 communications are transmitted over the common Telex-system (COREU).
- The political directors, who have the best information about the work and operations of the various foreign ministries, usually meet twice a month in the "Political Committee" of the Political Cooperation structure.
- Common working groups of national diplomats analyze important international problems in more than 100 sessions a year.
- Diplomats of the EC in third countries and in international organizations consult regularly, in order to coordinate their positions and their actions.
- Declarations on areas of international tension are made on behalf of the EC member states.
- The Ten are represented by one delegation at international conferences and in international organizations.
- The foreign ministers have developed a well-organized system of different meetings for an intensive and flexible treatment of foreign policy questions.

- The heads of government meet three times a year in the European Council, where they also discuss issues of Political Cooperation. Up to now, they have confined themselves to highly confidential exchanges on international conflicts and to declarations of prepared documents.
- Third countries increasingly approach the EC as an accepted and important actor on the international scene.(16)
- The Ten have used their new form of cooperation with variable success in different situations: in crisis situations (Cyprus), in conferences (CSCE, Euro-Arab Dialogue), in the direct geographical neighborhood (Cyprus, Portugal), as well as in more distant conflict areas (Southern Africa).

THE EC AS ONE ACTOR – INTERNAL FUNCTIONS OF POLITICAL COOPERATION

Information and Consultation: Coordination Reflex

The steady flow of information and constant exchange of views among the Ten has led to a routine which is described as "coordination reflex." "The main success of political cooperation consists of having injected the reflex into diplomatic behavior that it is useful to get to know what the partners are planning before one's own position is defined."(17) As a result of this reflex, the foreign policies of the other member states become more transparent and predictable. The number of surprising changes of position decreases. Also, in cases of open disagreement, this mechanism produces an internal group pressure for adjustments of divergent positions.

The practice of reciprocal information and consultation is of major importance among diplomats of the Ten in third countries, at international organizations, and during international conferences. Diplomats of the Ten emphasize the comforting value of mutual support in the UN General Assembly. The coordination is of central significance for the conference management of the Ten. For the CSCE and the subsequent Belgrade Conference as well as for the Euro-Arab Dialogue, a time-consuming procedure was developed which integrated national and Community officials into a negotiating machine that worked surprisingly well.

The cooperation among embassies in third countries functions with varying intensity and effectiveness. In a number of countries, ambassadors and respective experts of the Ten meet regularly with the result that their positions develop into some form of common views that can be identified as "European" positions by the host governments.   In important capitals, however, "special relationships," the search for national profiles, and the "direct" diplomacy of heads of governments and ministers make the regular exchanges less significant.

Despite this progress, the proper conditions for establishing common embassies of the Ten do not yet exist. Differences of political priorities and the increasing role of embassies as "sales" agencies for national products also complicate matters. The exchange of information and news is part of the daily bread of diplomats. The coordination reflex within and through the PC has, however, achieved a special intra-European quality far beyond levels previously achieved.

Toward a "Communauté de Vue"?

Information and consultation, which lead to an effective coordination reflex, are necessary but not sufficient instruments for achieving a "harmonization of views." Contrary to the thesis that PC just replaces political substance by method, it is possible to identify a harmonization of views in important areas of international relations. In questions of the Atlantic Alliance, in detente − above all, during the CSCE and the subsequent Belgrade Conference − in relations with the Arab countries and in declarations on the Middle East, during the Cyprus crisis and in declarations on Southern Africa, as well as in several positions in the General Assembly, the EC developed some stock of common "political achievements" ("acquis politique"). The "acquis politique" is not defined as unambiguously and as bindingly as the "acquis communautaire," which results from the Community treaties and subsequent legislation. In spite of common declarations, differences arise time and again in the day-to-day handling of diplomatic affairs. Common views on some aspects of an issue still do not necessarily mean agreement in concrete diplomatic work or on all diplomatic fronts. Compared to the position at the beginning of the 1970s, it is possible to share the conviction of many ministers and officials that PC has led to considerable and substantial progress. Such positive results, however, are more likely to be explained by the evolution of the national and international environment than by the effects of the new structure itself. The PC, in any case, is a useful form which helps such a process.

This harmonization of views is seen as a growing trend for the future. The process of approximation may well lead to a community of common basic conceptions, a "communauté de vue." Governments "learn" to harmonize their positions in more and more areas of international politics, so that they develop a broad and basic consensus on the global role of Europe. Even if no common European Foreign Office is established, national foreign policies and the external relations of the Community would have the same conceptual basis.

This notion presumes that the coordination of positions influences the fundamental concepts of national foreign policy and, at the same time, brings about a stability that can survive serious crises within the member states. Neither condition has been met by the PC. Despite a number of declarations on fundamentals (for example, in Copenhagen on European Identity in 1973), the basic conceptions of the international role of Europe still differ to a large degree. With regard to political stability, it is clearly disadvantageous that cooperation within the PC is limited to foreign ministers and diplomats. Social and political forces are not involved, actively or passively. The discussions with the political committee of the European Parliament and the even more sporadic discussions in national Parliaments are of no significance for an involvement in Political Cooperation. The public debate on the relevant chapters of Tindeman's Report, which was to serve as a blueprint for the construction of a European Union, showed, once again, that strong controversies on the international role of the Community continue to exist among political forces in the member states. The confidentiality of Political Cooperation is – in the short term – one of the most important factors behind the unproblematic mode of operation. In the long term, however, it might handicap a common foreign policy which should be based on political consensus.

The new form is, thus, not suitable for the establishment of a "communauté de vue." As far as this future task is concerned, the directly-elected Parliament and the European party federations are expected to initiate a comprehensive debate on foreign policy questions and thus perhaps contribute to a basic consensus on foreign policy goals. However, it is quite possible that such debates could accentuate intra-European controversies which might have quite disturbing side effects on Political Cooperation.

Crisis and Support Functions

The close relations among the member states, inside and outside the framework of the Community, are constantly subject to various international pressures, which are particularly heavy in the case of international crises and outside challenges. Diverging national reactions, which appear "logical" and "natural" to governments in accordance with their understanding of national interest, can endanger the Community itself, policies of the Community, or the general relations between the member states. Thus, the effects of the different reactions to the Arab oil boycott in 1973 led to considerable tension among the member states and threatened the existence of the Community. In cases like that, PC offers an extensive and familiar system for the internal management of crises ("consultation d'urgence"). Also, in less serious cases, PC helps neutralize "divide and conquer" policies at an early stage.

The coordination effects support and reinforce proper Community policies in the field of external relations. Political questions that are closely related to Community policies are discussed within PC. This supplementary and reinforcing role becomes particularly important when third countries link economic, monetary, trade and, in some instances, military demands so that neither the Community nor the member states alone could react appropriately. Within PC, the EC member states could reduce the deficiencies of their internal coordination and improve the coherence of their strategies. Nevertheless, new difficulties between the two structures, external relations of the Community and Political Cooperation, arise from time to time.

THE INTERNATIONAL ROLE AND CAPACITY OF THE TEN –
EXTERNAL FUNCTIONS OF POLITICAL COOPERATION

Partners in Diplomatic Trade

On the diplomatic stage, the member states were confronted with the
problem of introducing themselves under a new label, while at the same
time keeping their national and Community "hats." The international
involvement of the Ten led to a gap between expectations and possibilities. On the one hand, the member states do not want to place all
foreign policy instruments at the disposal of the PC; on the other hand,
they are identified as one "power" by many countries which, to a
certain extent, have big expectations regarding particular policies and
actions on the part of the EC.

The daily routine work of international diplomacy consists mainly of
flows of information, policy inputs, and the painstaking process of
adjusting different positions. With the new form, the member states
have a mechanism to participate in this diplomatic trade. PC lives
within and by means of the traditional diplomatic apparatus of the
member states, whereas the Community itself does not dispose of an
appropriate diplomatic infrastructure and cannot – apart from legal
competence – participate in most essential aspects of the diplomatic
trade.

To make the EC an accepted partner in the diplomatic routine is
particularly apparent in international conferences (CSCE, Euro-Arab
Dialogue) and in the General Assembly of the UN. The EC as an entity
has become fully integrated into the negotiating and coordinating
process. Outside of institutionalized procedures, the EC has been
increasingly involved in the daily diplomatic business.

The role within the diplomatic trade is of considerable value, even if
it has not yet shown spectacular results. The EC is increasingly
regarded as a single unit which cannot be easily divided.

A Diplomacy of Declarations

The most visible signs of PC activities are official declarations on
behalf of the member states. Declarations are common instruments of
international diplomacy, which are especially used by international
groups; the Group of "77," the group of non-aligned countries, NATO,
OECD, and the Warsaw Pact countries use declarations in order to
voice demands, express warnings, and indicate new policy directions.
Frequently, these declarations are primarily issued to form a consensus
within the group. PC is no exception to that rule. A number of
declarations have served mainly to harmonize positions within PC.
These declarations do, however, also represent points of reference to
which national diplomats refer in their day-to-day work, and behind
which national governments can "hide" if external and internal pressures make it useful. In some cases, declarations (such as those

concerning the situation in the Middle East and those concerning South Africa) clearly signal that the positions of the member states change or become firmer. It is difficult to estimate the effect these declarations have on the states or groups of states to which they are addressed; the influence largely depends on the importance which these states attach to the position and to the potential of the EC. Nevertheless, it is obvious that attention is being increasingly paid to the positions of the EC. In questions concerning the Middle East, the governments involved comment on declarations of the EC, and even urge the EC to publish declarations or hold them back.

The Levers of Political Cooperation

The role of the EC in the diplomatic routine, and the respect which its declarations are paid on the international stage are, to a high degree, dependent on the "power" and influence of the member states. Within the range of positive and negative sanctions, the EC has only direct diplomatic tools at its disposal: demarches, declarations, support or rejection at international conferences, and votes in the General Assembly of the UN. The deployment of these common instruments has proved particularly useful in multinational negotiations, compared to the more limited capabilities of the individual member states.

Beyond the utilization of direct diplomatic tools lies a realm in which the employment of positive or negative sanctions is unclear and unpredictable, especially with regard to the economic potential of the Community itself. The instruments of the Community are not simply arms at the easy disposal of PC; they are part of policies which gain their significance by the separate aims of the Community. The pillars of the Community's external relations are formulated in treaties which cannot be mobilized for political and diplomatic interventions. Central areas of the Community, such as tariff, trade, and association policies, can be politically used only during the negotiating phase. Financial aid granted under particular political conditions has proved a flexible instrument. Presenting the prospect of Community membership as an incentive for outside states to behave democratically cannot be used as a general sanction. The prospect of EC membership was, indeed, a significant factor in the domestic political development of Greece, Portugal, and Spain, and was exploited by the member states. At the same time, however, the Community was obliged to honor the given promises.

In treaties in which possible membership might be useful (Lomé, association agreements, European Free Trade area), the rules on entry are more or less fixed so that it is not possible to demand any particular behavior for the attainment of immediate foreign policy goals. The member states can also place instruments and channels of influence at the disposal of PC, which lie exclusively or primarily under national control. Breaking or entering into diplomatic relations, special bilateral relationships, arms exports or embargoes, military and development aid are potential instruments for the coordinated use of the EC. However, some of the member states seem consciously to cultivate such instruments outside PC.

NATURE AND CAPACITY OF POLITICAL COOPERATION

Taking the above criteria, Political Cooperation does fulfill the conditions for a foreign policy. There are rather differentiated working agreements on procedures, there is an "acquis politique" with respect to unity of goals on substantive matters, and there is some kind of purposeful actor, even if some incoherences and output failures continue to occur.

The new form, however, is not an independent and isolated form of European foreign policy. It is neither a substitute for all existing structures nor does PC create a new parallel instrument outside traditional forms – it represents an additional and supplementary level within a complex configuration of national, Community, and Atlantic policymaking structures. PC has successfully contributed to reducing difficulties of coordination between various levels and forms of European foreign policy, a success which is of benefit both to the external relations of the Community and to national diplomacy. The capabilities of the system to cope with "turbulences" were increased by a new, flexible structure.(18) With PC the EC has extended, differentiated, and strengthened the instruments of European foreign policymaking – both internally and externally. Internally, the "coordinated reflex" and the "harmonization of positions" furthered a process toward a "security community."(19) In the international system, the EC established itself as an accepted partner in daily diplomatic affairs, a partner whose common declarations and other means of diplomacy are taken into account. The influence of the Community and of the member states has increased – especially in international organizations and conferences. PC has served to strengthen the West European role as initiator, vetoer, controller, and broker in international organizations.(20) The model case reflecting all these modes of influence is the CSCE.

The member states have developed and upheld positions in conflict areas in which no common European voices were heard before; in many cases, some member states had not even formulated positions, or would not have developed them explicitly without stimulations generated within Political Cooperation. Compared to the carefully formulated Luxembourg and Copenhagen Reports, PC has developed a broad and differentiated structure.

As to the capacity of PC, experience also shows clear limits. The Ten are less flexible than other international actors. Diplomacy can often be reactive only to developments in the outside world; thus, PC has to be used primarily to minimize cost and contain conflicts. Preventive conflict resolution in all areas of tension which could affect Western Europe goes far beyond the capacity of the Community and its members. Nevertheless, the internal processes of information and coordination delay actions and, thus, decrease the effectiveness of PC. In a number of cases, the cost in terms of organizational burden and time compares unfavorably with the benefits of a common approach. PC also shows tendencies toward selectivity and discontinuity in the treatment of international problems. If sensitive and crucial interests of individual member states are touched – above all in times of election campaigns – then solutions to problem areas are either impeded or are completely excluded. The capacity to react to international challenges is further limited by political "accidents" and national frailties. Political considerations of the Ten frequently may necessitate nonbinding and ambiguous declarations. Discrepancies between diplomatic declarations on the one hand and closely-related Community policies on the other often exist; defense and security questions generally remain outside Political Cooperation. These problems will remain as long as the coordination among political problems, defenses, and Community processes is not improved on the European and on the national level.

So far, we have looked at Political Cooperation from a European level and tried to assess its quality as a mechanism creating a "European actor." Looking at it from the national level, this new form offers a perfect model for strengthening and refining national foreign policies. With the help of this additional "European channel," national governments get support for their own policies and can shape their policies more ambivalently and, thus, less vulnerably. Political Cooperation offers an alibi function, if external or internal pressures lead to dilemmas. The use or non-use of this new form is still subject to national cost/benefit analyses; there is – aside form interest group pressures – no obligation to put one's interest into this common form. The choice for extra-PC options remains open; whereas, for many Community policies, there are legally no more alternatives open. Thus, the satisfaction of many national actors with the status quo of PC can also be understood in terms of this self-interest.

To summarize, with PC, the member states have, up to now, developed a structure for mutual exchange of information and for common analysis and assessment rather than for decision making and action. Neither from its structure nor its performance can PC be regarded as a foreign policy structure of a third superpower. Rather, PC must be judged as an incomplete and painful attempt to extend the role of the Community as a "civilian" power in the field of international diplomacy.

POLITICAL COOPERATION – THE INTEGRATIVE ASPECT

The usefulness of PC lies in its direct task and function as a means of foreign policy formulation. Quite often, however, Political Cooperation stirs up controversies because of its integrative qualities or "defects." We now turn from an analysis of PC as an international actor to an assessment in terms of its contribution to the integration process.

PC is frequently characterized as an intergovernmental process which is clearly distinguished from the "Federal" or "Community" model. In order to identify the integrative quality, the structures of Political Cooperation and of the Community will be compared. Both structures display essential similarities in central features. Decisions are made after painstaking and, frequently, long processes of consultation, negotiation, and coordination in a dense interbureaucratic network among the member states. Both rely on a vertical hierarchy at the national level with the foreign ministers or heads of governments as the main agents of decision making. The functioning of the machinery is made possible by close horizontal contacts between the various corresponding levels of officials and politicians. Transnational coalitions which break the national monopolies for taking the final decisions are not existing in PC. In the Community, transnational interest groups and parties have developed a new political infrastructure, but their influence on decisions is limited to only a few sectors (particularly agriculture). The national monopoly remains dominant in all essential domains. PC decision processes are, thus, completely subordinate to the political control of national governments – just as Community processes are, to a large extent and in most essential respects.

Apart from these identical or similar elements, these structures show clear differences – even if taking into account that the actual decision-making processes in the Community vary from sector to sector and according to the actors involved. The rules of the Community treaties often fix the procedures of decision making to a considerable extent. The rules of the Luxembourg and Copenhagen Reports are more flexible and less binding. These differences are also due to the nature of the outputs. While PC concentrates mainly on informal consultations, the work of the Community bodies consists of passing acts of a legislative nature. The outputs of the Community are binding, whereas diplomatic declarations are usually characterized by flexibility. The political inputs into the Community are also rather different from those which influence PC. The Common Agricultural Policy (which directly affects politically active groups) or industrial policies (which have consequences for whole branches of industry) attract more attention and stronger political controversies than even delicate items within the PC framework.

In the EC, political bodies are involved which have no equivalent in the PC. Within PC, there is no Commission as a "motor," "guardian" of the treaties, and executive body which can rely on a bureaucracy with continuity, experience, and specialized knowledge. This is also true for important functions of the European Parliament and the European Court of Justice.

Two conclusions can be drawn from this comparison. First, PC is not a regression to an obsolete anachronism (Metternich style), but a method for common policy formulation, which shows similar elements to those of the Community. PC is a part of European integration, and not the relic of an historical epoch. A second conclusion modifies the standard classification of PC as "intergovernmental." It is correct that governments work together within an informal framework strictly applying the rule of unanimity and producing legally nonbinding declarations. Even if PC shares all these conceptual elements with historical and familiar forms of intergovernmental cooperation, the intensity and quality of PC activities go beyond these categories.

An essential feature of PC lies in its interdiplomatic structure which does not simply limit cooperation to the highest level, but anchors it firmly in the diplomatic machinery of the Ten. These direct institutionalized intercommunications have different intensity and mobilization effects than other forms of multilateral diplomacy. PC also has some forms of binding effects: "A kind of law of custom has emerged between the countries of the Community which naturally does not envisage sanctions but which has nevertheless taken on the character of a recognized rule, which can be occasionally broken, but whose existence is still recognized."(21) Even more, the habit of cooperation and the self-obligation (coordination reflex) imply sanctions which are not based on legal rules but on group expectations of mutuality. In spite of other forums for political concertation and in spite of all turbulences, some stable expectations and attitudes of governments have created a rather solid mechanism for formulating foreign policies.

Finally, the regular reference to unanimity points to only one aspect of reality; the consensus principle does not mean a stiff inflexibility of national positions, but it leads to dynamic adaptations. The national control is, however, strictly kept. Thus, characterizing PC as purely intergovernmental is inappropriate and misleading. The essential integrative quality of PC can be described as an interdiplomatic mobilization process without supranational effects, but with increasingly binding character.

By accepting this characteristic feature for PC, it seems also clear that "external federators" have generally only limited integrative force. In Political Cooperation, pressures of the international system are at their peak; integrative effects in the classic sense of federalization, however, have been weak. External pressures are not taken as common challenges, but as tasks for national governments. Their perception of the challenge, their interest, and their choice for the appropriate forum make Political Cooperation a useful instrument, even though limited in its integrative potential.

An Institutional Model?

A number of actors and observers take the structure of PC as an institutional model for a European Union. The informality and the confidentiality of the diplomatic apparatus, as well as the first positive results and the experience that national influence in European decision making is not reduced or disturbed by "unpredictable" bodies (i.e., the Commission, the European Parliament, and the Court of Justice) make PC an attractive model for the defenders of national sovereignty. Experience, however, shows that the efficiency of this institutional procedure depends on its area of operation. The work and effects of PC are mainly determined by the specific qualities of diplomatic work. A mechanical transfer of this model into other sectors of European politics ignores the fact that the structure of PC has developed from specific needs of international diplomacy. Applying this procedure to economic and social policies could not achieve the same results and would probably even lead to counterproductive effects on common policies in these sectors.

For the medium term, however, it is not a question of an <u>alternative</u> use of the models, but the main and constructive task is to combine the advantages of both. In the long run, from the experiences with PC, a new institutional model could be developed.

A Strategy for Integration?

From the static consideration as an institutional model, a dynamic perspective of PC as a paradigmatic strategy for integration can be discerned. At first, a major fear was that PC could be used as a strategy aimed against the Community and its system and would thereby produce disintegrative effects. But after initial difficulties, PC can be seen as a refined strategy through which common positions can be developed in hitherto national sectors of "high politics." The recipe for success a la PC could be based on the following rules: a common European enterprise has to begin with a loose, nonbinding, and modest formula by which mutual trust can be initiated; ambitious and binding plans only lead to early controversies about integration doctrines, which block and overload the new structure; without these "disturbances," a "natural" procedure will develop; self-organization does justice to the individual interests of the participants and is flexible enough to avoid deviations and to adapt to special needs without an irreparable break. In this flexible structure, the actors can accumulate an increasing body of common positions if they are confronted with the "right" external challenges; ultimately, all these processes create the conditions for qualitative changes into a new integrative dimension.   With this perspective, PC could be assessed as a strategy to achieve preconditions for integrative change. Compared to the debates on the Fouchet plans at the beginning of the 1960s, or on Economic and Monetary Union in the 1970s, the PC method has proved itself to be a superior strategy to initiate and develop common endeavors in areas of high politics, different political constellations in the respective epochs not being taken into account.

Although it creates certain political and administrative conditions for further steps, PC will not move the integration process forward as a <u>federator</u> — a fact that can be derived from its weakness in creating a community of common conceptions. In relation to integration strategies, there is, again, no clear choice between alternatives but, rather, a plurality of strategies has to be used in parallel fashion. In this respect, valuable suggestions can be gained from experience with PC.

Some Notes on the Methods

When analyzing the structure of Political Cooperation and assessing its effects, we are confronted with major methodological difficulties. A central condition for analysis and assessment is an appropriate level of information. Compared to the majority of Community affairs, PC is surrounded by an unusually high degree of confidentiality.(22) A second and far greater difficulty lies in registering and explaining reciprocal or causal relationships between changes in national positions on the one hand, and developments in the common framework on the other.

To what extent can views held by the member states be traced back to effects of cooperation, or what changes in national constellations and the international scene are responsible for harmonizing views? The impact of external "power" and its effectiveness can be grasped in an even less satisfactory way. In order to know whether and how governments are influenced by the policies of the Community, information is required which usually is not available to an outside observer.

In assessing PC, the criteria are crucial. Frequently, PC is compared with a federal model, in which common institutions take and execute all necessary foreign policy decisions and, thereby, substitute themselves for previously existing foreign policymaking structures. This yardstick is not useful as it will not capture processes in which sovereign states try to work together. By dividing the functions of PC into internal and external ones, we do greater justice to the particular conditions and qualities of PC than by using such an ideal model.

To get an empirical basis for these assessments, we must heavily rely on case studies and the analysis of structures which must have a common framework of reference. Interviews with different actors must be put into a mosaic of information bits. Standardized interviews will "spoil" the diplomatic atmosphere, as simple indicators will be misleading about the real functions of PC.(23) The careful work of historical description has to be combined with systematic analysis. Nevertheless, major deficiencies in empirical testing remain.

THE FUTURE OF PC – THE LIMITS OF PRAGMATIC EVOLUTION

The PC has seen a cumulative growth process in the last few years. Unless major international crises in the next few years prove extremely disruptive, PC will cover more and more international topics of common interest. One consequence to be expected is a bureaucratic arteriosclerosis which endangers all larger, especially international, organizations. An increasing number of rules, of working groups, and a heavier burden for coordination will further militate against innovation and flexibility. Facing a diminishing rate of return for an increasing input, institutional adaptations will have to be taken if this structure will be of further use for the national governments.

New Challenges: Southern Enlargement and Direct Elections

Besides a mere extrapolation of trends, two new developments have to be taken into account: the direct elections to the European Parliament, which took place in June 1979; and the second enlargement, with Greece, Portugal, and Spain becoming members of the Community. These new developments will change the overall framework and might influence the functioning of Political Cooperation.

With direct elections, the European Parliament will demand more influence on all aspects of common policies. Concerning the diplomatic procedures, parliaments seldom play a major role. But the European Parliament may gain some weight as the result of meetings which the Political Committee of the European Parliament has four times per year with the foreign ministers of the member states.

The role of the Parliament could be more important in an indirect way. Debates and resolutions of the new Parliament might lead to a broader and deeper consensus on Europe's role in the world, thus furthering an evolution to a Communauté de vue. However, this process will be difficult, as major cleavages concerning Europe's future role exist at the present time. An increased polarization which could come about through the debates of the parliamentarians might have negative effects on Political Cooperation as the smooth working of the PC might then become the focus of public attention and controversy.

With the southern enlargement, additional and diverging interests of the "newcomers," as well as more conflicts, will also increase the number of problems. The already complex process of decision making will become more cumbersome and time consuming. Against these liabilities, certain assets need to be mentioned. The new members will bring in "special relationships" with Third World countries, especially in Latin America and Africa. They also are highly interested in common policies: Political Cooperation offers them a structure, through which they might have some influence in international affairs – a major reason for them to become members of the Community.

Institutional Reforms

The extrapolation of present trends and the new challenges indicate that the present institutional structure needs careful consideration. To keep Political Cooperation as a useful instrument, the Community has to reflect on reforms and adaptations of their common working methods. A total reform would bring the Community and the PC structures into a federal constitution through which clear rules for foreign policymaking are set up along usual federal patterns. This option has presently no realistic chance of being implemented.

A second line of reasoning suggests integrating all PC structures and topics into the legal framework of the Community, thus making it an exclusive Community instrument. This option has major disadvantages: as long as the Community does not dispose of its own experienced diplomatic service, the present mobilization effect of national diplomats is of a higher value. Furthermore, national opposition against such a heavy loss of sovereignty will prevent a large shift of powers from the member states to the Community. The pragmatic way is to improve the present division of labor between different structures and levels. First, the challenges lying ahead for Western Europe must be tackled by those bodies which are most experienced and competent for the respective tasks. Secondly, the mutual information and coordination tasks need further improvement; especially the role of the presidency of the Council and of the Political Cooperation mechanism need additional strengthening. A "political" secretariat for Political Cooperation, however, would be of no help as it would have negative implications for the mobilization of national diplomats and the involvement of the Commission. The limited reforms will be useful; however, the major shortcoming will remain in the lack of a basic consensus on the international role of the Community and on future institutional structures. To change this drawback, Political Cooperation as such is too weak.

NOTES

(1) Michael S. Dolan and James A. Caporaso, "The External Relations of the European Community," in The Annals of the American Academy of Political and Social Science (November 1978), p. 136; see also Werner Feld, The European Community in World Affairs (Port Washington, N.Y.: Alfred, 1976), pp. 308-325, especially pp. 313-315.

(2) See for these criteria, Dolan and Caporaso, "External Relations," p. 136.

(3) Pierre-Henri Laurent, "The Decade of Divergence and Development," in The Annals of the American Academy, p. 13.

(4) Press and Information Office, Federal Government of the Federal Republic of Germany, European Political Cooperation (Bonn 1976); Second Report of the Foreign Ministers to the Heads of State and Government of the Member States of the European Community, July 23, 1973 (Copenhagen Report), p. 52.

(5) William Wallace and David Allen, "Political Cooperation: Procedure as Substitute for Policy," in Policy-Making in the European Communities, ed. Helen Wallace, William Wallace, and Carol Webb (New York: John Wiley, 1977), pp. 241-244.

(6) This position is taken by some national diplomats and politicians not directly involved in common or coordinated procedures.

(7) See Kissinger's position when launching the "Year of Europe," in The New York Times, April 24 and 26, 1973.

(8) Ralf Dahrendorf, "Wieland Europa," in Die Zeit, Sept. 7, 1971, p. 3.

(9) See Claus Schöndube, "Der Konigliche Web," in Europa Union, Europaische Zeitung, February 1976, p. 6.

(10) The association agreements with Greece and Turkey were supposed to show the "open" character of the Community (after failure of the first British application for membership), and to strengthen the links of these countries with the Western world.

(11) See Alfred Grosser, "En Guise de Conclusion," in Les Politiques Extérieures Européenes dans la Crise (Paris: Presses de la Fondation Nationale des Sciences Politiques, 1976). The ambiguous role of these two powers remained; whereas they use the normal information and consultation procedures of Political Cooperation, they keep certain "world power" areas (Security Council, Berlin) out of the common web.

(12) See Ernst B. Haas, "Turbulent Fields and the Theory of Regional Integration," International Organization, 30, no. 2 (Spring 1976): 181; see also the annual reports of the Commission of the European Communities and the bi-annual reports of the President of the Council.

(13) The most sophisticated procedures of a sheer byzantine nature were developed during the CIEC: the internal position of member states (foreign office – economic ministry), bilateral relations (France – FRG), the Community decision making in Brussels and Paris, the coordination within the Western group, and finally the negotiations with the oil-producing and the developing countries, which had to be organized into a coherent process.

(14) Again, a high degree of sophistication was developed: e.g., a bipresidential representation (Presidency of the Council and Commission, whereby the Presidency sometimes included representatives of the former, the acting, and the incoming Presidents).

(15) See First Report of the Foreign Ministers to the Heads of State and Government of the Member States of the European Community, of October 27, 1970 (Luxembourg Report), and the Copenhagen Report, in Press and Information Office (Federal Government) European Political Cooperation (EPC), Bonn 1978, 3rd edition.

(16) The Russian ambassador to the United Nations addressed his West European colleagues as the "Mighty Nine."

(17) Vicomte Davignon, the founding father of Political Cooperation, quoted in William Wallace, "A Common European Foreign Polity: Mirage or Reality?" in New Europe, Spring 1977, p. 26.

(18) See Haas, "Turbulent Fields," p. 199.

(19) See the familiar concept by Karl W. Deutsch, Sidney A. Burrell, Robert A. Kann, Maurice Lee Jr., Martin Lichterman, Raymond E. Lindgren, Francis L. Loewenheim, Richard W. Van Wagenen, Political Community and the North Atlantic Area (Princeton: Princeton University Press, 1957), p. 7.

(20) See for these categories, Robert W. Cox and Harold K. Jacobson, The Anatomy of Influence (New Haven and London: Yale University Press, 1973), p. 12.

(21) The acting Council President, the Belgian Foreign Minister Simonet in the debate of the European Parliament, November 15, 1977.

(22) This is especially true for the involved services of the Commission.

(23) The voting behavior of the member states in the General Assembly is often taken as the main indicator for the performance of PC, disregarding the political substance and the tactical value of the votes.

3 Problems of Community Enlargement: The Accession of Greece, Portugal, and Spain

Christian Deubner

INTRODUCTION

The following is an exercise in speculation on probable perspectives of enlargement for the European Community: taking the EC as it is today, what are the possible consequences of the accessions of Greece, Portugal, and Spain to membership? Two of the dominating political goals of European Community politics can serve as criteria in measuring what may come about: a) stabilizing and advancing democracy and economic-political stability in the member states as an internal goal; b) securing and extending the Community's role as a framework for determining, formulating, and protecting the common foreign trade and foreign policy interests of the members vis a vis the outside world and reconciling this with a Community role as a factor of liberalization and development in global economic relations. Will enlargement of a status quo European Community assure these goals or bring us closer to them?

Whereas one might try to analyze these questions by comparing the Community of today with the newcomers — as the EC Commission has done in its analyses, for example — another approach seems to promise more relevant and realistic results. It focuses attention on the inequalities already existing between different national developments and

*This chapter is a substantially enlarged version of the views of the author formulated as part of a paper for a public hearing before the committee of foreign affairs of the Deutscher Budestag: Referat bzw. Stellungnahme der Stiftung Wissenschaft und Politik (Chr. Deubner, H. Kramer, G. Roth, R. Rummel) zur öffentlichen Anhörung des Auswärtigen Ausschusses des Deutschen Bundestages zum Thema "Die Erweiterung der EG nach Süden" May 29 and 30, 1978, in: Deutscher Bundestag, 8. Wahlperiode, Auswartiger Ausschuss, 3. Ausschuss, Protokoll No. 32 and 33, Teil II, S.705-747.

international relations within the Community as a source of strain on European integration and on the way these inequalities and their consequences might develop in the course of enlargement and, thus, affect the attainment of the goals of integration.

The central elements of the European Community are the customs union with the tradition of external liberalism, an increasing volume of common external trade policy, and a common agricultural market. In sum, these elements affect the conditions of external economic exchange of the member states, but they also restrain effective change and adaptation processes in the member states of a common market. It is well known that these central elements with their combination of liberalist and protectionist foreign trade principles, of liberalism and dirigism in domestic economic policy, constitute the historic balance of interests and power between the member states – countries which hold a different rank in the hierarchy of the international division of labor and whose economies are internationalizing in very different ways.

This traditional balance has changed in the past 20 years of the Community's existence. West Germany has emerged as the undisputed economic superpower of Western Europe whose interests and policies exercise a dominating influence on the character of intra-EC economic and political relations. Other member states' development did not keep up and disparities widened. West Germany's integration into the international division of labor and, therefore, its position and interests vis a vis the rest of the EC-group have changed.(1) This has, in the past, put considerable strain on the cohesion of the EC. Entry of Greece and the two candidates (Spain and Portugal) will widen internal EC disparities even more.(2) Portugal and Greece on the one hand, West Germany on the other, will constitute extremes which can hardly be reconciled under the roof of common policies of the kind constituting the EC. Therefore, it appears justified to analyze the upcoming enlargement in reference to this relationship of extremes.

In doing this, it seems appropriate to follow up the two questions at the beginning of this chapter with two related queries concerning West Germany's role, and taking into account two cardinal considerations with which West Germany political elites view the prospects of Western European integration policies today. These considerations are, indeed, not new: on the one hand, the realization that the Common Market and the rest of Western Europe has more and more become the most important area of West Germany foreign economic activity and expansion at a time when successful economic activity abroad is endangered from many directions; on the other hand the realization of growing tendencies towards dirigistic and protectionistic government interference in national economic growth and international economic exchange in Western Europe and beyond. In West German official thinking and from the view of industry, government interference in the economy cannot but impede and endanger West German progress on Western European markets. Thus, in West Germany there is a deep ambivalence in European policy attitudes, between stabilizing and enlarging the Western European market under the rules and institutions of the

European Community, and the controlling of its progress. One objective is to insure against the dangers of being bound up with a Western European group of protectionistic and dirigism-oriented states which could impede West Germany's economic progress abroad, and, indeed, even affect its own internal economic order.

This ambivalence may be seen in West German attitudes toward the new European Monetary System as well as in its enlargement interests and policies. Thus, when asking what the chances of economic-political stability through accession to the European Community are, the appropriate question in regard to West Germany would be: how far is this aim compatible with, or indeed a condition of, its aim of a stable and liberal Western European market? Moreover, in considering the problem of common Western European foreign economic policies, one ought to take a look at how enlargement may affect the Western European balance of liberalist and dirigistic forces and – thereby – West Germany's interest in reaping the fruits of unhindered participation in the internationalization of production and liberal world trade.

Seeing West Germany as representing the interests of the industrialized European metropoles in the process of EC enlargement, one cannot but mention the third important factor which is only indirectly connected with economic-industrial considerations: the political interests of stabilizing the southern flank of capitalist Europe. This interest is certainly one of all West European bourgeois governments (though not of all the important political forces in the region). But again, the West Germany position is crucial, not only because of the well-known and weighty influence of its government in being able to grant or withhold substantial economic or financial inducements or by serving as a middleman with privileged access to the United States administration, but also because of the enormous influence which West German political and social organizations (e.g., parties and trade unions) exercise at the level of subgovernmental, transnational, political processes in Western Europe due to their organizational and financial strength.

That this is not just a concern of purely West German national politics was demonstrated very clearly by the clash between West Germans and Americans on the strategies to be applied to Portugal after the 1974 revolution. It showed the West Germans and the governing Social Democratic Party defending, and in fact successfully applying, a specifically European method of action, which included these very instruments of transnational political processes and governmental diplomatic play with financial-economic inducements.(3) There can be no doubt that the West German actions were in the American interest as well. But they show, and indeed stress, that Western Europe is up to now essentially a "civilian superpower" (to use a term of Johan Galtung) which, if only for lack of military power in the Mediterranean, cannot rely on this form of power coupled with threats to retain control of Mediterranean affairs as the US appears to have done, but has to use the potent means of transnational processes and of inducements. Even the enlargement policy of the EC is, in the end, a clear political consequence of the fact that military force is not an available nor an acceptable way of bringing about intra-European stabilization or co-ercion today.

To say all this obviously begs the question of how – over and above the political decision of letting the three candidates into the EC – West German engagement in diplomatic and transnational political processes could contribute to or even mold stabilization policies in Greece and the candidate countries.

One more important point has to be stressed in this introduction: economic growth will probably make all the difference. If there is growth, and if it even approaches the dimensions it had in Western Europe during the 1960s, many of the foreseeable problems and contradictions of enlarging today's European Community might fail to have dramatic socio-political consequences; the acquis communautaire might be preserved in its substance without great problems. On the other hand, continuation of the current economic stagnation or even a slipping into a new recession could give alarming proportions and dynamics to the impending problems.

As concerns West Germany, which so vitally depends upon stable access to international economic exchanges, the ambivalence of its European policies might only result in international economic crisis, protectionism, and trade wars. There have been apprehensions about this in West Germany, and the foundations for a clearer Europeanist strategy have been providentially strengthened in the recent past – they only need the breath of life.

Keeping clear of both of these extremes, though, this author views the upcoming period mainly as one of halting, intermittent growth and stagnation.

THE INTERNAL PERSPECTIVE: SECURING STABILITY AND DEMOCRACY BY ENLARGEMENT

There is no doubt that integration into the existing structures of the Common Market would expose the new member states' industries to dangerous pressures of superior competition from the outside.(4) The protective barriers against this competition, which existed up to now in the form of high tariffs and national industrial policies, would have to be removed to a large degree. This statement is true even though a number of preferential trade agreements between the EC, Greece, and the candidate countries postulate far-flung liberal trade principles and have, in fact, led to a certain measure of tariff reductions which create – strongest in Portugal and least in Spain – the image of free trade between the two sides and, therefore, the impression that nothing much would change in the case of EC membership. A closer look reveals that this picture is strongly idealized. In fact, those areas in which the industrial and agricultural development of Greece and the candidates enters into spheres where they actually compete with already existing industrial and agricultural producers in the EC are heavily protected against imports by these countries. As these areas have to expand in the course of further development, protection will expand as well. Thus, it is only logical that Spain, with its relatively well developed industry, should have the highest degree of import restrictions and export aids. In Portugal, the relative absence of tariffs and quotas has temporarily been offset by substantial import duties introduced to combat the acute balance of payments deficit. All of this would have to end after entry into the EC if the status quo in the Community policy is to be preserved.

In relation to third countries outside the EC, the situation looks even graver: developing countries with low-cost labor, in the Mediterranean region and beyond, compete with their exports of consumer goods in the very areas where Greece and the candidates have their principal export strengths as well – and their production costs are lower. Upon accession to the EC, these countries would have to lower their present high protection rates and, thus, open themselves on two fronts to superior competition.

Evidently, the counterweight to these risks is seen in the opening of EC markets to Greece and the candidates with the perspective of substantial export increases. But here again, a closer look reveals that, in fact, the additional opening of the EC to imports over and above the preferences they already enjoy will not be very big. Substantial effects may only come about in the field of very specific low to medium-quality manufactured goods where the EC industry is in a crisis and where imports of these countries have been subjected to a protectionist EC import regime with quotas imposed also on imports from overseas developing countries. Candidates may have the chance of complementary division of labor with the present EC in these fields. But if Greece and the candidates want to use this chance, they would have to have a wage level which remained very substantially below the rest of Western Europe; in fact, somewhere in the neighborhood of the Third World countries. Alternatively, they might press for higher EC import tariffs and for decreased import quotas to keep the lower-cost Third World imports off EC markets and make room for themselves. This would, at the same time, give them a better chance to protect their domestic markets against the threatening Third World import wave. Neither of the two alternatives is in accordance with EC aims for enlargement, though; the first would maintain an intolerable gap in incomes and standard of living within Western Europe, and the second would have to come about at the price of reducing the Third World countries' chances for development by exports. However, both of these alternative strategies seem to materialize in current policies of Greece, Spain, Portugal and the EC, as the next paragraphs will try to show.

In the face of these highly unattractive perspectives, there seems to be only one overriding economic reason for entering the EC: staying out might be even more disadvantageous. Spain and Portugal are already in very intensive and expanding economic exchanges with the European Community countries and, thus, directly or indirectly subject to most Community policies, though without a voice in their making. The advantages of admission to the EC and participation in EC policymaking, as well as of intra-EC transfers of subsidies, might, under these circumstances, override the clear and unavoidable disadvantages. (Perhaps, though, a "special relationship" with the EC might also render some of these advantages, but without all the disadvantages.) Some of the conditions under which this strategy might have a chance of success will be outlined later in this chapter.

In speculating about the foreseeable effects that integration might have in Greece and the candidate countries, one must differentiate between two main factors: only a relatively small sector of industry and of large-scale agriculture is internationally competitive, with Spain being in the best position; and most capital and labor is located in small and medium-scale industry and small agriculture, which produce at costs that are, due to low technology and/or productivity, too high to be internationally competitive. For both of these sectors, past growth has been possible only on the basis of protected national and colonial markets and national industrial policies with high subsidies. The second sector has not yet learned to stand the wind of international competition without these crutches. A liberalized inflow of goods from the European Community's industrial centers into these countries would, thus, mean a severe crisis for this, by far the largest, sector of the three Mediterranean economies. The large majority of capital owners, workers, and small farmers in all of the three countries is, thus, liable to suffer big losses in profits and wages, their very means of subsistence, by integration into the Common Market.(5)

The smaller sector of internationally-competitive industry which exists mainly in Spain, and only to a small degree in Portugal or in Greece, seems, indeed, to have outgrown the need for state subsidies of all kinds. Often, these industries have started to assert themselves on the continental and overseas export markets; and, frequently, they are based on heavy foreign capital investment from the Western European and the North American centers.(6) But even the success of these industries seems in large part due to the existence of cheap labor in all three Mediterranean countries, combined with modern technology and marketing. Can this success continue and expand under conditions of Common Market integration? If one looks at the perspectives of the basic conditions of this success, namely the inflow of foreign capital and the presence of cheap labor, one is inclined to be pessimistic.

As for foreign capital inflows to create export-oriented industries, Spain, Portugal, and Greece have to compete in increasing measure with the lower-cost countries of the Third World. Access to the Common Market might give them an additional edge over their overseas competitors on the EC markets, which would be about equal to the cost differences in transports and EC import tariffs which these third country producers have to surmount to reach the EC customers. But continuing success in this field would mean lowest labor costs and continuing complementary exchange with central Western Europe. This seems to be a very undesirable perspective. As for those capital inflows which were motivated by assuring themselves of free access to the growing internal markets of the three Mediterranean economies themselves, integration into the EC will remove the most potent incentive for engagement.(7) In sum, foreign capital investment might stagnate or even partly decrease after the accession of the three countries.(8) As for the labor cost differences which existed between the three countries and the industrial center of Western Europe, they have been reduced during the past few years with the social policy advances made in the course of democratization.(9) In the meantime, though, austerity policies in Greece and the candidate countries have let this gap increase again very substantially.

There is no assurance at all that a prolonged adaptation period (during which trade barriers between the three countries and the EC would be mainly reduced in favor of Greece and the candidate countries, while EC trade toward these countries would continue to meet higher barriers for a period of up to ten years) would actually suffice to neutralize the impending problem. Experience with more than 20 years of European integration, within a community with internal structural differences much smaller than those looming ahead with the Mediterranean countries' entry, are very disillusioning. International and interregional differences in development have increased, not decreased, within the past 20 years.(10)

This economic scenario spells trouble for political development within the three countries, once they are members. Very probably, only a small minority of the population would profit from the integration into the Common Market with its opening of borders. The vast majority would have to accept substantial disadvantages. Internal differences of income, as well as social and political tensions in these countries, are liable to increase.(11) In the not so distant past, tensions of this kind were contained by dictatorial regimes in all of the three countries. Obviously, this is not an acceptable solution either today or tomorrow. It is the very centerpiece of EC enlargement policy to assist in a democratic solution to these problems and to win democratic majorities for integration into the EC. It is doubtful, though, whether democratic majorities can be won on the medium term for a policy which implies, as has been shown above, pressures on wages and high unemployment, reduction of buying power and increasing disparities in income, destruction of small and medium industry, and accelerated concentration on industry and agriculture. On the other hand, there would be a small social minority which would be interested in a development of this kind, and which might be tempted into more or less covert forms of authoritarian regimes in order to guarantee it. After all, institutions as well as potential leaders and political supporters of such a course are still present in all three countries. The very forces that made democratization possible in these last few years, be it the articulate part of the labor class or a growing portion of the middle class and the capital owners,(12) would thus be pushed back, and their political mobilization obviated. The only alternative to a course of this kind might be leftist radicalization on the part of the majority of the population and the election of a leftist government which might then proceed to cut the new bonds to the EC and to try an autonomous or regionally-limited development model on the basis of stabilized or expanded mass buying power and/or reduced disparities of income.

POLITICAL PARTIES AND THE INTEGRATION PROCESS

Looking at the position of the political parties in the three countries today, one wonders about their obvious and forceful support for entry into the European Community, even though alternatives to EC membership seem to be out of sight. One important explanation seems to be that they definitely expect protection from potential authoritarian backlashes in their countries as a result of EC integration. The second one would be that they or their leaders underestimate the socio-political effects which EC accession may have. In regard to this second point, though, learning processes seem to be taking place and a certain note of alarm has been creeping into the more recent utterances of politicians when speculating about the degree of public support which EC accession and membership may enjoy in the future. Thus, the potentially destabilizing effects of integration in the socio-political arena must not be ignored. A closer look at the relations between political parties and economic conditions may help to clear up this point a bit further.

Today, almost all large parties in the three countries, including the leftist socialist parties of Spain and Portugal and the communist party of Spain, firmly support entry into the EC.(13) Of the important parties, only Greece's socialists (PASOK) and communists (respectively, 25 and 9.4 percent of the 1977 vote), and Portugal's communists (19 percent of the 1979 vote) are opposed up to now. For the others, their support may not simply be taken for granted in the future either. There seems to be a potential for change which may be analyzed in three points:

- the relatively high concentration of political opinion-making at the party-leadership level or in political elites in general;
- the relatively low degree of political mobilization within the wage-earning population up to now; and
- the contradictions inherent in the support which the parties give to EC entry.

Existing analyses on the first point seem to show that political-economic discussions at the membership level of the parties hardly exist.(14) The party leaderships have been conceded credibility by the masses so that their arguments for EC integration were not questioned. This may be explained by the past years of dictatorship or by the general socio-economic underdevelopment. But it is not to be expected that this state of affairs will continue and that the vast majority of the population will accept the discrepancies between the promises of the EC entry propaganda and the foreseeable disadvantages of entry itself without generating political dissatisfaction.

As for party membership and voters, their attitudes have as yet not been thoroughly researched. But there are good reasons to believe that party membership of all relevant parties, including the socialists and communists, is more or less dominated by the countries' professional, economic and intellectual elites, whereas the broad masses of the population, the small and medium farmers as well as the workers, are frequently underrepresented if represented at all.(15) This could change as well, bringing parties into closer touch with the material needs of the population. Finally, and most importantly, party support for entry into the EC is determined by very different and sometimes outright contradictory motives. Up till now, these contradictions have been kept in the background, but they may come to the fore and unfold after entry into the EC.

For the socialist and communist parties, except the Greek PASOK and the Portuguese and Greek communist parties or party-wings, integration into the EC seems to promise a stabilization of democratic rule and an improvement of social norms and industrial relations as well as a rise in the standard of living for workers. Conservative and Liberal parties, all of them staunch supporters of EC entry, want to head in a different direction. For them, entry into the Common Market promises on the one hand political support against the expansion of socialist and communist ideas in their countries. On the other hand, they hope that the opening of their national markets might lead to improved inter-national competitiveness of domestic firms. Improved competitiveness is conceived in the context of a European division of labor, in which the Mediterranean economies concentrate upon the medium, consumer-oriented, or semi-finished goods and technologies.(16)

This economic model is strongly export-oriented. Considering pre-sent developments, the international division of labor will probably function only at the cost of keeping down or even lowering earnings and rights of the working population in the Mediterranean countries. Ob-viously, this would run contrary to the expectations of the socialist and communist parties, and would reverse the trends in the recent period of democratization. In the course of time, the parties will hardly be able to keep aloof of these contradictions. It is impossible for EC member-ship to serve the ends of both sides at the same time. Consequently, one has to face the prospect that at least one of the two sides, probably the leftist forces, will be frustrated in their intentions, and hence may develop stronger resistance to EC membership, while favoring autono-mous development policies for the future.

SUGGESTIONS FOR A REVISED ENLARGEMENT POLICY OF THE THREE COUNTRIES AND THE EC INDUSTRIAL CENTER

Meanwhile, a broad debate has begun in the Federal Republic of Germany and at the EC level on possible counterstrategies which would guard against the risks inherent in full application of existing EC rules to the candidate countries. Suggestions have been made either to slow down the application process or change the structures and rules of the European Community itself(17) in a qualitative way. The common aim of these counterstrategies is, for the most part, a reduction of the disadvantages of EC membership mainly in the economic field, and an increase in the advantages resulting from the closer relationship with democratic and highly developed industrial states by consolidating their influence on democratic structures within Greece and the candidate countries and by possible support of the economic development. The demands flowing from this discussion aim at three levels: (1) the structures of the European Community, (2) the political-economic interests and structures of the old member countries, and (3) those of the three countries.

On the level of the Community, the role of the political institutions and the democratic process must be substantially expanded and deepened. The well-known democratic and political deficit of the Community has to be reduced. One step in this direction is the direct election of the European Parliament.(18)

Within the three countries, the socio-economic momentum generated by the opening of their markets must be blocked by effective measures of protection. There must be considerable efforts not only to create the capital funds necessary for future industrialization, but also to increase mass buying power and, thereby, the internal market for industrial products. This would probably have to take longer than the 10 year-adaptation period contemplated at present. The small and still dominant group of capital owners and the middle class within these countries and an economic policy based upon the "autonomous forces of the market" certainly do not seem to be a sufficient social and ideological bases for this strategy. Cooperation of trade unions and possibly of the communist parties seems unavoidable in the longer run. In addition, strong elements of a dirigism- and plan-oriented economic policy would have to be implemented. The second leg of this strategy would have to be massive capital transfers from the industrial centers of Western Europe, a kind of "Marshall Plan" for Southern Europe.(19)

For the old Community member states, this might require a reappraisal of possible communist or left-socialist participation in the prospective countries' governments. They may have to modify their basically negative attitudes.(20) The economic forces hoping to profit from the enlargement of the Western European market would have to be restricted and channeled in such a way as to allow for an optimal development effect in the new member states.

Is there a chance that these demands can be wholly or at least in part fulfilled? Most analyses agree that there is little chance that this will happen without serious economic, social, or political upheaval forcing decision makers in this direction.(21) Up to now, there seems to be no realistic perspective on how the potentially disruptive effects of integration of the Mediterranean countries can be neutralized (the existing inequalities in Western Europe leveled out) in time.

THE ROLE OF THE FEDERAL REPUBLIC OF GERMANY

It appears obvious that the Federal Republic of Germany would have to play an important role in any realignment of EC integration policies, considerig the sheer weight of West German industry in Western Europe and the momentum of this industry's economic-political interests in European economic policies. These interests are strongly reflected in West German attitudes toward EC enlargement as well. Due to its specialization in investment goods, West German industry stands to gain the most from liberalized economic exchanges with the prospective member countries. There is open and mounting pressure by industrial trade associations on the government to insist on open and unhindered access to the Mediterranean markets in the enlargement negotiations.(22)

In addition, trade associations are almost unanimous in their opposition to any dirigistic measures of industrial policy in the candidate countries; they have clearly spoken out against any undue subsidization of Southern European industrial development projects, such as might be financed out of the so-called "Marshall Plan for Southern Europe." Only recently, under the influence of the economic crisis which has not spared the West German internal and foreign markets, discussions have begun within West Germany and abroad, which might give cause to foresee a revision of the basic West Germany orientation toward exported growth and dependence on foreign markets. Reflections about Keynesian stimulation of the internal market by trade unions, leftist political groups, and independent researchers have implicitly pointed to strategies of stronger orientation toward the internal market of the Federal Republic and toward public and private services instead of industry.(23)

Certainly, perspectives of this kind would provoke serious problems. As Andrew Shonfield put it recently, "Is the West German 'bee,' structurally specialized on the production of 'honey,' viz industrial goods, especially investment goods, for the international market, at all able to produce 'milk,' like, for example, services?"(24) But, in spite of these justified doubts, thinking of this kind could indicate a path for economic policy which would lead away from West Germany's structural dependence on open access to stable export markets in Western Europe and elsewhere. Thus, it might point to a chance to revise the dominant West German position and to allow a more effective policy of improving the relative positions of the less developed community members (i.e., the new members-to-be).

However, looking closer at this debate, it quickly becomes evident that, up to now, no relevant grouping in West Germany would be prepared to jeopardize accustomed advantages of export orientation by really following up the above reflections to their logical conclusions.(25) The basic West German orientations have not changed.

If the validity of these arguments is accepted, then there is no escaping the conclusion that the Federal Republic might, on some not so distant day, on the basis of its dominant European position, and in defense of its well-established Western European political and economic interests, become the preceptor of a policy which runs counter to her declared economic and political aims in the Mediterranean EC countries. First, as far as the aim of stable economic expansion is concerned, the IMF rules laid down for Portugal – and clearly co-designed and supported by West German policymakers as the most important creditors – give a clear indication that, for them, the international solvency of Portugal as an importer has priority over the expansion of mass buying power and economic expansion on this basis.(26)

In addition to the EC-coordinated financial help for Portugal or for the other candidates, there has been notable West German material assistance. The above-mentioned so called "Marshall Plan" or "Solidarity Programme" for Southern Europe which was hatched out in the Social Democratic Parliamentary Group of the Federal Parliament and became publicly known in 1978, had run aground by year's end; party sources seem to agree that financial restraints were put forward against the program by the Chancellor and the Minister of Finances and that the acceleration of enlargement negotiations had tempted the government to draw the program into the negotiations themselves. An exact interpretation does not yet appear possible; but it seems as if the present silence must not necessarily spell the end of the Program. After all, it remained part of the Social Democrat Party platform on the direct elections to the European Parliament and will probably be invoked by party members and groupings.

The balance sheet of West German actions in the candidate countries, therefore, shows clear priority for effective measures of political stabilization on a moderate, middle-leftist line. At the levels of transnational party and union activities, these are carried out by all the relevant political forces of the Federal Republic, but with clear preponderance of the Social Democrats. The West German presence in this area far outweighs that of other Western European countries, and it is the Germans who exert the most important outside influence in party and union building on the Iberian peninsula.

Aside from infrequent and isolated murmurings of discontent about this, there seem to be no negative effects so far – in a 1978 political opinion poll in Portugal,(27) West Germany figured as that foreign country which most Portuguese considered as their foreign "model country," very closely followed by Sweden. But difficulties are clearly ahead, especially in Portugal and Greece as the two less developed countries. Both of them combine a need for financial resources and industrialization as well as infrastructural programs with a grave lack of qualified planning staffs and so called "absorptive capacity" for capital inflows. So, even if there were enough funds to satisfy the capital hunger of these countries, the need for foreign engagement in Greece and Portugal would remain, especially for purposes of creating the necessary development programs inside these countries via foreign expertise. Here again, transnational strategies at the party level are tried by the West German Social Democrats, for example, by financing and prestructuring an institute for socio-economic planning and research for the Socialist Party of Portugal. This represents a risky course in the long run, which ought to be changed to a multilateral one with the EC as the guiding spirit, so as not to put West Germany into the position of appearing to be mingling into the internal affairs of the three countries in neo-imperialist fashion.

Secondly, as to the political aims, West Germany, in the course of this policy, risks becoming an ally of those very forces within the three Mediterranean countries which were earlier identified as potential supporters of a possible backlash to authoritarian regimes. The afore-mentioned public opinion poll in Portugal might be a hint in this direction: the majority opting for West Germany as a "model" belonged to the upper class with an overproportionate percentage of CDS voters among them.(28)

THE EXTERNAL PERSPECTIVE

Will enlargement advance the chances for common interest formulation and of a liberal platform vis a vis the outside world? Relations with third countries, especially in the developing world, are the second field in which EC enlargement will pose serious dilemmas for the Community. As with the prospective problems of EC internal developments under the stress of enlargement, the field of external relations will also fall under two headings: (1) the relations between the EC and third countries, especially in the Third World, since mainly Third World countries create problems by industrial competition for the candidates; and (2) the specific dilemmas of West Germany in this context.

Preferential external economic and political relations of the Community exist or are planned with countries of the southern and eastern Mediterranean, and with the ACP countries. They have, in the recent past, become pivotal points of the EC's external politics, be it in the North-South Dialogue or the energy question.(29) Very probably, enlargement will pose a serious danger to the continuation of these EC policies because the Mediterranean countries, themselves members of the developing countries' group, compete on EC markets with the same specific product range offered by newly industrializing countries in the South. Enlargement forces the EC into a clear differentiation in the kind of access to EC markets which it grants to developing countries: through membership or by preferential arrangements. As demand for specific products stagnates within the EC and may well continue to stagnate in the foreseeable future, any such decision would probably be made at the expense of one of the two parties' future access. For example, a solution favoring the prospective members' rights to free access to EC markets, and perhaps even granting them additional protection against outside competition, would threaten the position of external competitors with traditional preferential access. This could be the case even if they compete with lower labor costs and prices, thus keeping them at their present market shares or even reducing them. Present trends point to relative increases in the candidates' share of EC

trade compared with the nonoil-producing developing countries. Whereas the share of these latter countries in EC exports shrank from 22.4 to
19.4 percent between 1970 and 1976, and their share of imports
decreased from 21.4 to 17.6 percent,(30) the Mediterranean's share in
EC exports and imports remained at approximately 10 percent and 5
percent respectively.(31)

Secondly, Greece, Spain and Portugal compete with other developing
countries for development aid funds from the Community countries.
There have been agreements on growing preferential EC capital aid for
non-EC countries in the last decade, mainly for the already mentioned
groups of states. Here again the demands of the prospective members
might only be supported at the expense of these other nascent aid
programs, the more so because funds of the EC states for internal and
external structural aid are liable to stagnate, and new demands cannot
be satisfied by increment. Moreover, it is precisely these aids which
frequently serve the construction of those industries whose export
orientation sharpens competition on the overflowing markets of Western Europe.

Thus, comparable to internal EC problems, dilemmas will crop up
from external EC relations out of the enlargement as well, if enlargement is not coupled with new policies. Status quo policies in external
EC relations, especially toward the South, would mean a serious
restriction to full implementation of the internal aims of enlargement
and vice versa.

WEST GERMANY'S ECONOMIC IMPACT

The compromise which has to be found between the internal and the
external priorities of aiding and subsidizing the candidates' full integration into the European Community on the one hand, and of preserving
preferential, or at least liberal, exchange relations between the EC and
industrializing countries on the other, will depend very much on the
balance between the regionally-oriented protectionist forces and the
world market-oriented liberalist forces in the EC itself.

Weighing West Germany's position in this matter will serve to put
into focus the current balance of these forces and their possible effects
on external versus internal priorities. As table 3.1 shows, among the
Community countries, West Germany conducts the most important
overall import-export trade with the three countries. Its total exports
to each of them surpass those of any EC competitor by a clear margin,
and this margin is even larger when only trade in finished and semifinished goods is considered. West Germany's total imports from all
candidate countries were larger by about 35 percent than those of the
next biggest importer, France, even though, in trade with Spain and
Portugal, as evidenced in table 3.1, the French and British were the
bigger buyers. This meant also that the French and British respectively
accepted higher shares of the manufactured goods exports of Spain and
Portugal.

Table 3.1. Trade of Greece, Spain, and Portugal with West Germany
Compared with Their Trade with the Next Biggest EC Trading
Partner in 1975 [in percent of imports and exports of
manufactured goods (SITC 5-9) and of total trade].

Country		Imports from			Exports to		
		West Germany	Competitor		West Germany	Competitor	
Spain	total	10.4	France:	8.4	10.7	France:	13.7
	manuf.	20.6		14.2	9.7		13.1
Portugal	total	11.4	Great	8.7	10.2	Great	21.2
	manuf.	19.7	Britain:	14.3	11.1	Britain:	23.0
Greece	total	15.8	Italy:	8.2	21.1	Italy:	8.3
	manuf.	27.0		12.8	21.0	France:	9.1

Source: Computed from H. Hasenpflug and B. Kohler, eds., Die
Süderweiterung der Europäischen Gemeinschaft (Hamburg:
Verlag Weltarchiv, 1977), tables A-1 – A-12.

West German trade with the three brings high surpluses to its own
economy and high deficits for the latter. With a West German share of
imports of the three from the EC of 32.8 percent in 1971 (31.8 percent
in 1975), and of their exports to the EC of 28.4 percent in 1971 (29.2
percent in 1975), West Germany's share of the total EC-trade deficit of
Greece, Spain, and Portugal amounted to 36.3 percent in 1971 (35
percent in 1975). There are, though, surpluses from tourism and foreign
labor in these countries which neutralize or outweigh the trade deficits,
as in Spain with approximately 2.4 billion DM in 1978. (Figures
computed from current trade statistics.)

Whereas the economies of the three have deficits in trade with all
of the EC countries with very few exceptions (1971-1975 having been
analyzed), the deficits versus West Germany are by far the highest.

Taking trade in one of the typical products or industrialized
countries as an example, the same phenomenon can be shown. In
textiles and garments the Community countries substantially increased
their imports from the three between 1970 and 1974. Their share of
exports from these countries grew from 49.4 to 60.5 percent (Spain),
from 42.6 to 51.4 percent (Portugal) and from 95.4 to 96.2 percent
(Greece). Only West Germany's share of these exports decreased in the
same period. By contrast, West Germany's share of textile and garment
exports from other developing countries outside the EC increased. In
fact, they increased slightly quicker than the respective share for all
EC members.(32) This could create the impression that trade with the
candidates played a lesser role in the foreign trade of the Federal
Republic than in the foreign trade of other EC member states. This
was not the case. On the contrary, the share of exports from the three
was clearly higher in West German imports than in the imports of the

whole EC (these respective shares were 2.4 percent vis a vis 2.07 percent in 1975).(33)

In a second step, West Germany trade with extra-EC developing countries must be compared to the trade with Greece, Spain and Portugal. Here it is important to exclude oil and other raw materials since they are irrelevant to the trading position of these countries, as well as in regard to competition between intra- and extra-EC developing countries. Intermediate and finished goods, standardized and on medium levels of technology, are the main foreseeable areas of competition. Looking at imports from developing countries in 1978, one finds that nonoil imports represented a much larger part of West German imports than was the case for the other EC member states: intermediate and finished goods made up 21 percent in West Germany versus 9 percent in France and Italy, 10 percent in the Netherlands, 19 percent in Great Britain, and 22 percent in Belgium in 1976.(34) These imports to West Germany, having grown by 80.7 percent between 1973 and 1976, by far outdistanced the increase in comparable imports of all other EC countries which rose by only 50.5 percent in the same period. As a consequence, West Germany accounted for 32 percent of these EC imports in 1976, compared to 27 percent three years earlier. [Oil imports from developing countries accounted for 56.2 percent of imports to Common Market countries in general, but only for 39.9 percent of imports to West Germany.(35)] The result of these trends in the past was a reduction in West German trade surpluses in this product range vis a vis the nonoil-producing countries and, since 1976, a West German deficit of 3.3 billion deutsch marks.(36)

Taking a closer look at a number of manufactured products in international trade in 1975 will illustrate these tendencies in more detail. These products are among the most important export goods of the candidate countries.(37) A first impression may be gained by comparing the amount the industrial centers of the EC imported from Greece, Spain and Portugal with the amount they imported from their two most important Third World supplier countries in the same time period, placing the imports from the three at the 100 mark and expressing the imports from the two Third World countries in proportion to it.(38)

The most important point to note is that the economy of France, as second largest importer of the Community, has consistently been oriented to high imports from Greece, Spain and Portugal. The four other principal trading powers in the Community — West Germany, Great Britain, Italy, and the Netherlands — all have much more important suppliers outside Western Europe. The figures of Table 3.2 gain added significance when one considers that Great Britain's share of finished and semifinished imports from the Third World countries has been dropping, and that it is still in the process of detaching itself from its Commonwealth affiliations, while increasing its exchanges with Western Europe. Italy's share of Third World imports (excluding oil) is diminutive as the table shows.

Table 3.2. Comparison of Imports

Subject	West Germany	France	United Kingdom	Italy	Nether- lands
(1) Index of Third World imports versus candidate-imports in 1975*					

SITC No.**	Goods					
599	Chemicals	8	14	6	6	7
651	Threads, yarns	87	28	35	173	47
653	Noncotton textiles	101	19	113	459	46
678	Steeltubes, etc.	36	3	13	793	25
719	Nonelectric machinery	74	20	26	72	14
729	Electric machinery	99	79	161	161	34
732	Road vehicles	124	7	11	28	28
841	Garments, nonfur	403	98	667	143	375
851	Shoes	39	29	79	-	22

Subject	West Germany	France	United Kingdom	Italy	Nether- lands
(2) Imports of finished and semi-finished manufactured goods from developing countries in billion DM, 1976	9.4	4.0	7.1	2.8	2.3
(3) Imports of finished and semi-finished manufactured goods from Greece, Spain and Portugal in billion DM, 1975	2.7	2.5	1.5	0.6	0.6
(4) Proportion of these imports from Greece, Spain, and Portugal in total imports of finished and semifinished goods, 1975, in percent	2.6	3.4	2.2	1.6	2.4

* Candidate countries imports = 100
** Standard International Trade Classification

Sources: United Nations Yearbook of International Trade Statistics 1976, New York, 1977 (author's computation from 1976 figures); Presse-und Informationsamt der Bunderegierung, Aktuelle Beitrage zur Wirtschaftspolitik, no. 92 (1977); H. Hasenpflug and B. Kohler, eds., Die Suderweiterung der Europaischen Gemeinschaft. (Hamburg: Verlag Weltarchiv, 1977).

Finally, it can be shown in textiles and garments, but probably in other fields as well, that developing countries have been taking away substantial market shares from EC countries in West Germany. Thus, West Germany's orientation toward low-priced imports from the Third World has been, in the last decade, at the expense of other EC members.(39)

The reasons for these differences seem to lie in the structural differences between West Germany and the other big EC member states. West Germany's economy is more highly competitive as well as more flexible. Therefore, it is easier for it to export and compete on a global scale in most modern industrial fields than it is for other West European competitors. Because of this, the internal economic effects are not as great and not as negative, and the socio-political effects of global trade not as weighty and as dangerous as for the other big EC countries. Moreover, trade unions have been more willing than elsewhere to put up with a high measure of low-cost, Third World imports in limited sectors. Finally, stability and competitiveness of West German prices rest to no small degree on lowest-cost imports.

In sum, West Germany seems to be the Western European country with the strongest orientation — now and in the future — toward the lowest-cost international suppliers of finished and semifinished goods. Its economic structure and perceived advantage work in this direction, while putting the three countries at a disadvantage. For the other big EC partners, the developing countries' share in imports constitutes a bigger load — in balance of payment terms and in regard to socio-political problems. In France, for instance, a clear limitation of extra-European exchanges in this field has been the answer, whereas exchanges with the candidates, especially Spain, with their relatively higher costs and less dangerous competitive positions, have been reinforced.

The problem of harmonizing these different interests between the different EC member states appears at least as big as the problem of conflicts between the European Community and the Third World countries. The trends seem to point to an enlargement constellation in which some EC countries, together with the three, would pressure actively for increasing protectionism; and West Germany would figure as the leader of a smaller coalition of EC states opposing this kind of strategy.

There is no easy and clear-cut way out of this dilemma of conflicting interests. In the end, though, it seems probable that a factual compromise will be found on the side of more regionalist orientation and protectionism for Western Europe, even though lip service will be paid to the principles of liberalism by the enlarged Community. This tendency to consolidate EC protectionism vis a vis the outside world after enlargement might well entail the risk of weakening its internal structure. Its central elements, the customs union and a common foreign trade policy, could, in the end, be essentially endangered because West Germany capital will not accept a continuing and deepening integration on terms where it would have to accept a reduction of its worldwide economic commitments.

NOTES

(1) There is no room here to go into the details of this development. For figures and interpretation, see for example, Michael Kreile, "West Germany: The Dynamics of Expansion," International Organization 31, no. 4 (Autumn 1977). More detailed work has been done in the last two years on the subject by a project group at the University of Constance (Christian Deubner, Gerd Junne, Udo Rehfeldt, Friedrich Schlupp) under the responsibility of Professor Gilbert Ziebura in a project called "Internationalisierungsprozess, Staatsintervention und gesellschaftliche Entwicklung in Westeuropa am Beispiel Frankreichs und der Bundesrepublik Deutschland." Results were published in Christian Deubner, Udo Rehfeldt, Friedrich Schlupp, "Deutsch-franzosische Wirtschaftsbeziehungen im Rahmen der weltwirtschaftlichen Arbeitsteilung, Interdependenz, Divergenz oder strukturelle Dominanz?" in Deutschland, Frankreich, Europa, edited by Robert Picht (Muchen/Zurich: R. Piper and Co., 1978). For an American interpretation cf. Fred Bergsten, "The United States and Germany: The Imperative of Economic Bigemony," in Toward a New International Economic Order, edited by F. Bergsten. (Lexington, Mass.: Lexington Books, 1975); for a French interpretation see G.R.E.S.I. (Groupement de Reflexion sur les Strategies Industrielles du Ministere de l'Industrie et de la Recherche), La Division Internationale du Travail, 2 Vols., Paris: 1976.

(2) Per capita gross domestic product at market prices in 1978 of the EC candidate countries, and the U.S. are as follows: (in thousand US dollars) Denmark 9,0; Germany, F.R. 8,4; Belgium 8,1; Netherlands 7,7; France 7,2; UK 4,4; Italy 3,5; Ireland 2,9; Spain 3,1; Greece 2,8; Portugal 1,7 (OECD Observer, March 1979); see also Klaus Esser, Guido Ashoff, Tilo Becker-Fahe, Cordula Gaschuetz, Portugal, Industrie und Industriepolitik vor dem Beitritt zur Europaischen Gemeinschaft. Deutsches Institut fur Entwicklungspolitik (German Development Institute), Berlin 1977; EC-Commission, Ubergangszeit und institutionelle Fragen der Erweiterung (1978) Brussels 1978, p. 149.

(3) Angela St. Yergin, "West Germany's Südpolitik," Orbis 23, no. 1 (Spring 1979): 51-72.

(4) See among others, Hajo Hasenpflug, "Industrie-und agrarpolitische Probleme der Beitrittskandidaten. Ein Uberblick," in Die Suderweiterung der Europaischen Gemeinschaft, edited by H. Hasenpflug and B. Kohler, Hamburg: 1977; also the written statement for the public hearing before the Bundestag by H. Hasenpflug, Welt Archiv Verlag, pp. 760-78 (Hasenpflug represents the influential HWWA Research Institute for World Economics); Klaus Esser (Deutsches Institut fur Entwicklungspolitik) written statement and oral testimony, Teil and oral testimony, Teil II, pp. 998-1,016 and Teil I (Klaus-Werner Schatz represents the influential Kiel Institute of World Economics), Olav Sievert, written statement and oral testimony, Teil II, pp. 1,019-1,027

and Teil I (Sievert was a member of the Economic Experts' Council for Assessment of the Economic Situation, officially counseling the Federal Government).

(5) See for a general assessment, for instance, the statement of O. Sievert, Ibid. There is no great hope that emigration to the EC industrial centers will immediately become liberalized under the treaties of accession to the Community, thus easing at least the pressures of unemployment. There seems to be agreement among the old member governments not to liberalize labor migration for the newcomers – trade unions have vociferously argued against this possibility – and the economic crisis in Europe would probably reduce the attractiveness of the center for potential immigrants from the candidates. For Greece, see Wilhelm Hummen, Griechenland und die Europäische Gemeinschaft. Probleme und Lösungsansätze im Bereich der Industrie (Berlin: Deutsches Institut Fur Entwickelungs politik, 1977), pp. 101 ff; P. Kravaritou-Manitakis, "Problèmes sociaux et adhésion," in Colloques Européens: La Grèce et la Communauté, Problèmes poses par l'adhesion (Bruxelles: Editions de l'Universite de Bruxelles, 1978), pp. 114 ff; for Spain see Stefan Musto, Spanien und die Europäische Gemeinschaft (Bonn: Europa Union Verlag, 1977), pp. 146 ff; for Portugal see Esser, Portugal.

(6) See for Portugal, Luis Salgado de Matos, Investimentos estrangeiros em Portugal, 3rd ed. (Lisboa: 1973) (Seara Nova), Esser, Portugal, pp. 177 ff; Luigino Scricciolo, "Spain and Portugal on the Threshold of the EEC," Lo Spettatore Internazionale 12, no. 3 (1977): 215-38; for Spain see J. Munoz, S. Roldan, and A. Serrano, La Internacionalizacion del Capital en Expana (Madrid: 1978) (Cuadernos para el Dialogo), concerning MNCs in Spanish exports see pp., 224 ff; M.V. Montalba, La Penetracion Americana en Espana (Madrid: 1974); Musto, Spanien, pp. 152 ff.; for Greece see Karl-H. Buck, Griechenland und die Europäische Gemeinschaft (Bonn: Europa Union Verlag, 1978), pp. 159 ff.; D.J. Chalikias, "Foreign Capital in the Development of Greece," in Colloques Européens, pp. 105-12.

(7) The West German chambers of commerce summed up the incentives for direct investment in the Mediterranean candidate countries for a recent (1978) inquiry by their national association, the DIHT (Deutscher Industrie und Handelstag). Leading the list were: low wages and social costs; low emission control and costs; protectionist import tariffs; lower raw materials prices; better penetration of the internal markets; and better accessibility of certain export markets, perhaps in former colonies). All of these incentives will certainly deteriorate after accession to EC.

(8) For the conditions and motivations of MNCs in Western Europe, see for instance, Lawrence Franko, The European Multinationals (London: Harper & Row, 1976).

(9) I.L.O. (International Labour Organisation), Yearbook of Labour Statistics, Geneva 1977 gives figures for "hourly earnings in manufacturing, all industries," expressed in percent of West German earnings of candidate countries changed from 1970-1975: Spain from 35% to 46%; Portugal from 23% to 32%; and Greece from 32% to 27%. (Calculations from I.L.O. figures are the author's.)

(10) Concerning the duration of an adaptive period suggested by the EC Commission, see EC Commission, Ubergangszeit. The durability of interregional differences in the Community was documented in EC Commission, Erster Jahresbericht uber die Tatigkeit des Europaischen Fonds fur Regional Entwicklung im Jahre 1975 (Brussels 1976), p. 3.

(11) See note 5 above.

(12) Obviously, one of the most crucial and intriguing problems in this context is the question of the potential for a new type of authoritarianism. The potential supporters of new authoritarian regimes cannot be seen in direct continuity and identity with the old dictatorships in Portugal and Spain. To ignore this would imply a complete misunderstanding of the problems which led to the overthrow of the old regimes and the social groups which supported this overthrow. The specific mechanisms of the old Iberian dictatorships were designed to serve the interests of those fractions of agricultural, industrial, and financial capital that would or could not adapt to the conditions of modern internationalized capitalist production and competition and that wanted to conserve the structures of power and exchange which would protect them therefrom. Thus, there were growing parts of the bourgeoisie in the modern sector and the intellectual professions which worked against the old regimes, even if the unrest of the labor class made the latter appear as the most visible opponent. One of the open questions up to now has been which measure of change in the regime would suffice to satisfy the aspirations of these dissident bourgeois groups, and what kinds of modernized authoritarianism they might underwrite if the pressures of crisis and a mobilized labor class made the attainment of their hopes under a liberalized pluralist regime impossible. As for Greece, the picture is slightly different because here open dictatorship was introduced only in 1967, with the explicit aim of consolidating conditions for internationalized, modern sectors of industry. See Nicos Poulantzas, Die Krise der Diktaturen: Portugal, Griechenland und Spanien (Frankfurt: Sur Kamp Verlag, 1977); Lothar Maier, Spaniens Weg zur Demokratie (Meisenheim am Glan, Anton Hain, 1977); Robin Blackburn, "The Test in Portugal," in New Left Review, No. 89 (1975).

(13) See Musto, Spanien, p. 87; Buck, Griechenland, pp. 93 ff; Luis E. Insula's written statement for and oral testimony at the public hearing of the Deutscher Bundestag, Teil II, pp. 921-56 and Teil I, p. 254; written statement and oral testimony of Carlos Beaumont, Ibid., Teil II, p. 921-56 and Teil I, p. 256.

(14) See for example Antonio Lopez-Pina, "Die politischen Parteien und die Errichtung der Demokratie in Spanien," in Berichte zur Entwicklung in Spanien, Portugal und Lateinamerika, No. 11 (May/June 1977), pp. 17-35; Werner Herzog, chapters on Portugal and Spain in Die politischen Parteien in Westeuropa, edited by J. Raschke (Reinbek: Rowohit 1978), pp. 437 ff.; E.M. Leon, "The Spanish Communist Party," in Lo Spettatore Internationale 13, no. 3 (1978): 199-226; Ilias Katsoulis, chapter on Greece, in Raschke, Die politischen Parteien, pp. 221-227.

(15) For the Spanish Communists, see Leon, "The Spanish Communist Party": "due to the paucity of reliable data, it is impossible to present a detailed analysis of PCE member strength. . .little is known about the social composition as no general breakdown has yet been released by the PCE" (p. 199; see also pp. 200 ff). For the Greek parties see Katsoulis, Griechenland: "the Greek party system of today is in its formative phase. . .only weakly anchored in its constituency" (p. 222, translation is the author's).

(16) For Greece, very explicitly G. Spentsas, "Le développement industriel en Grece dans la perspective de l'adhesion," in Colloques Européens, pp. 105-12; Buck, Griechenland, pp. 94 ff.

(17) See for example EC Commission, Ubergangszeit; Deutscher Budestag, Teil I and II.

(18) For the hopes and speculations connected with direct elections to the European Parliament, see the speech of EC Commission President Roy Jenkins to the Cercle de l'Opinion in Paris on October 6th, 1978, documented in Europa-Archiv 33, no. 24 (1978).

(19) For instance, a temporarily muted project with this name is being discussed within the Social Democratic Party in West Germany and is expected to be realized in bilateral or multilateral form. Obviously, this transfer would have had functions of expanding and stabilizing export-markets for West German industry, and it is an open question which end it would serve better: this one or that of developing the competitiveness of the candidates' economies. See Karsten Voigt, "Solidaritätsprogramm für Südeuropa," in Die Neue Gesellschaft 25, no. 4 (1978): 321-23; Sozialdemokratische Partei Deutschlands (SPD), Programm der SPD für die erste europäische Direktwahl, Bonn 1978.

(20) This attitude has in the past been documented on many occasions; for example in Rolf Stender, Reaktionen und Einflussnahme der SPD auf die Entwicklung in Portugal vom April 1974 bis zum April 1976. Schriftliche Hausarbeit zur Diplomprufung im Herbst, Free University of Berlin, Dpt. of Pol. Sci., Mimeo 1977 (1978), especially pp. 33 and 54 ff.

(21) See among others, written statement and oral testimony of Ralf Dahrendorf at the public hearing of the Deutscher Bundestag, Teil II,

pp. 748-59 and Teil I, p. 752; written statement of Sievert, Teil II, p. 1021.

(22) Deutsches Institut für Wirtschaftsforschung (DIW), "Ausfuhrinduzierte Beschäftigung," in DIW-Wochenbericht, 1978, no. 42 (1978): 400 ff; mainly Volker Hauff and Fritz Scharpf, Modernisierung der Volkswirtschaft (Frankfurt/M.: Europäische Verlagsanstalk 1975; Christian Deubner, "Internationalisierung als Problem alternativer Wirtschaftspolitik," in Leviathan, 1979, no. 1 (1979). Note the clear preferences declared by the Federation of German Industry (Bundesverband der Deutschen Industrie [BDI]) in its written statement for and oral testimony at the public hearing of the Deutscher Bundestag, Teil II, pp. 840-54 and Teil I. The same is true of the Federation's member associations, as internal documents show. See the written statement of the Deutscher Industrie und Handelstag (DIHT), Ibid., Teil II, pp. 855-70 for the German Diet of Chambers of Commerce's position.

(23) See, for example, Deutscher Gewerkschaftsbund (DGB), Vorschlage zur Wiederherstellung der Vollbeschäftigung (Dusseldorf 1977); Deutsches Institut für Wirtschaftsforschung, "Eine mittelfristige Strategie zur Wiedergewinnung der Vollbeschäftigung," in DIW - Wochenbericht 1978, no. 15 (1978); Memorandum, Alternativen der Wirtschaftspolitik, Cologne: Bundverlag 1978; Wilhelm Hankel, "Focal Points and Perspectives of German Economic, Financial and Monetary Policies of the 80s." Paper presented at the Bologna Center Conference: The Economic Political Role of the Federal Republic of Germany in the European Community, at the Johns Hopkins University Bologna Center (October 5-7, 1978).

(24) A. Shonfield made these remarks in discussions at the recent Bologna Center Conference, ibid.

(25) See Deubner, Internationalisierung.

(26) See, for instance, the account of the IMF-negotiations in Portugal, in The Financial Times, (March 30, 1978), p. 2. Meanwhile, there have already been clear effects of the deflationary austerity recipes of the Fund. Unemployment is mounting and real incomes are sinking in Portugal.

(27) Mario Bachalhau, Os Portugueses e a Politica Quatro Anos depois de 25 de Abril, Lisbon 1978 (Ed. Meseta), p. 131.

(28) Ibid.

(29) For a general and well documented discussion of these questions see EC Commission, Dossier sur l'interdependence Europe-Tiers Monde. Document du Travail, Direction Generale de l'Information, Division Development (481/X/78), Brussels, 1978.

(30) The EC-associated ACP countries, with 26 percent of their exports to the EC being oil, barely held their own with approximately 6.5 percent of exports and imports of the EC.

(31) "The EEC-Third World Trade Picture 1970-1976," in The Courier, 1977, no. 45 (1977), 31-38.

(32) Deutsches Institut für Wirtschaftsforschung (DIW), "Textilimporte der Bundesrepublik Deutschland im Rahmen der EG-Politik," in DIW-Wochenberichte 1977, no. 38 (1977).

(33) See Hasenpflug and Kohler, Die Suderweiterung, table A-20.

(34) Presse-und Informationsamt der Bundesregierung, Aktuelle Beiträge zur Wirtschafts-und Finanzpolitik, No. 92 (1977).

(35) Eurostat, Beilage zu Monatsbulletin der Aussenhandelsstatistik, 1979 (for January-September 1978; calculations by author).

(36) See Presse-und Informationsamt der Bundesregierung, Aktuelle Beiträge.

(37) See Musto, Spanien; Esser, Portugal; Buck, Griechenland.

(38) UN Yearbook of International Trade Statistics 1976 (New York 1977).

(39) For textiles and apparel see DIW, Textilimporte: 1970-1976 the EC share of imports shrank from about 70 percent to about 48 percent.

4 Lomé II: The Evolution of the Relations Between the European Community and the ACP Countries

Michael B. Dolan

Four years after the signing of the Lomé Convention, the European Community and the ACP states joined in negotiations for the successor to Lomé. Perhaps predictably, the EC pushed for an agreement closely modeled after Lomé, advocating only incremental changes, while the ACP negotiators called for much more radical changes. Symbolic of their differences, there was even disagreement over the name for the new convention. The EC, in keeping with its desire for incremental change, refers to the negotiations as "Lomé II," while the anglophone ACP states, in demanding more radical change, wanted the signing of the convention held in a nonfrancophone country, and Khartoum and Nairobi were volunteered. In addition to the tensions caused by these interbloc differences, there were also important intrabloc differences. In this study we examine these various bargaining positions, and the conditions that engendered them. Finally, future EC-ACP relations are discussed in reference to the rest of the developing world.

The Lomé Convention was intended to link Western Europe and Africa more closely together, or at least to shore up a weakening relationship. The ACP states did not view closer links with Europe as the final goal, but as a means to advance their economic development. In the attempt to understand the respective bargaining positions in the negotiations for the new convention, it is important to know the effects of the Lomé Convention on economic relations between Europe and Africa from the point of view of both sides. The mechanisms of linkage in the Lomé Convention were aid, trade, and investment; but the

*Part of the research for this chapter was funded by the Social Sciences and Humanities Research Council of Canada. The author also wishes to acknowledge the help of Hans Van Beek, Christine Desloges, Richard Couturier and Dan Mayhew in the compilation of the trade data, and the School of International Affairs at Carleton for providing these research assistants.

primary concern was with the fostering of trade through the reduction of barriers.(1) Before turning to the bargaining positions, then, let us first examine the trade relationship of the last four and a half years for which data are available.

EC/ACP TRADE ANALYSIS: 1974 TO 1978

The Lomé Convention reduced trade barriers in several ways. The Yaoundé Conventions eliminated tariff and quota barriers on industrial goods between the EC and the 17 African associates; but the Lomé Convention extended these to the 46 (now 57) African, Caribbean, and Pacific signatories. The Lomé Convention also eliminated almost all of the tariff and quota barriers on agricultural products. At the same time, the Lomé Convention reduced the reciprocal preferences given to European exports in the Yaoundé Conventions to that of most-favored-nation treatment. Thus, if all other factors are held constant, we should expect an increase in ACP exports to the EC, and a decrease in EC exports to the ACP countries. Of course, since we cannot control for the other determinants of trade, bear in mind that we cannot directly test the impact of the Lomé Convention. If a decrease in trade occurred over the post-1975 period, it could be argued, probably correctly, that the decrease would have been even greater if the Lome Convention did not exist. But the relevant quesiton is whether the ACP's trade situation is worse in an absolute sense, either in comparison with the pre-Lomé period or across the post-Lomé period, or worse relative to the comparable situation of the rest of the developing world. Regardless of the merits of the Lomé Convention, if the ACP's trade situation has deteriorated, then this is an argument for more radical change in the new convention. We address this question through an examination of quarterly trade data from 1974 through 1978, which are presented in figures 4.1-4.7. The trade provisions of the Lomé Convention, signed in February 1975, became effective in July 1975. Therefore, the analysis includes six pre-Lomé quarters and ten (and in some cases twelve) post-Lomé quarters.

The value of ACP exports and the exports of the rest of the developing world(2) to the EC are presented in fig. 4.1.(3) The ACP figures show that in 1977 the value of exports finally surpassed the pre-Lomé 1974, but since these are current values, the real total value of ACP exports was lower than it was before the Lomé Convention. There was an upward trend until the middle of 1977 but a downward trend since then. In contrast, the exports of the rest of the developing world to the EC are growing more rapidly, although the recession in Europe has also affected these exports since 1977. A more direct comparison between the two is made in fig. 4.2 where the ACP exports are graphed as a percentage of the total exports of the developing world to the EC. From a pre-Lomé average of around 17 percent, the percentage dropped to a low of around 14 percent in 1976 and then increased back up to about the same level as in 1974. After the middle of 1977, the ACP's

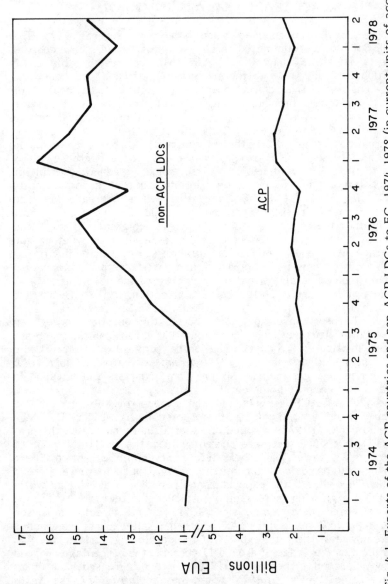

Fig. 4.1. Exports of the ACP countries and non-ACP LDCs to EC, 1974-1978 (in current units of account)

Source: Supplement to the Monthly External Trade Bulletin, various issues.

56

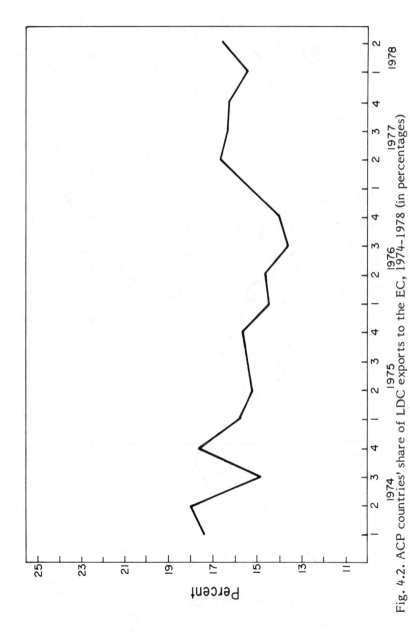

Fig. 4.2. ACP countries' share of LDC exports to the EC, 1974–1978 (in percentages)

Source: Supplement to the Monthly External Trade Bulletin, various issues.

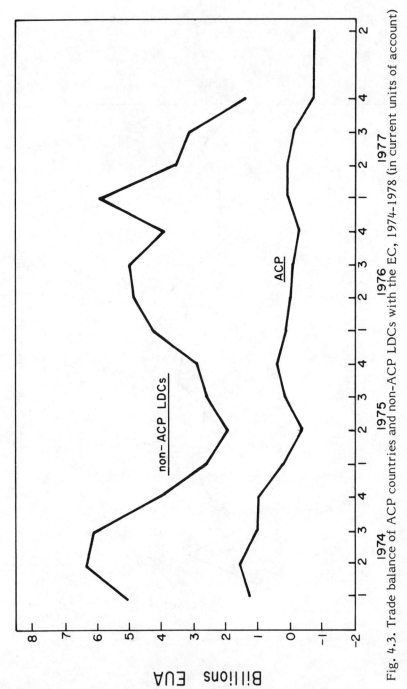

Fig. 4.3. Trade balance of ACP countries and non-ACP LDCs with the EC, 1974–1978 (in current units of account)

Source: Supplement to the Monthly External Trade Bulletin, various issues.

58

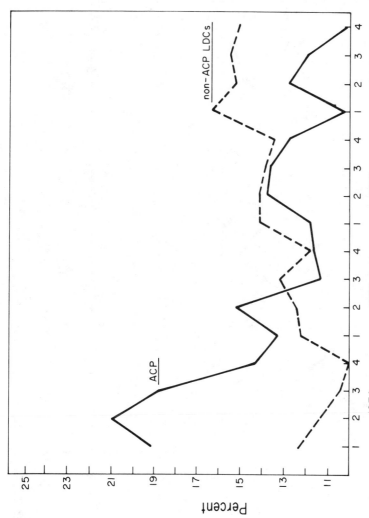

Fig. 4.4. Manufactured product exports as percentage of total exports of the ACP countries and non-ACP LDCs to the EC, 1974-1977.

Source: Supplement to the Monthly External Trade Bulletin, various issues.

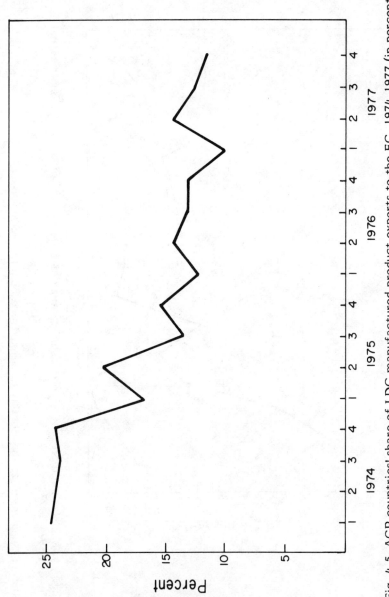

Fig. 4.5. ACP countries' share of LDC manufactured product exports to the EC, 1974–1977 (in percentages)

Source: Supplement to the Monthly External Trade Bulletin, various issues.

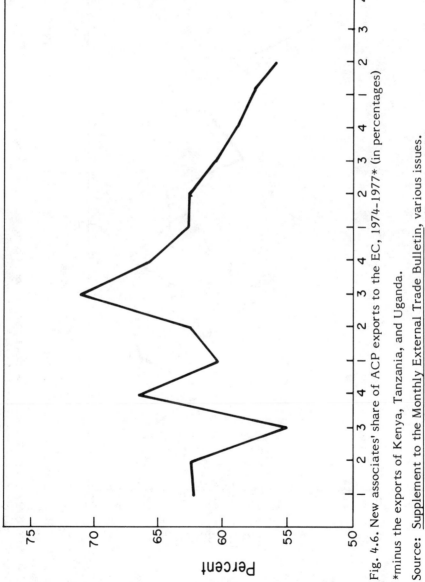

Fig. 4.6. New associates' share of ACP exports to the EC, 1974-1977* (in percentages)

*minus the exports of Kenya, Tanzania, and Uganda.

Source: Supplement to the Monthly External Trade Bulletin, various issues.

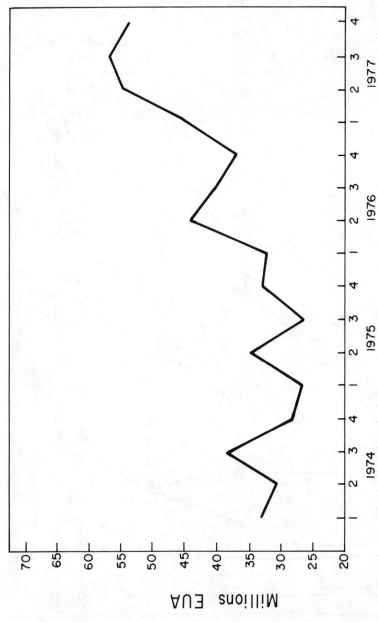

Fig. 4.7. Manufacturing product exports of seven leading ACP countries to the EC, 1974-1977* (in current units of account)

*Nigeria, Ivory Coast, Mauritius, Madagascar, Gabon, Cameroon, and Congo.
Source: Supplement to the Monthly External Trade Bulletin, various issues.

share of Third World exports again decreased to about 16.5 percent. The ACP's relative decline is partly a result of having only one major oil exporter in the ACP group, but even ACP exports in non-fuel products as a percent of Third World non-fuel exports to the EC decreased from 27.1 percent in 1974 to 24.3 percent in 1976. In sum, the data from figs. 4.1 and 4.2 do not allow optimistic conclusions; the real value of ACP exports to the EC has decreased, although the ACP states were almost holding their own vis a vis their Third World competition, at least in 1977.

The trade balance between the ACP and the EC blocs is presented in fig. 4.3. From a pre-Lomé average quarterly surplus of about 1.3 billion EUA, the ACP trade surplus over the 1975 to 1977 period was just above the balance point. A trade deficit was experienced from the last quarter of 1977 through the first half of 1978 (an average deficit of about 350 million EUs over the three quarters). Thus, the ACP bloc has gone from a strong trade surplus to a moderate trade deficit. In comparison, the trade surplus of the non-ACP Third World countries with the EC increased over the post-1975 period, although this surplus decreased substantially in the latter half of 1977. Other factors, then, have prevailed over the Lomé clauses that decreased barriers to ACP exports and eliminated the preferences given to EC exports.

The Lomé Convention was also intended to assist the development of industry in the ACP through aid and preference measures. The data in fig. 4.4 show that manufacturing products(4) as a percent of total ACP exports to the EC have decreased over the period. From an average of about 18 percent in 1974, the percentage of manufactured exports decreased to about 12 percent in 1977.(5) In contrast, the same percentage of the rest of the Third World has increased from an average of about 11 percent in 1974 to about 16 percent in 1977. A direct comparison is made in fig. 4.5 which shows that the ACP manufactured products as a percentage of the total Third World manufacturing exports to the EC decreased from an average of about 24 percent in 1974 to about 13 percent in 1977. Clearly then, ACP manufacturing exports to the EC are slipping relative to their other exports, and also relative to the EC's imports of manufactured goods from the rest of the Third World.

Thus far, the discussion has focused on the ACP as a group, but as indicated in the introduction, many different bargaining pressures were evident within the ACP bloc. One important difference was the more lukewarm attitude of some of the anglophone countries, and the less critical attitude of most of the francophone countries. There are many historical reasons for this difference, but it is evident that the francophone countries have been associated with the EC since its inception (and later through the Yaoundé Conventions); and, perhaps, they are both more at ease with, and psychologically dependent upon, the EC. However there is evidence that, in terms of exports, the francophone countries have benefited more from Lomé than have the anglophone countries. Since the anglophone countries were not signatories to the Yaoundé Conventions, the reduction of trade barriers in the Lomé Convention were more than incremental for them, and, therefore, we could expect that their exports to the EC would increase relative to the francophone countries. Fig. 4.6 presents the percentage of ACP exports contributed by the 26 countries that were associated with the EC for the first time in the Lomé Convention (primarily the anglophone countries). Kenya, Uganda, and Tanzania are omitted from this figure because they are, as a result of the 1968 Arusha Convention, something of an in-between group. The graph indicates that, since 1975, the exports of the anglophone countries as a percentage of ACP exports to the EC have declined substantially − from a high of 71.3 percent in one quarter of 1975 to a low of 56.7 percent in the middle of 1977. Undoubtedly, this accounts for part of their more lukewarm attitude toward the Convention and toward the EC in general.

Another illustration of differential growth is in the manufacturing sector. The diminishing importance in the composition of manufactured goods in the ACP's total exports was discussed above. However, in certain countries and in certain product lines, there has been considerable growth. In fig. 4.7, we see that the value of the manufacturing exports of the seven ACP countries (Nigeria, Mauritius, Ivory Coast, Cameroon, Madagascar, Gabon, and Congo) that produce most of the EC's textile, clothing, plywood and veneer imports from the ACP, has increased substantially since the first half of 1975.

Table 4.1 focuses on the relative market importance of the EC and the ACP to each other over four years, 1972 and 1975-1977. It shows that the ACP is very dependent upon the EC market, while the EC's percentage of exports directed toward the ACP countries is of only marginal importance. This relationship has not substantially altered for many years, but this relationship stands in contrast to the growing importance, for the EC, of the non-ACP Third World market. Over the 1972 to 1977 period, the non-ACP Third World market has grown from 21.9 percent to 30.3 percent of EC exports (excluding intra-EC trade).

It was noted in the introduction that the EC wanted the new convention to be modeled on the Lomé Convention while the ACP wanted a radical break with Lomé. While these were obviously bargaining strategies − the EC wanting to minimize its costs and the ACP bloc wanting to maximize its gains − this trade analysis gives empirical support for their respective positions. Relative to the rest of the developing countries, the ACP market has become less important to the EC member states, including Germany, France, and the United Kingdom. Thus, even though the EC needs the raw materials supplied by the ACP region, the EC did not want to radically increase its assistance to the ACP, which would have come at the expense of the rest of the Third World. From the EC's perspective, it was preferable to keep the ACP on a string while increasingly diversifying its aid and preferences (through the Generalized System of Preferences, GSP) to other developing countries. The long-term problem for the EC is to placate both sides − a difficult task at best − but the immediate problem was to minimize its costs in the new convention.

Table 4.1. Export Destination of EC and ACP States,
1972, 1975, 1976, and 1977.

	1972	1975	1976	1977
EC exports to ACP as % of total exports*	5.9	6.9	7.2	7.6
EC exports to non-ACP LDCs as % of total exports*	21.9	29.8	29.7	30.3
ACP exports to EC as % of total exports	48.5	40.3	38.2	42.6

*excludes intra-EC trade

Source: The Courier, No. 52 (November-December 1978), p. 48.

In light of this bargaining position, then, the trade figures are an embarrassment to the EC. The EC's rationale for incremental change — that little change was needed — is refuted by the data. The real value of ACP exports has decreased; the percentage of Third World exports to the EC accounted for by the ACP is less in the post-Lomé period than it was before Lomé; the ACP manufacturing exports, with some exceptions, is of diminishing importance in terms of its total exports and in terms of the manufacturing exports of the rest of the Third World; and finally, the ACP's trade surplus in the pre-Lomé period has changed to an average position of approximate parity and, most recently, to a trade deficit. It is difficult to blame the Lomé Convention for these changes; indeed, without the Lomé Convention, the picture might be even more bleak. But from the ACP's perspective, these figures are arguments not for incremental change but for a more radical approach. With this background, let us turn to the negotiations and a discussion of future European-African relations.

BARGAINING POSITIONS: INTER- AND INTRABLOC COALITIONS

The Negotiating Climate

The economic climate and predisposition of the EC and ACP states were important factors affecting the negotiation process. As with the 1974 Lomé negotiations, the shadow of economic recession cast a pall over the recent negotiations. The effect in 1975 was a spartan aid package of 3,500 million units of account (EUA), a far cry from the 8,000 million EUA pressed for by the ACP states, and a substantial real per capita decrease from previous EC development funds. However, in 1974 the EC member states feared and expected that the success of the

OPEC cartel could be realized in other raw materials, and their felt need to ensure access to these supplies increased the bargaining power of the ACP bloc. As a result, the EC, in the end, compromised more than it had originally intended. The situation in 1979 was remarkably different: the fear of raw materials cartels had dissipated, and the economic recession in Europe was perceived to be exacerbated, if not caused, by Third World manufacturing product imports. Thus, in contrast to 1974, the effect of Europe's present economic problems was an inclination not to be forthcoming to the ACP, but to be more guarded and protectionist. An illustration of this mood is the new Multifibres Arrangement between developed and underdeveloped countries which, at the EC's insistence, is more protectionist than its predecessor.

Adding to this protectionist mood was the upcoming enlargement of the EC to include Greece, Spain, and Portugal. The inclusion into its midst of three developing countries that have considerable industrial output and potential (especially Spain) is going to be costly for the EC in terms of regional aid and loss of jobs in several sectors. The EC, then, was disinclined to give the ACP a significant increase in aid or a real boost to their industrial exports. This was especially true since there were increasing pressures within the EC to direct more of the aid to the rest of the developing world.(6)

The bargaining powers of the EC and the ACP states were grossly unequal in 1974. The Lomé Convention existed only because the EC desired it. The changed climate in 1979 reduced further the bargaining power of the ACP states. There had also been changes in the ACP states which, when combined with their reduced bargaining strength, did not augur a smooth and speedy negotiation process. Their expectation and hope in 1974, that a real interdependence could be achieved, gave them a unified confidence at the negotiating table. In the intervening years this confidence dissipated. The ACP states had seen their margins of preference decrease as the EC continued to increase the preferences given to other developing countries. As the trade analysis revealed, their trade position weakened. Finally, the EC's intransigence on many issues in the administration of Lomé convinced the ACP states that the EC's behavior was not in the spirit of the Lomé Convention. The effect of these perceptions could have been either resignation or anger; in the ACP there were both responses. Generally, the francophone countries were more resigned to the situation, perhaps because they had a longer history with the EC and knew what to expect. Many of the anglophone countries, who were still uncomfortable with their new relationship, were frustrated with the EC and were likely to be more uncompromising. The upshot of this is that the ACP countries did not present a force as unified as it was in 1974. This could only further increase the gap in the respective bargaining strengths. A last minute threat by the dissatisfied countries to leave the relationship unless substantial changes were forthcoming could have been fruitful, or may have left them with nothing.

From this set of uncompromising background factors, we turn to an examination of bargaining positions and the various coalitions.

EC Bargaining Positions

The attitude of the EC toward the negotiations was expressed by the President of the European Council of Ministers (Mr. Genscher of Germany) at the outset of the negotiating period in July 1978:

> We are prepared to continue and extend further the cooperation launched over the Lomé Convention. The Convention has proved itself in practice. The negotiations will therefore not deal with sweeping changes or renovations, but with adjustments and improvements.(7)

The EC's primary goal, then, was to keep costly changes at a minimum. In keeping with their expressed desire for only incremental change, the shopping list that the EC brought to the negotiating table was small. One change that the EC wanted, but did not press for because of fear of strong ACP rejection, was that the new convention would be of unlimited duration with five year review periods. The EC correctly viewed each new negotiating process as a means for the underdeveloped associates to exact greater costs from them. A convention with unlimited duration would have been a constraint upon the ACP's attempt to continually better their position. The preferential agreements with the Mediterranean countries also are of unlimited duration. The EC's attempt to incorporate unlimited duration had been rejected by the ACP in the Lomé agreement, so this time the EC decided to have sympathetic ACP countries introduce the issue. Therefore, at the ACP-EEC Consultative Assembly in June 1978, the rapporteur for the annual report on Lomé, Mr. Guillabert from Senegal, suggested a new treaty of unlimited duration so that the relationship could become "more permanent."(8) This is only one illustration of cross-bloc coalitions.

The most publicized demand that the EC made was that a human rights clause be included in the new convention. There had been a huge outcry of public opinion in Europe against the mass deprivations in Uganda, especially, but also in Equitorial Guinea and in the Central African Empire. Britain and the Netherlands, who strongly supported inclusion, wanted to suspend aid to the countries in which violations occur. There would have been operational problems in this since it would have meant the EC's intrusion into ACP domestic matters. Sensitive to neocolonial penetration, the ACP states were firmly against this proposal. Their argument was that, while they are committed to human rights, the UN rather than a multilateral economic agreement is the appropriate place for discussion of the issue. Some anglophone ACP countries bitterly said that a human rights clause could "boomerang" because of the maltreatment of ACP nationals working or training in Europe, and because of Europe's less than wholehearted attack on apartheid in southern Africa. Apparently, the EC de facto solution is to suspend aid to the human rights violators, except for the STABEX payments which they are locked into.(9)

An issue which the EC's Commission had supported for some time was an investment guarantee clause. Pressed initially by mining companies whose new investments in Africa have dwindled drastically,(10) the Commission pressed the Council of Ministers for an EC-level investment insurance plan for EC multinationals, and the ACP for a guarantee against nationalization and expropriation. Both the Council and the ACP resisted; the member states feared the economic costs and the political intrusion (the member states have their own guarantee plans), while the ACP states sensed a neocolonial tinge to the idea. The ACP states also have their own laws protecting foreign investors, and they did not want to give European MNCs special advantages over other potential investors. The ACP states argued that in the past they had moved to regulate foreign investment when it was inappropriate for development, and that there was nothing in the Lomé Convention to channel European investment into projects beneficial to the ACP countries.

The last, but not the least, of the important demands of the EC was to protect some of its failing industries, especially in textiles and to a lesser extent shoes. As a group, the ACP states export relatively few textile and clothing products to the EC (less than 1 percent of EC imports in this sector); but, as was noted earlier, the export capacity in several countries, such as Mauritius and Ivory Coast, is growing rapidly. As one European textile representative put it, "To the extent that they [the ACP] export, they are part of the problem."(11) Through the safeguard clause in the Convention, the EC could stop these imports, but implementation of it could be politically embarrassing, as the EC found out after it felt compelled to invoke the safeguard against Tunisia and Morocco not long after the 1976 economic agreements. Until recently, the EC gave the ACP states unlimited access, but in October 1978 unilateral restrictions, in the form of quotas on certain textile products, were placed on ACP states.(12) The EC wanted a somewhat clearer statement of the safeguard clause, and they also wanted to make the consultation procedures in the present Convention obligatory. Essentially, the EC wanted to regulate and direct the industrialization process in the ACP countries. Given their previous actions, the modified clauses would have only legitimized the de facto situation.

Regarding the element of protection, the Commission suggested that business and labor be brought into the ACP-EC institutions, but both the EC member states and the ACP states resisted this move. The member states wanted the "social partners" to use them as their voice, and the ACP states feared that inclusion of European associations would make it even more difficult for them to deal with the rising protectionism in Europe.

EC Bargaining Strategies

There appear to have been at least four distinct elements to the EC's bargaining strategy. The first was, in essence, a reminder to the ACP states that they received an inordinate share of the EC's development aid, and a warning that this fact need not be permanent. Soon after the beginning of the negotiations, the Council of Ministers held an infrequent series of meetings on overseas development in which the discussion was limited to the non-ACP developing countries.(13) Since the negotiating team for the EC did not have a full mandate, the ACP states could have expected that the Council would have at least included discussion of the ongoing negotiations. Aid to the nonassociated developing countries(14) has increased substantially over the last few years (20, 45, and 70 million EUA per annum over the 1976-1978 period), although this is a miniscule amount compared to the aid for the ACP countries. In the middle of the negotiations (in December 1979), Mr. Cheysson, the EC's Commissioner for Development, signed agreements awarding 65.6 million EUA to 13 non-ACP countries.(15) The message of the EC appeared to be for the ACP to go easy because there were limits to the exceptional benefits that the ACP receives, and that there was another group more solicitous of EC assistance.

The second element was the reinforcing of the value of the Lomé Convention to the ACP states. What better way to do this than to award large sums of aid at critical moments. In December 1978, the largest loan under the Lomé Convention (a 25 million EUA soft loan) was given to Nigeria.(16) The support of Nigeria, by far the most important of the ACP countries, was critical for a satisfactory outcome of the negotiations. The loan was made to the Nigerian Industrial Development Bank of which the Nigerian government is the largest shareholder.

Rushing the negotiations was another element to the EC's bargaining strategy. The EC pressed for a wrap-up of the negotiations by April and the signing in May 1979. Their argument was that the Lomé Convention would expire in February 1980 and the intervening period was necessary for ratification by the signatories. The EC realized that the longer the negotiations continued, the more likely that the ACP would elicit concessions from them. The negotiations for the Lomé Convention lasted 18 months, and the EC was not entirely satisfied with the results. This time, the EC attempted to limit the negotiating period to six months. The EC also feared that, if the negotiations continued past the UNCTAD V, held in May 1979, the ACP might become more demanding and intransigent.

The final element was to use sympathetic ACP governments to intercede on the EC's behalf. The EC thought that its proposals would stand a better chance if they were introduced by ACP states, or if they could suggest uncompromising amendments to EC proposals already on the table that would render them acceptable to the more recalcitrant ACP states. This technique had been used in the Lomé negotiations. Obviously, though, the support of the larger and more important ACP countries was critical for a successful culmination to the negotiations. To this end, Commisioner Cheysson visited a number of African capitals in the autumn of 1978.

ACP Bargaining Positions and Coalitions

Commensurate with their general commitment to a more radical change in the next convention, the shopping list that the ACP brought to the bargaining table was much more extensive than the EC's – a list of changes in 28 areas. The discussion here is limited to the major issues, and they can be grouped under the headings of aid, trade, and industrialization.

The trade problem was the greatest concern of the ACP states. The trade analysis at the beginning of this chapter revealed that even with the preferences contained in the Lomé Convention the outlook on their overall trading pattern was gloomy. Their former trade surpluses with the EC had become deficits, and their share of developing country exports, especially in manufactured products, was decreasing. The reasons for this relative decline are many and include the facts that Africa is not oil-rich, except for Nigeria and to a lesser extent several others,(17) and is generally at a lower stage of growth than are many Southeast Asian and Latin American countries. But there are more immediate reasons why the Lomé Convention had not been more beneficial. The Convention offered the negative benefit of removing import barriers on about 99 percent of ACP exports, but little positive assistance, except aid which would have taken longer to affect ACP exports. However, about 75 percent of ACP exports had duty-free access simply from most-favored-nation status, so this leaves only 25 percent of ACP exports that receive real preferential treatment. Also the EC's GSP which is given to almost all of the developing countries had progressed to the point that even without the Lomé Convention, 95 percent of ACP exports would have entered duty-free.(18) Thus, the elimination of duties in the Convention gave the ACP countries few real benefits.

As the ACP's margin of preference was diminishing, not only from the GSP but also from Mahgreb and Mashrek agreements, they wanted to build into the new convention means to maintain or increase this margin. In the past, the ACP states have caused tensions in the Third World by attempting to block the increases in the GSP preferences.(19) Their tack for the recent negotiations included a demand for consultation before GSP changes were made, but their emphasis was upon more positive measures. What the ACP states wanted was to maintain their margin of preference through EC compensation for any increase in the preferences given to other countries. Because direct compensation would not be considered by the EC, the ACP states approached the matter in a variety of ways: exemption from the variable levy of the EC Common Agricultural Policy (CAP) (i.e., to remove the barriers that still exist on ACP exports), elimination of the safeguard measures (which were used against ACP beef and veal in the past), and aids to production (such as were intended in the Lomé's banana protocol but never materialized), and marketing (the Lomé Convention already contained a chapter on trade promotion, but it had had little impact). Early in the negotiations, the EC negatively replied to the first two demands. Within the ACP bloc, some of the anglophone countries were opposed to attempts to maintain their margin of preferences by blocking preferences in the GSP. Later, however, their position gravitated toward that of the ACP as a whole, that is, GSP preferences should be increased only if compensation were given to them.

The issue of industrialization and the exporting of manufactured and semimanufactured goods to the EC is perceived by some ACP countries to be crucial for their development. Complementarity is a concept espoused by both the EC and the ACP states, but they define the term differently. To the EC, complementarity in their relationship refers to their manufactured goods being exported to the ACP in return for raw materials. To the ACP states, the term refers to their development in certain sectors (textiles, wood, shoes) while the EC specializes in other sectors. Many of the ACP states are relatively unconcerned about the EC's rising tide of industrial protectionism, an indicator of the low state of industrialization characterizing the ACP bloc, but as fig. 4.7 indicated, there is a small group of ACP countries that has begun to increase the level of industrial exports, and they are very upset and frustrated with the EC over the new de facto textile quotas. Their frustration is heightened by the fact that textiles often are the first stage of industrial development, and they have spent years building up this sector. Their basic demand was that any treatment of industrial development in the new convention be complemented with clauses relating to industrial restructuring and reconversion within the EC. This call for the EC to set its own house in order was galling to the EC because the Commission had been calling for just this type of complementarity between the EC's overseas development policy and industrial policy, whereas the EC has accomplished little in this area. In fact, outside of the Netherlands, the member states have no systematic restructuring policies. Thus, while the ACP's logic of relating the two was impeccable, their chance of success was extremely low. The EC's commitment to industrial development in the ACP region appears rather shallow. The CAP products have always been protected because the ACP region was competitive in the agriculture sector. In contrast, the EC eliminated the industrial barriers because the ACP states were not competitive; but as soon as they reached a competitive level, the EC warning flags flew and the barriers went up.

Two areas of their industrial package that were more likely to be successful were the rules of product origin clauses and a separate fund for industrial development. In the Lomé Convention, if less than 50-60 percent of the value of a product was added within the ACP region, the product did not receive preferential treatment.(20) The ACP states argued that this was unduly restrictive and that it even affected edible goods (e.g., a can of fish is not an ACP product if the container has to be imported). Regarding the separate industrial fund proposal, the ACP states were disappointed that hardly any aid was given to manufacturing projects that might then compete with EC manufactures. While about 20 percent of the Lomé fund has been allocated to industrial projects [compared with 5 percent in the pre-Lomé funds(21)], the specific targets have been chosen with EC rather than ACP interests in mind. The EC was against the proliferation of funds, but such a splitting off in itself need not have been costly to the EC; the EC could have used it as a showpiece to the world as an indication of their "real" concern" for industrial development in the Third World.

The issue of aid was, of course, extremely important to the ACP states but the EC chose to be reactive on this issue. Initially, the ACP itself was rather quiet about the size of its demand, perhaps because of the embarrassment of the Lomé negotiations which left them with 3,500 million EUA out of a demand for 8,000 million EUA. As a result, the real per capita aid of the Fourth European Development Fund was less than that of the previous fund. The ACP states spoke of the 0.7 percent of GNP that the member states are committed to achieve. This would have meant a substantial increase in aid by most of the EC member states, and the Commission had already reminded them of their pledge.(22) However, the 0.7 percent of GNP refers to all aid, and the EC's Development Fund represents only about one-fifth of total aid by the member states. Citing interminable delays and other administrative problems, the ACP states also want to be included in the management of the new fund. Over 40 percent of the aid given to rural projects has been allocated to large agro-industrial projects concentrating on export products needed by the EC, rather than on domestic processing which is needed by the ACP.(23) Again, the emphasis was given to EC interests rather than ACP needs.

ACP Bargaining Strategy

The bargaining strategy of the ACP states seemed to be modeled after the Lomé negotiations. They found that prolonging the talks was to their benefit then, and it appears they repeated this tactic.(24) An ACP/EC ministerial meeting was held in December 1978 and the next meeting was scheduled for April 1979 to conclude the negotiations.(25) But the negotiations moved slowly, and the ACP states noted another working ministerial meeting would be required before the talks could be concluded.(26) In contrast to the EC, the ACP states were not anxious to bring to the May UNCTAD meeting a new convention containing sections that would be roundly criticized by other developing countries.

There was also an attempt by the ACP bloc to maintain their cohesiveness. This was most notable among the anglophone countries which, as a result of their embarrassment over the preferential treatment they receive at the expense of other developing countries, had argued for a more "globalist" EC development. It was expected that they would only accept new preferences if the nonassociates could benefit as well. (There was even talk by some anglophone countries of not joining in the successor to Lomé.) This would have been very divisive because the francophone countries are much more comfortable and experienced with the EC's regionalist approach. However, the anglophone countries did not press for similar benefits for nonassociates, and appeared to want the GSP liberalized only if the ACP states received compensation.

Another element in their strategy, if it can be called that, was Directorate General VIII (DG VIII) of the European Commission. DG VIII, the development directorate, was the most sympathetic voice that the ACP states had in the EC camp. The ACP states, or various groups therein, found support from individual member states, but this support varied depending upon the issue. In contrast, DGB VIII felt responsible for the Lome Convention and similar development agreements, and as in other policy areas a strong development policy enhances its prestige (and the prestige of DG VIII within the Commission). Outside of lobbying within the EC, DG VIII helped the ACP states by indicating changes which they felt were desirable. An illustration was the sugges- tion in a working paper to inflation-proof the STABEX scheme, a suggestion that was rejected by the Council.(27) However, this signaled to the ACP states that the EC was soft on the issue, and after some negotiating the EC agreed to modify the scheme. The problem for some of the ACP states is that they are often too reliant upon, and accepting of, the good offices of the Commission. This reliance is particularly irksome to those anglophone countries that suspect the motives of Commissioner Cheysson.

THE NEW CONVENTION (28)

After the negotiations were terminated successfully, the new conven- tion very much in the Lomé mold and dubbed Lomé II, was signed in that city in Togo on October 31, 1979. The EC's Commissioner for Development, Cheysson, characterized the new convention as a "signif- icant step forward" which contrasted to the "despair and disappoint- ment" of the ACP countries.(29) All of the ACP countries signed the new convention but several, including Nigeria and those in the Carib- bean region, had seriously considered foregoing the new convention. The obvious reason for the ACP's displeasure is that they were unable to exact significant changes from the EC. The aid package is 5.6 billion EUA over five years, about half of the ACP's 11 billion request. In comparison with the Lomé aid, the 1.12 billion EUA aid per annum in the new fund is 30 percent greater than the .86 billion EUA aid per annum (3.44 billion EUA over four years) in the Lomé Convention. However, this increase is in nominal terms; due to the effects of inflation, the real aid difference is negligible. Also, this new sum will be divided by 56 and not 45 countries as in the Lomé Convention (Nigeria was not an aid recipient). On trade matters, the EC refused to discard the safeguards clause or to substantially amend the rules of origin. The ACP acceded to EC demands for most-favored-nation treatment although, in certain commodities, some Mediterranean coun- tries receive more favorable treatment from the EC than do the ACP countries. The EC refused to establish an industrial fund as requested by the ACP. With STABEX, the EC refused to index the price of agricultural imports from the ACP to the price of their manufacturing exports to the ACP. Thus, the new convention does not contain the major changes requested by the ACP negotiators. Instead, the EC contented itself by allowing several minor revisions such as increasing the number of products covered by STABEX from 34 to 44 and reducing the dependence threshold (the percentage of export earnings for specific products compared to total exports to all destinations) and the trigger threshold (reduction in earnings compared to average earnings during the last four years) to 6.5 percent from 7.5 percent (from 2.5 percent to 2.0 percent for the least developed ACP countries). Also, the ACP countries now have a two-year grace period before repaying the EC's STABEX transfers.

The major change in the new convention is in an area which concerns the EC at least as much as the ACP. In the minerals sector, there will be a regime to ensure Europe's access to several important minerals (copper, cobalt, phosphate, bauxite, aluminum, manganese, tin, and iron ore). If annual production capacity or exports to the EC markets fall by 10 percent as a result of a decline in export earnings, or force majeur of any description, soft loans (1 percent, 40-year term, 10-year grace period) would be obtainable from the EC. The EC also undertakes to provide financial and technical assistance for mineral exploration, and the risk capital for the launching of mining and energy projects which are considered by the EC to be of joint EC/ACP interest. The EC, in conjunction with participating ACP countries, will provide specific investment protection for private EC investments in the mining sector.(30) The ACP must accord mineral (and industrial) investments from EC member states treatment that is no less favorable than that received by the most-favored EC member state – to allay fears of discrimination against the smaller EC countries that do not have bilateral investment protection agreements with the ACP countries as do Britain, France, and Germany. The major ACP exporters (Zambia, Zaire, Mauritania, and Papua) "were very outspoken in there [sic] response to the proposals, saying that they served the interests for no-one but the EC itself: 'maintaining the production equipment which keeps them supplied with raw materials'."(31)

THE FUTURE OF EUROPEAN RELATIONS WITH THE DEVELOPING COUNTRIES

It was suggested by Robin Sharp(32) that the ACP states had three alternatives: to oppose the renewal of Lomé and to advocate a global policy; to accept a new convention only if the nonassociated countries were accorded similar treatment; or to negotiate a new agreement with the goal of getting as much as they could for themselves. The first alternative was rejected outright. Although some anglophone countries had talked of terminating their association after the Lomé Convention expired, apparently all of the Lomé signatories will go for more. In this regard, the Lomé Convention has been very successful; the original 46

ACP countries have grown to 57, as new countries have become independent, and Angola and Mozambique are expected to join the new convention. The second alternative also was rejected; there was apparently little talk coming from the ACP group about the needs of the nonassociated countries. In fact, the ACP states decided to maximize their own benefits. In terms of self-interest, this choice may not be surprising, but actually it is, considering the voiced concern of some ACP countries for their nonassociated brethren over the years since Lomé. Apparently, the concern of those ACP states was inversely related to the concern of the EC. In the period when the EC focused its attention and aid upon the ACP states, they could generously voice their concern for those countries left out. As EC interest has begun to shift somewhat toward the nonassociated (through the agreements with the Mediterranean countries, a more liberal GSP, and more aid), the ACP's concern for these countries has dissipated.

What does this analysis tell us about the new convention and the form that it could have been expected to take? First of all, we could have expected that there would be a new convention because the EC and most of the ACP states wanted or needed to continue the relationship. The ACP states might have stalled, and perhaps even threatened to withdraw if the EC gave no ground at the negotiating table, but in the end they would have had to accept what the EC offered. But the EC wanted the new convention enough not to politically embarrass the ACP states into walking out. So a modicum of substantive change in the new convention was expected, but only a modicum because the superiority of the bargaining power of the EC and the economic climate in Europe would not allow more. However, the ACP states conveniently presented enough satisfiable demands (on petty, inconsequential issues) that would allow the EC and many of the ACP states to hail the new agreement as an important step forward toward the growing interdependence of North and South.

But why is there a new convention given the complaints of many ACP states and the relative lessening market importance of the ACP region for the EC? This is a fundamental question that concerned both parties – for Europe its relations with Africa and the rest of the developing world; and for Africa, its development choices. As for Africa, and the ACP states more generally, they have chosen to attempt to develop through interaction with the developed countries rather than through a strategy of self-reliance. Once that choice was made, they attempted to get as much external assistance as possible. Since they are historically related to much of Europe as former colonies, it was natural that the greatest offers of aid came from their former colonizers. In sum, the ACP states have no comparable alternative to relationship with the EC. COMECON recently agreed to give aid to Ethiopia and Angola, and already gives aid to 34 African countries and 44 other developing countries,(33) but COMECON, because of the low level of development characterizing most of its members, presents no real trade and aid alternative to Western Europe (although it might be chosen for political or ideological reasons). The United States is a potential alternative but it has disinclined to increase its aid to Africa substantially. As Africa is becoming increasingly dependent upon the European market and aid, the lack of an alternative necessitates maintenance of the relationship with the EC, even if it is destined to remain unequal and imperfect.

The EC, for its part, also wants to maintain the relationship with Africa and the rest of the ACP region. Although the EC is becoming more interested in other developing regions (notably the Mediterranean and the Middle East, as their market importance increases), it remains tied to the ACP states in several ways. Only about 10 percent of imported raw materials originate in the ACP region, but the EC depends upon the region for certain critical materials: in 1977, 96.2 percent of thorium and uranium imports to the EC were from ACP states; 46.7 percent of the copper ore; 68.9 percent of the cobalt; 59.2 percent of the aluminum ore; and 19.5 percent of calcium phosphates and iron ore.(34) Also, the ACP market for EC goods is increasing even if the increase is somewhat smaller than that of exports to other developing countries (see table 4.1). Perhaps more important for the EC is the heavy concentration (37 percent) of European MNCs in the ACP region – a region which has a population about half that of India.(35) In sum, the EC has a vested economic interest in maintaining its ACP relationship.

Finally, there are important noneconomic reasons for the EC to remain tied to the ACP; traditionally, Africa has been within its sphere of influence. Neither the Soviets nor the Americans have been truly effective in Africa, although the recent reassertion of the USSR's interest in the area has drawn American concern. Through its "civilian power" as well as sporadic French, British, and Belgian military action where requested,(36) the EC can maintain its influence in Africa.

A few years ago, one scholar described the Lomé Convention as a step in the decolonization process, a means through which the African countries could free themselves from their postcolonial dependence.(37) It is, therefore, ironic that Europe appears to be outgrowing Africa more so than the reverse. It is likely that for the foreseeable future the EC and the ACP states will remain married together even as unequal partners, while the EC increasingly courts also its new interest – the other developing countries.

NOTES

(1) For a listing of some of the articles analyzing the Lomé Convention, see footnotes 2 and 6 in Michael B. Dolan, "The Lomé Convention and Europe's Relationship with the Third World: A Critical Analysis," Journal of European Integration 1, no. 3 (May 1978): 369-94.

(2) The "rest of the developing world" refers to the countries in Class 2 (all non-communist developing countries) minus the ACP countries.

(3) The sources of the trade data are the Supplements to the Monthly External Trade Bulletin, Statistical Office of the European Communities, Luxembourg, 1974-1978. The unit of account changed from the EUR to EUA at the end of 1976. (One EUA is worth $1.44 as of January 31, 1980.) All the data have been changed to EUA at the exchange rates listed in Monthly General Statistics Bulletin, 4/6 1978, Statistical Office of the European Communities, p. 169.

(4) Manufacturing exports are defined as trade in the Standard International Trade Classification (SITC) categories 6-8, that is, "machinery and transport equipment," and "other manufactured goods."

(5) These percentages are high because SITC categories include semifinished products such as refined copper which are often excluded. Under a more restricted definition of manufactured goods, roughly five percent of ACP exports are manufactured goods.

(6) Robin Sharp, "EEC/ACP: One more time? – A Critical Guide to the Renegotiation of the Lomé Convention," EuroAction - ACORD (Amsterdam, 1978), p. 18.

(7) Europe/Documents, no. 1017 (July 27, 1978), p. 1.

(8) Draft Report on Annual Reports of the ACP-EEC Council of Ministers, Mr. Guillabert, Rapporteur, the ACP-EEC Consultative Assembly, CA/CP/41/rev., August 23, 1978, p. 33.

(9) West Africa, no. 3198 (October 30, 1978), p. 2126.

(10) In 1961, 57 percent of EC mining investment was in the developing countries; by 1973-75, the percentage was down to 13.5 percent of total investment. Europe/Documents, 985 (February 2, 1978), p. 2.

(11) Private interview conducted in June 1978.

(12) Carol Cosgrove Twitchett, "Toward a New ACP-EC Convention," The World Today 34, no. 12 (December 1978): 479.

(13) Europe, no. 2537 (October 12, 1978), pp. 4-5.

(14) The countries excluded by the term, "nonassociated" are, in addition to the ACP states, the Mediterranean countries that have preferential agreements with the EC. The latter are sometimes referred to as the "semiassociates." The Mahgreb and Mashrek countries and Israel have been allotted 339,270 and 30 million EUA, respectively, over the five year period, 1976-81. Commission of the European Communities, "The Development Cooperation Policies of the European Community" (Brussels, April 1977), p. 21.

(15) Europe, no. 2586 (December 22, 1978), p. 7.

(16) Europe, no. 2583 (December 18/19, 1978), p. 11.

(17) The ACP region supplies the EC with only six percent of its oil imports; 84 percent of ACP oil is supplied by Nigeria and the rest comes from Gabon, the Bahamas, Trinidad and Tobago, and Congo. The Courier, 52 (November-December 1978), p. 65.

(18) Abby Rubin, "Lomé II: The Renegotiation of the Lomé Convention," The Catholic Institute for International Relations, London, England; and Trocaire, Catholic Agency for World Development, County Dublin, Ireland, 1978, p. 5.

(19) Dolan, "The Lomé Convention," pp. 387-88.

(20) See Protocol 1 (Annex II), ACP-EEC Convention of Lomé.

(21) Sharp, "EEC/ACP: One more time?" p. 27.

(22) Commission of the European Communities, "The European Community and the Developing Countries," 2nd ed., 1977/1, p. 9.

(23) Rubin, "Lomé II: The Renegotiation of the Lomé Convention," p. 11.

(24) Sharp, "EEC/ACP: One more time?" p. 31.

(25) Ibid., p. 28.

(26) Europe, no. 2686 (December 22, 1978), p. 5.

(27) Sharp, "EEC/ACP: One more time?" p. 21.

(28) While the rest of the chapter was written largely in the fall and winter, 1979, this section was written after the negotiations broke off in late June, 1979. Because the text of the new convention was not available for analysis, the discussion in this section rests heavily upon the summaries and coverages of Europe and the European Report (see especially Europe, nos. 2708-2709, June 28 and 29, 1979; and European Report, no. 608, June 30, 1979.).

(29) European Report, no. 608 (June 30, 1979), pp. 6-7.

(30) The European Commission's attempt to generalize this protection to private investment in the industrial sector succeeded to the extent that the EC member states allowed a clause effectively deferring a decision for about a year.

(31) Europe, no. 2708 (June 28, 1979), p. 6.

(32) Sharp, "EEC/ACP: One more time?" p. 59.

(33) New African (January 1979), p. 94.

(34) The Courier, 52 (November-December 1978), pp. 105-106.

(35) This figure is computed from data contained in "Survey of Multinational Enterprises," Volume 1, Table E, Commission of the European Communities, July 1976.

(36) The French military presence in Africa is discussed in "Saints Return," New African (January 1979), pp. 45-46.

(37) William Zartman, "Europe and Africa: Decolonization or Dependency?" Foreign Affairs 54 (January 1976): 325-43.

5 The View From the Urals: West European Integration in Soviet Perspective and Policy *
Robert M. Cutler

This chapter concerns Soviet relations with West Europe. It deals with West Europe as a unit and does not emphasize the relations of individual countries with the USSR. Since we can better understand Soviet policies toward West Europe by first attending to Soviet views of world politics, the introductory section of this chapter sketches the basis for those perspectives. The second section analyzes Soviet attitudes specifically toward economic, political, and military integration in West Europe in the 1970s.

In the third section, I address Soviet foreign policy proper, paying special attention to the role of East Europe in Soviet policy toward Europe generally, and as an intermediary between West Europe and the USSR. Two subsections compose this section: one provides necessary background by reviewing events between the end of World War II and the beginning of the 1970s; the other concerns that decade recently ended. The final section of this chapter provides an evaluation and criticism of Soviet perspectives and policies toward West Europe, drawing some conclusions therefrom.

INTRODUCTION

Soviet Thinking About World Politics

After having been eclipsed for the better part of the 1950s, inter-national studies reemerged during the last years of that decade as a

*I wish to thank Zachary Irwin, for comments on an earlier version of this chapter; Morris Bornstein, for direction to and discussion of the economic literature; and Lawrence Brainard and William Zimmerman, for access to forthcoming works.

legitimate subject for scholarly inquiry in the Soviet Union. Soon thereafter, international relations began to be considered a separate field, distinct from diplomatic history and global economics. Studies at the reopened Institute of World Economics and International Relations (IMEMO) expanded in scope, and that Institute spawned a number of more specialized research institutes devoted to the study of world politics. Two of special note here are the Institute of the USA and Canada and the Institute of the International Workers' Movement (IMRD). Each institute publishes its own research journal: IMEMO, Mirovaia ekonomika i mezhdunarodnye otnosheniia (The World Economy and International Relations); the USA Institute, SShA: ekonomika, politika, ideologiia (USA: Economics, Politics, Ideology); and IMRD, Rabochii klass i sovremennyi mir (The Working Class and the Contemporary World).(1) The researchers at these institutes also publish monographs on world politics. Those in positions of administrative responsibility contribute to the formation of Soviet foreign policy by writing not only in their specialized publications but also in the daily Soviet press, as well as by consulting with responsible officials in the Soviet government.

The opinions of these Soviet policy advisers often diverge markedly among themselves, as well as from those expressed by writers in, for example, the military press. Responsible cadre in the research institutes also hold political positions: e.g., the director of the USA Institute, G.A. Arbatov, is a member of the Central Committee of the Communist Party of the Soviet Union (CC CPSU). He and his colleagues work closely with Foreign Minister Gromyko on strategic matters. Likewise, V.V. Zagladin, who works in the International Department of the CPSU as chief assistant to the man responsible for relations with nonruling (including West European) communist parties, publishes fairly regularly in the IMRD journal. Thus, the relationship between these institutes and the Soviet government is not unlike that of American "think tanks" to the US government. Institute researchers have even, on occasion, been appointed to serve in Soviet embassies abroad as political attaches.

Although Soviet researchers' interest in Western political science increased during the late 1960s, the field of comparative politics remained little developed in Soviet writings. The title of the 1975 English-language book published by Soviet authors for general foreign distribution, Fundamentals of Political Science, would mislead the Westerner. The last word of the Russian title, znanii, is more akin to the German Wissenschaft than to the English "science."(2)

However, the detente between the US and the USSR has increased the importance which the Soviets attribute to the ideological struggle. That has, in turn, provided an impetus in the 1970s for the serious study of the domestic politics of capitalist countries. Thus, shortly after the close of the Twenty-Fourth Congress of the CPSU in 1971, at which was launched the foreign policy initiative called the Peace Program, one Soviet research journal pointedly editorialized that "Soviet literature on state and law clearly lacks work devoted to the analysis of reformist concepts regarding the problems of state and law, and of the influence of these concepts on the practice of the Social-Democratic governments which are coming to power."(3)

As military force is progressively devalued in world politics, the ideological struggle becomes more important. In that struggle, the Soviet Union attempts to use public opinion in capitalist countries (but not just in capitalist countries) as an instrument of Soviet foreign policy.(4) In the age of linkage between a state's domestic politics and its foreign policy, the Peace Program would play upon their connections. One Soviet scholar stated the matter this way:

> The grafting together of internal and international relations in the age of imperialism makes it possible, to a certain degree, to change the methodology of approach to the socialist potentials of the revolutionary masses. The success of socialist changes within national borders may at the outset be determined specifically by the state of worldwide productive forces and also by the state of class forces on a world scale. . . .

> [Because, in Brezhnev's words, "socialism has become the dominant trend in the development of humanity"]. . ., the narrow "country-by-country" approach is increasingly being invaded in Marxist sociology by an approach based on consideration of the possible grafting of social relations within a country to the international relations in which that country is actually participating.(5)

A Note on Terminology

There are two sets of terms to be clarified: Atlanticism/Europeanism and microintegration/macrointegration. Atlanticism refers to the belief in or condition of cooperation between the US and West Europe, in contrast to Europeanism, which refers to West European autonomy in world politics and economics. Microintegration refers to the extension of contacts and cooperation among subnational units across national borders (e.g., of the various national Social-Democratic parties) or to that within transnational nongovernmental units (e.g., transnational corporations), whereas macrointegration refers specifically to intergovernmental contacts and cooperation. As used in this chapter, both may occur in the economic, political, and military spheres with reference to West Europe and Europeanism. The distinctions between this usage and Soviet terminology are indicated where appropriate.

Assumptions of the Soviets' Analytical Framework

That capitalism – and its foreign policy, imperialism – is in perpetual crisis is axiomatic to Soviet analysts. The "general crisis of capitalism" goes through cyclical phases, and since 1945 we have been living in the epoch of its "third stage." Soviet writers attribute to the scientific-technological revolution (STR) those developments since 1945 which Western political economists attribute to the liberalization of global trade: the internationalization of capital, the intensification of the international division of labor, and increased inflation and unemployment in the capitalist countries. In the Soviet perspective, the first two of these aspects produce capitalist macrointegration in the economic sphere, resulting in the third aspect. By this reasoning, inflation and unemployment are expressions of the deepening of the third stage of the general crisis of capitalism.(6)

The first two stages each ended in a world war, but the third "began and developed under qualitatively new conditions," i.e., imperialist states conducted mutual relations with socialist states.(7) This fact is exhibited as a manifestation of the "Leninist principle of peaceful coexistence" (a doctrinal innovation, in fact, of J.V. Stalin which was given its present connotation by N.S. Khrushchev), which is itself asserted to be the "principal factor" in bringing about changes in the "correlation of forces" between socialism and capitalism. In West Europe, the result of these developments is the tension between Atlanticism and Europeanism, the former decreasing in influence while the latter has increased.

The existence of "interimperialist contradictions" is the second axiom of Soviet analyses of contemporary international affairs. The STR deepens interimperialist contradictions and intensifies the general crisis of capitalism. In particular, it has brought about a situation where the United States has lost its controlling influence in the capitalist world system but remains the leading capitalist state. As a result of the disintegration of the United States as the major center of world capitalism, two other centers – Japan and West Europe – have risen.(8) However, the establishment of a West European "grouping of powers" (gruppirovki derzhav) as one of the three centers of interimperialist contradiction "by no means signif[ies] the elimination of contradictions among the members of this same grouping."(9)

SOVIET ANALYSES OF WEST EUROPEAN INTEGRATION

Economic Integration

Reflecting the two opposing motive forces in Soviet foreign policy – the desire of the CPSU in keeping with its revolutionary heritage to transform the world; and that of the USSR qua superpower to preserve at least some aspects of that world – Soviet writers on capitalist integration in Europe differ concerning its importance. Those whose main concern is to argue that socialist (East European) integration is superior, are more likely to contend that "the EEC . . . has no real future."(10) Those, however, who make capitalist integration their primary concern and thus consider it at greater length, tend to the view that, on the macrolevel in the economic sphere, it "appears not as a temporary or accidental phenomenon, but as a long-term tendency" which, moreover, the international communist movement must fully consider in developing its strategy.(11)

There is, nevertheless, a consensus among Soviet analysts that capitalist economic integration occurs on both the macrolevel and the microlevel. But because these analysts write out of an intellectual tradition which treats economic phenomena as the cause of political phenomena, they find the fact "paradoxical" that macrointegration is made more difficult by microintegration.(12) In fact, those two terms were recently dropped from the lexicon of "creative Marxism-Leninism," perhaps because they seemed too derivative of bourgeois political economy; actually, they had been proposed in the beginning by a Hungarian scholar.(13) At any rate, three senior Soviet analysts have indicated their strong preference for the distinction between "integration on the state-monopolist plane" and "integration on the private-capitalist plane." But these two phrases mean the same thing as macrointegration and microintegration, so what does the difference matter? According to the same three authors, the contradiction between the two forms of capitalist integration – that is, the fact that economic microintegration inhibits economic macrointegration – may be resolved and eliminated by the realization of the goals of Soviet foreign policy. Therefore, this evolution of terminology is an example of creative Marxism-Leninism in action, an instructive study of how empirical categories can acquire normative content.(14) Here I retain the original pair of terms for parsimony's sake and apply them as well to the political and military spheres.

How is this contradiction between microintegration and macrointegration supposed to operate? One Soviet writer explains their dynamic this way:

> Under the prevailing scientific and technological revolution, organs of state power have been more and more actively involved in the competitive struggle of the monopolies. In fact, the outcome of this struggle largely depends on the degree of support offered to monopolies by the state. Thus the scientific and technological revolution is raising the contradictions between monopolies to the level of interstate ones.(15)

In this perspective, the earliest result of the STR affecting economic macrointegration in West Europe was opposition to the European Economic Community (EEC) and the European Free Trade Association (EFTA), which is assumed by Soviet analysts to represent the antagonism between France and West Germany on the one hand and Great Britain on the other.(16) By the same token, "the competition of the US super-giants" has impelled the firms of both small and large countries in West Europe to merge their capital with that of corporations in neighboring countries. But since, in Zakhmatov's words, "American monopolies used the foundation of the 'Common Market' to expand further their export of capital and to strengthen their economic position" in West Europe,(17) the two economic blocs there could not last. Competition from American companies, by forcing mergers among European firms, merely prepared the ground for the enlargement of the Common Market.(18) The leading Soviet analyst of capitalist economic integration in West Europe believes that the competition between American and European governmental economic policies is the most acute contradiction in the contemporary capitalist world.(19)

The very transformation of the Six into the Nine, however, provided American capital new access to European markets via its bases in Britain.(20) The Eurodollar market, centered in London, gained correspondingly greater influence on West European monetary integration.(21) One might conclude, therefore, that West European economic integration proceeds, in Soviet eyes, along Atlanticist lines on both the microlevel and the macrolevel. This inference is only partially correct, however, for the Soviet analyses do not ignore the opposition to economic Atlanticism generated in West Europe by those very developments. The countries of West Europe see, Gromeka writes,

> . . . that their economic, scientific, and technical dependence upon the USA can be, and in fact is being accompanied by serious losses. . . . Consequently, the struggle waged by West European capital for a larger measure of independence in general – and in the advanced technological sectors of industry in particular – enjoys the support of the respective governments.(22)

This would seem potentially to be an example of how economic microintegration works in favor of economic macrointegration, rather than against it.

The prospects for microintegration, according to this analysis, are little short of inevitable. Shakhnazarov puts it this way in this Soviet argot: "whatever obstacles, objective and subjective, arise on the path of West European [economic micro] integration . . . , influential circles of monopoly capital are as determined as ever to give this process a new impulse."(23) But those circles – primarily the monopolistic national bourgeoisies of Britain, France, and Germany – are no less mutually rivalrous, for transnational monopolies within the European Communities (EC) are nationally based. Truly multinational monopolies (i.e., controlled by more than one country) are, the Soviets think, unlikely to arise because the EC member states follow their own national economic interests; and even if multinational European monopolies did arise, they would still evolve in opposition to the USA-based transnational monopolies.(24)

The significance of these developments extends beyond the continent. One Soviet writer claims, for instance, that German monopolies are trying to acquire some of the influence which British and French monopolies exercise in the Third World, but find themselves checked by Anglo-French preponderance in the political and military spheres.(25) It is, thus, appropriate to turn here to Soviet evaluations of political and military integration.

Political Integration

Soviet analysts agree among themselves that cooperation among West European governments in political matters – which they do not call, but which we may, political macrointegration – stems from the need to resolve and regulate the contradictions, or disagreements, arising from economic integration. But, just as Soviet observers disagree among themselves on the significance of economic macrointegration, so they disagree on that of political macrointegration. Thus, for instance, within six months of each other, one of the pioneers of the Soviet study of West European integration affirmed that "the European Economic Community is now not only an economic but also a political reality,"(26) and a colleague of his asserted that "The ambitious programs [behind the foundation of the EEC] for the creation of an economic, monetary, and later political union have now to all intents and purposes come to a total standstill."(27)

In fact, political macrointegration among capitalist countries is difficult to explain within an intellectual tradition which posits the irreconcilable mutual opposition of ruling national bourgeoisies. Those Soviet writers who believe capitalist political macrointegration to be impossible and to have failed emphasize its nature not only as a response to contradictions issuing from strictly economic microintegration among nationally based European monopolies, but also as a European response to a unilateral US global strategy. On the other hand, the adherents of that school of Soviet analysis which gives greater weight to the reality of political macrointegration tend to be more thorough-going and imply that political macrointegration mutes the conflicts arising not just from economic microintegration but also from economic macrointegration, and therefore, results from the STR having raised contradictions of economic microintegration to the inter-governmental level.

Still, all Soviet attempts to understand the dynamics of political integration in West Europe have a common basis. That basis is the emphasis on the "London-Paris-Bonn 'triangle'," to the almost total exclusion of all other national capitals. This emphasis on Britain, France, and Germany in the analysis of political macrointegration derives mainly from the perceived dominance of those countries' national bourgeoisies in West European economic microintegration (and macrointegration, when this is acknowledged). So French support for British admission to the EC was interpreted as having been motivated in part by a desire to "neutralize the supranational principle" supported by Germany, France having favored since De Gaulle the confederative principle of West European political integration.

Both leading political parties in Britain support the confederative principle, in alliance with French ruling circles and in opposition to West Germany. Britain, according to this mainstream Soviet analysis, used to advocate that the West European Union (WEU) be revitalized as the center of West European cooperation, but since joining the EC has dropped that insistence, treading lightly in matters of institutionalized cooperation in order to maintain its independence in world affairs.

Ruling circles in the FRG, this line of analysis continues, have always favored a federative political union, based on the supranational principle, in the hope that Germany might play a leading role in a unified West Europe. After the Grand Coalition of the late 1960s, however, this principle ceased to animate West German diplomacy which, nevertheless, rejects the WEU as an instrument of political cooperation because it would face there a France and an England which would make common cause to limit German influence. British-German relations have nevertheless ameliorated, particularly as their industrial and financial interests have grown closer; even though London and Bonn are mutual competitors, they are both interested in furthering the integration of West Europe. Despite their economic competition with one another, they are both still "tied politically to US imperialism."(28)

As may be inferred from the foregoing, Soviet writers primarily have foreign policy coordination in mind when their discussions turn to political integration in West Europe. Mel'nikov has opined that it was impossible to say West Europe had a "truly efficacious common diplomatic activity" before Britain joined the Community in 1973. But, he continues, there are so many "factors complicating the elaboration of a single foreign policy course . . . that such countries as England, France, and the FRG, as well as other members of the Community, cannot agree to the total subordination of their own interests to any supranational organ."(29) This position is consistent with past Soviet analyses.(30)

The formation of a directly-elected European Parliament is believed to have resulted not from the wishes of the states concerned but rather from those of the transnational corporations, which "need a special parliament with a supranational basis to pass legislation that could be to their advantage." The EC Court of Justice is viewed similarly.(31) Soviet writers have noted the formation of European political parties within the European Parliament, but the attention accorded it is more polemical than analytical.(32) In this respect, it is treated like the renaissance of neofascism in the mid-1970s, though by no means as vehemently. It is convenient to call this sort of West European integration "political microintegration" – occurring across state borders rather than among national governments; the Soviets, however, do not use this term.

The most significant aspects of political microintegration in West Europe are Eurocommunism and Social-Democracy. The Soviets' concern with these issues falls under the rubric of the ideological struggle. Their interest in the matter is directed as much toward East Europe as toward West Europe; the Soviets have demonstrated in 1956 and again in 1968 their concern to prevent a breakdown of Marxist-Leninist political forms in East Europe. They wish to prevent the Finlandization of East Europe, at least as strongly as some in the West wish to prevent the Finlandization of West Europe. For, albeit that Finnish foreign policy is hardly at cross-purposes with that of the Soviet Union, Finland is a multiparty parliamentary democracy.(33) As trade and diplomatic barriers between East and West have become more penetrable, the Soviets have given increased attention to the ideological struggle both in order to keep their bloc in line and in order to influence West European opinion (particularly the West European left). Thus, Shakhnazarov combines tactical objections to West European political macrointegration with objections to political microintegration which could also be intended for East European elites' ears:

> Is it not obvious that [the big European bourgeoisie] would not act against its own interest ... ? The situation in Western Europe now differs from country to country, and the preconditions for the further development of the revolutionary process also vary. . . . In these conditions the creation of a West European confederation could lead to a weakening of the positions of the Left-wing forces in those countries where they have gained much ground.(34)

Rusin expresses the mainstream interpretation of the American response to these events when he writes that "Washington's strategists are planning to make use of the EC countries' dependence on their military and political obligations to NATO to prevent the further foreign policy isolation of the West European center and to consolidate US relations with its NATO partners."(35) It is, therefore, appropriate to pass here to the consideration of military integration in West Europe.

Military Integration

Using NATO to put a rein on the potentially more independent political and economic aspects of European integration means expanding NATO's scope of competence and giving it additional functions. Such was the motivation Utkin detected behind Kissinger's call for a New Atlantic Charter.(36) Washington's concept of "mature partnership" was also seen as an instrument of American control; to the Soviets, this idea meant the conservation of the American right to make unilateral decisions about NATO's strategic nuclear weapons at the same time that responsibility for preparing and maintaining the bloc's nonnuclear military forces was devolved upon the West European allies.(37)

Military integration of an intergovernmental nature in West Europe generally means one of two things to the Soviets: either the reinforcement of a USA-dominated NATO or the establishment of a separate West European force; and any form of the latter they usually expect to reflect the desiderata of American policy. The Soviets see each project to be at cross-purposes with the other, and both are anathema to them. Utkin, however, thinks it possible that military macrointegration in West Europe may diminish the collective military dependence of the West European states on the USA.(38) Although Soviet observers do not use the term "military macrointegration," one writer allows that "the formation of a [n intergovernmental] military coalition may be viewed as a particular form of military and military-industrial integration."(39)

The military coalition called the Eurogroup is double-edged to the Soviets, for it can serve either an Atlanticist or a Europeanist function – or even both. In fact, the Soviets, though they are not explicit about this, appear to believe that Eurogroup is Atlanticist on the macrolevel, for in their eyes it was organized "with Washington's consent" and is "led by Britain"; and Europeanist on the microlevel, as it has the potential to enhance cooperation among the national military industries of the EC states.(40) Eurogroup, thus, appears to one leading Soviet analyst as an instrument which Britain uses to attain a leading position among West European powers in the military sphere. Because the FRG does not have nuclear weapons, it is militarily dependent on its NATO allies, and British ruling circles want to use NATO to limit Germany's powers.(41) Moreover, Britain (this analyst continues) desires that the Eurogroup "conduct France's course, on maintaining the military-political independence of Western Europe, over onto anticommunist rails," even though France's refusal to participate in the Eurogroup "has placed definite limits upon its development as a major center of military cooperation between the West European powers."(42)

Although it appears that West Germany and Britain, in contrast to France, share the desire to maintain their ties to the USA through NATO,(43) Madzoevskii and other analysts believe that Bonn views the Eurogroup as the kernel of a West European military unity parallel to economic and political unity. Still, they caution that the "two (Bonn, London) for – one (Paris) against" interpretation of West European attitudes toward the Eurogroup is too simple. For one thng, London originally preferred to reactivate WEU, or to establish a new structure outside both WEU and NATO, as an instrument of West European military macrointegration; for another, some French military and political figures have supported contacts between France and the Eurogroup for the purpose of using the Eurogroup to Europeanize NATO. But since a revitalized WEU would serve both British and French interests by maintaining West Germany's military inferiority, Bonn rejects WEU as an instrument of military cooperation, preferring the Eurogroup, where she need deal only with London.(44) Despite the cautions by Madzoevskii and others, some Soviet writers persist in the belief that the United States is drawing West European military integration into the bounds defined by NATO, neutralizing both the Eurogroup's potential autonomy and continued French independence.(45) One author goes so far as to say that the Eurogroup's main achievement has been

> ... the elaboration and wide propaganda of programs of in-creased military expenditure by its members, designed to prove to the US Congress and to American public opinion that Western Europe is assuming a greater share of the cost of the Atlantic alliance.

> In other words, its principal activity has been in the limited field of bribing the United States not to reduce the present level of its armed forces in Europe.(46)

Military-industrial microintegration is to Soviet analysts but one aspect of economic microintegration generally. They predict that military microintegration, like industrial cooperation in West Europe generally, will not become supranational. The division of labor among national military-industrial complexes is regulated, in their eyes, by the European Program Group (EPG). But the Soviets perceive the EPG to fall under the supervision of NATO and thus of the USA, even though it is not formally connected with NATO and includes France as a member. The EPG thus appears to some Soviets as "the nucleus around which [macrolevel] eforts to create a West European military-industrial complex are being concentrated"; such a complex, however, can be built only upon a foundation of "intergovernmental monopolist corporations," which Ovinnikov has deemed unlikely to evolve.(47) Indeed, the examples adduced to lend credence to this fear – such as the British-German-Italian development of the multirole combat aircraft, the Franco-German development of the Milan missile, and the Anglo-Franco-German development of the Jaguar airplane – tend to substantiate the EPG-as-divisor-of-labor hypothesis. There is no joint West European military force for which these projects have been developed. More accurate is the view that the EPG has the potential to unify its members' strength "in the struggle with [their] transoceanic partner."(48)

SOVIET POLICIES TOWARD WEST EUROPEAN INTEGRATION

From the End of World War Two to the Beginning of the Seventies

Soviet Foreign Minister Molotov at first responded favorably to the prospect of Soviet participation in the Marshall Plan, but Stalin vetoed the idea. Instead, the Council for Mutual Economic Assistance (CMEA, better known as COMECON) was established in 1949, including the USSR and other communist countries in East Europe, except Yugoslavia. Until Stalin's death, COMECON was largely a device by which the industrial capacity in East Europe which the war had not destroyed was transferred, often factory by factory, to the Soviet Union.(49) Although COMECON remained relatively dormant until 1955, it was used to coordinate the blockade against Yugoslavia and to organize production for the Korean War. Rapid industrialization in East Europe during the 1950s depended heavily, with the exceptions of Poland and Romania, on Soviet supplies of raw materials. Both Soviet preferences and Western embargoes during the period encouraged that development. As a result, the economies of the countries in East Europe developed relatively autarchically; because parallel production capacities were constructed in the different countries, specialization and division of labor in the region were inhibited.(50)

The major economic groupings in Europe seem to have consolidated and drawn inward in the years following Khrushchev's "secret" anti-Stalin speech in 1956, but that "regional polarization" seems largely to have been caused by the increasing preoccupation of European Community members with themselves.(51) It is quite possible that the Soviet Union would have been receptive to Western overtures for economic and even political cooperation during the mid-1950s, after Khrushchev established his primacy and before the Treaty of Rome was signed. One Western student notes that "the USSR made proposals" at the April 1956 session of the Economic Commission for Europe (ECE) "for developing East-West trade, in particular the preparation of an Agreement on All-European Economic Cooperation and the creation of an ECE organization for developing the peaceful uses of atomic energy." Not only did the Soviets believe that the West European integration efforts would be an obstacle to these proposals, but they also feared that they would hinder German reunification, enhance West German economic capabilities, and enable West Germany to obtain nuclear weapons.(52) Probably there were at least two tendencies among Soviet policymakers and policy advisers at the time: the disadvantaged (light industry and consumer goods) economic managers, including those who supported Malenkov's New Course after 1953, plus some international relations analysts and East European elites, on the one hand; and the CPSU ideologists and heavy-industrial managers, who had no cause for complaint about the economic status quo, on the other. The former would have encouraged contacts with West Europe, and the latter would have discouraged them. A disagreement along these lines would have coincided with and exacerbated the division between Malenkov (whose criticisms of Stalin's arrangements in East Europe were primarily economic) and Khrushchev (whose criticisms of them were primarily political). Khrushchev's openness to contacts with West Europe after his defeat of Malenkov would be understandable as a maneuver designed to reinforce his own domestic political base; as such, the tactic would duplicate the pattern of Stalin's behavior during the succession crisis after Lenin's death.

The continued expansion of NATO dampened Soviet pleasure over the foundering of the European Defense Community in the French National Assembly. NATO's counterpart, the Warsaw Treaty Organization (WTO), "represented the single most important formal commitment binding the states [of East Europe] to the USSR, officially limiting their scope of independent action, and legalizing the presence (and hence the political influence) of the Soviet troops stationed in some of them."(53)

COMECON was revived in the mid-1950s, partly in response to the successful operation of NATO but also partly in response to the dissipation of Stalinist international relations in East Europe.(54) After the 1956 revolt in Hungary and its Polish echo, the Soviets began extending credit to those two countries. COMECON's purposes were later redefined to include (1) the facilitation of mutual exchanges of experiences and techniques, (2) the promotion of an international division of labor and of specialization of industrial production, and (3) coordination of investment in subsequent five-year plans. Even if these intentions were not entirely realized, they represented a new emphasis on the mutuality reflected in COMECON.

During the late 1950s and early 1960s, integration in Europe proceeded within the two political-economic blocs but not between them. It is worthwhile to review some salient features of East European integration. The USSR, in its attempt to stimulate COMECON integration, found trade bilateralism (i.e., the desire of centralized nonmarket economies to balance debits and credits individually with every given foreign trade partner) a hindrance. After some experimentation with multilateral financial techniques in the late 1950s, the COMECON countries agreed in Moscow in October 1963 to establish the International Bank for Economic Cooperation (IBEC). The unit of account within IBEC is the "transferable ruble" (perevodnyi rubl'), sometimes erroneously called the "convertible ruble." The latter term is imprecise because IBEC does not sell hard (i.e., convertible or Western) currencies or gold for transferable rubles. But transferable rubles remain, for the most part, transferable not among all COMECON countries but only between the USSR on one side and other COMECON countries on the other.(55) McMillan concludes from an analysis of trade figures that, between 1963 and 1970, "indices of multilateral balancing . . . show no evidence of an increase in the multilateral content of   COMECON bloc trade."(56) Clark's index, which in the absence of political changes depends over time only on its previous value, remains unchanged after IBEC's creation. Because Clark wishes to use his foreign-trade index as a measure of political integration, he suggests that this finding reflects COMECON's rejection of Khrushchev's 1962 proposals for supranational planning. But it is equally interpretable, in light of McMillan's conclusion, as a confirmation of IBEC's failure to influence significantly the trading patterns within COMECON.(57)

During the 1960s, political and military integration within the Eastern bloc – as measured by the frequency of contacts between top leaders of the various ruling parties, by military collaboration and contacts, by the conclusion of cultural and scientific agreements, and by intra-COMECON tourism – increased.(58) Although the USSR was able, by emphasizing the specter of West German access to nuclear weapons, to persuade the "northern tier" of Poland, Czechoslovakia, and East Germany to assist in strengthening the WTO, it was less successful in convincing the Hungarians, Bulgarians, and Romanians of a threat from the West.(59) And after the failure, against Romanian objections of Khrushchev's initiative to transform COMECON into a mechanism for supranational planning, the USSR relied increasingly on East Germany and Czechoslovakia for long-term bilateral trade deals. The possibility of West European economic support to Romania made the threat of a COMECON trade embargo against that country less powerful.

Beginning with increased West European interest in East European markets, contacts between the two halves of Europe increased in the late 1960s. The USSR and her East European allies soon discovered that capitalist commercial and economic organizations were prepared to take steps to accommodate socialist idiosyncrasies. "So the USSR seems to have decided to allow her allies a policy of sauve qui peut in dealings with Western capitalist states and trading organizations, provided that they did not prejudice the solidarity of the Soviet bloc or contradict the main line of Soviet foreign policy (for example by official recognition of the EEC)."(60) This resumption of East-West trade was very much a part of the contemporaneous attempt in East Europe to modernize and reform the various national economic systems. In fact, the renovation of interbloc trade was so successful that by 1968 the USSR was seriously concerned over the divergence of the COMECON economies. Trade between East and West European countries had so encouraged national economic roads to socialism in East Europe that plan coordination within COMECON was significantly complicated. Also, collaboration among COMECON countries excluding the Soviet Union had increased. The national political elites in East Europe – particularly those of Hungary, Czechoslovakia, and Romania – were being pressured by their economic planners, some of whom saw COMECON as an obstacle to their national economic reforms. Moscow was increasingly concerned about the growing technological gap between East and West, but continued to balk at large-scale involvement in Western markets. East Europe, thus, became (as it still remains to some degree) a conduit for technology transfer between West Europe and the USSR.(61)

The invasion of Czechoslovakia in 1968 was, thus, a response as much to the increasing threat of COMECON disintegration as to that of political and ideological apostasy. As occurred after the invasion of Hungary twelve years earlier, COMECON cohesion increased and was pursued more assiduously, the limits of Soviet indulgence toward East European economic and commercial liberalization having been underlined.

The 1970s in Perspective

In order better to understand relations between West Europe as a unit and the Soviet Union, it is useful first to survey relations within the East bloc and then to examine relations between the East and West blocs in their light. In the years after 1968, the USSR retrenched in East Europe, reinforcing its position and its influence. The Comprehensive Program of Socialist Economic Integration, a broad 15-20 years framework which COMECON adopted in 1971, represented a compromise on Soviet terms between the "market integration" formula advocated by reform economies in East Europe (notably Poland and Hungary) and the Soviet concept of "planned integration." That program, however, was not a "plan," for it was essentially a set of proposals and contained few specific suggestions for their implementation. This is probably because a relatively high level of abstraction was required to surmount Soviet-East European disagreements. Marsh judges that program to have contained major Soviet concessions to market principles and to have boosted the USSR's foreign policy goals. "Taken as a whole," he concludes, it "represented the sum total of agreement possible between states with conflicting economic and political interests."(62)

The early 1970s were not easy years for relations between the USSR and its East European allies. The contradictions between market integration and planned integration were, one might say, raised to a higher level. The issue was transformed into a question of how, institutionally, to regulate international economic cooperation: by multinational sectoral planning or by transnational coordination on the enterprise level. The model statutes which COMECON published in 1975 provide for both kinds of collaboration. The relative importance attached to the two forms varies in the Western literature, some of which betrays confusion over the distinction between them. Although the former (mezhdunarodnye ekonomicheskie organizatsii) provide a potential source of control over the latter (mezhdunarodnye khoziaistvennye organizatsii), it is not clear that the creation of the two forms makes such control inevitable.(63) The proposition is tenable, for instance, that the purpose of the decentralization incorporated into the 1973 Soviet economic reforms was to reestablish some symmetry between Soviet economic structure and that of the East European states.(64) In this perspective, the Soviet reform in 1973, which created "trusts" or "industrial associations" at a level between the ministries and the enterprises, is a delayed effect of the extension of economic ties, beginning in the mid-1960s, between the member states of the EC and the East European members of COMECON; for the latter "the decision[s]to liberalize the economic systems and to expand trade with the West ... were closely interrelated."(65) This interpretation in turn suggests that Pindak's contention (adopted by Abonyi and Sylvain) that the post-1971 COMECON "set-up closely resembles the Soviet ministerial system of planning and management as it has been reestablished by the Brezhnev-Kosygin leadership since 1964," requires closer scrutiny.(66)

If the replication of that planning and managerial structure on a regional scale is a Soviet goal, its realization or failure is influenced by forces and events outside COMECON, including those in West Europe. Marsh states a consensus view when he writes that "the Soviet Union [was able] to resolve some of the major points at issue between the COMECON member states very much in its own interest" between 1973 and 1975 "only with the aid of three external developments – the emergence of a common EEC policy towards the COMECON states, the onset of the Energy Crisis and the Western recession."(67) Likewise, Marer, listing seven elements which hinder COMECON integration, mentions only intra-COMECON factors; but of the thirteen factors which he says promote COMECON integration, most involve economic and political events in West Europe and the West generally.(68) One specific example that we can point to is the activity of the International Investment Bank (IIB), established by COMECON in 1971, which has come to play a significant role in COMECON integration by borrowing convertible currencies needed to realize joint integration projects on capital markets in West Europe and North America.(69)

Military and political integration in East Europe was also reinforced after the Prague Spring was expunged. This fact helps to explain the renaissance in the 1970s of a strong Soviet foreign policy despite the ignominious invasion, an otherwise enigmatic phenomenon. Thus, the events of 1968 not only did not weaken WTO but strengthened it as an instrument of political integration in East Europe.(70) Although coercion for membership in WTO continues, however, recent events confirm Starr's conclusion that WTO members have some freedom to determine the size of their defense contributions to it.(71)

Capitalist stagflation, beginning in the mid-1970s, made less likely the hot pursuit of trade agreements by the EC with the USSR or other COMECON members. However, increasing competition from the United States and Japan for East European markets, coupled with the Treaty of Rome's deadline for adoption of a common commercial policy, motivated the EC to turn unofficial contacts with COMECON into actual negotiations. The USSR was also ready to pursue the matter, for its East European allies had been adversely affected by rapidly rising world market prices for energy and raw materials during the first half of the 1970s. Increased East European trade with the West generally and with West Europe in particular could diminish the Soviet burden of subsidizing the East European national economies and free up raw materials for Soviet export to the West in return for hard currencies.(72)

The main sticking-point resisting clarification in the matter of East bloc trade with the Community is the important political issue of the respective competencies of COMECON on the one hand and of its member states on the other; for the USSR's solicitude of interbloc agreement is also motivated by a desire to supervise East European relations with West Europe.(73) The Final Act of the Conference on Security and Cooperation in Europe (CSCE) did not provide for a European Trading Organization, as the Soviets had desired, but the USSR has pursued other arrangements to establish (in Brezhnev's words) "some forms of business relations between the inter-state trade-economic organizations on which exist in Europe, COMECON and the 'Common Market'," under the condition that members of the latter "refrain from any attempts at discrimination in connection with the other side and facilitate the development of natural bilateral links and all-European cooperation."(74) Some Soviet officials might even favor interbloc cooperation on large-scale projects in order to encourage EC competition with the United States, but the EC Council of Ministers has declined to establish a Community export bank to issue and provide export credits. On this, Pinder comments, judiciously, that

> . . . Community industries without Community financial support will be unable to match the scale on which the Americans can operate; and the Soviet Union will draw political conclusions from the Community's inability to act in common in matters which are much more important, in this context, than the common commercial policy.

> . . . The Community's political weakness, the Soviet Union's political strength, and the lack of economic interest of either in

trade negotiations present the most unfortunate combination that could have been devised to present difficulties for East Europeans who have real economic problems over on which to negotiate with the Community.(75)

One reason the Soviets have little interest in negotiation with the EC is the nature of their exports to the Community: mainly raw materials, which are not subject to large import duties. Although the Soviets' exports of manufactured goods are continually increasing, their concern with transition among their political leadership is conducive to the maintenance of the status quo in the matter. For the same reasons, the USSR is not likely to join the General Agreement on Tariffs and Trade (GATT) in the near future. It has not, however, prevented Czechoslovakia, Poland, Romania, and Hungary from acceding to GATT. Romania has even become a member of the International Monetary Fund (IMF) and has taken out loans from both it and the International Bank for Reconstruction and Development (IBRD).

It is outside the scope of this chapter to analyze West European trade with the East European COMECON countries.(76) But Tables 5.1 and 5.2 suggest the changing importance to the Soviet Union of trade with the West. Table 5.3 provides a different perspective on the more recent figures. These figures are only suggestive, however, for to assess their real significance would involve analyzing their breakdown by economic sector. That analysis has been well performed elsewhere, and there is little to add to it here.(77)

CONCLUSION

Evaluation of Soviet Analyses

The point of departure of this evaluation is my earlier criticism that the dropping of the term "macrointegration" in favor of "integration on the state-monopolist plane," and that of "microintegration" in favor of "integration on the private-capitalist plane," has not enriched the analysis of West European integration. Let me discuss the Soviet analyses in terms of macrointegration and microintegration, each having separate economic, political, and military manifestations.

In general, the Soviets take microintegration in West Europe more seriously than macrointegration, perhaps because trepidation over the latter inhibits reasoned consideration of it. But economic integration in West Europe is taken seriously on both the macrolevel and the microlevel. Economic microintegration is seen as a result of the STR, economic macrointegration as the result of attempts to resolve the contradictions of economic microintegration exacerbated by the STR. Political microintegration is then seen as the result of attempts to resolve the contradictions (1) of economic macrointegration itself, and (2) between economic macrointegration and economic microintegration.

Table 5.1. Exports to the USSR by Selected Countries in the
Industrialized West, in Millions of Dollars

Country	1960	1965	1970	1975	1976
United States	38	45	118	1,837	2,308
France	116	72	273	1,143	1,119
West Germany	185	146	422	2,824	2,685
Sweden	38	50	131	294	280
United Kingdom	150	129	245	464	432

Source: United States Congress, Joint Economic Committee, Western
Perceptions of Soviet Economic Trends (Washington, D.C.:
U.S. Government Printing Office, 1978), p. 19.

Table 5.2. Imports from the USSR by Selected Countries in the
Industrialized West, in Millions of Dollars

Country	1960	1965	1970	1975	1976
United States	23	43	77	280	221
France	95	146	203	770	915
West Germany	160	275	342	1,313	1,703
Sweden	63	72	156	526	477
United Kingdom	210	333	528	900	1,193

Source: United States Congress, Joint Economic Committee, Western
Perceptions of Soviet Economic Trends (Washington, D.C.:
U.S. Government Printing Office, 1978), p. 19.

Table 5.3. Soviet Trade with Selected Countries in the
Industrialized West, 1976

Country	1976 Exports to USSR*	1976 Imports from USSR*	Total Turnover*	Percent of all USSR Trade with Capitalist Countries
United States	2,308	221	2,529	10.5
France	1,119	915	2,034	8.4
West Germany	2,685	1,703	4,388	18.2
Sweden	280	477	757	3.1
United Kingdom	432	1,193	1,625	6.7

*In millions of dollars.

Source: United States Congress, Joint Economic Committee, Western
Perceptions of Soviet Economic Trends (Washington, D.C.:
U.S. Government Printing Office, 1978), p. 19; and Vneshniaia
torgovlia USSR v 1976 g. [USSR Foreign Trade in 1976]
(Moscow: Statistika, 1977).

At this point, the logic founders. The problem is that Soviet analysts appear to asume that macrointegration of any kind requires the existence of international governmental organizations (IGOs). Although that assumption is basically correct with respect to relations among Marxist-Leninist political systems, it can be incorrect where transnational microlevel interactions are not regulated by macrolevel structures. In fact, transnational microintegration in the West can by itself assume macrolevel significance.

A case very much to the point involves the political integration of the European peripheries into the European center. The Soviets acknowledge only one form of political macrointegration in West Europe, and that is the EC foreign policy (which, let it be pointed out, is more economic than strictly political). Nowhere have they seriously discussed in print the EC's stabilizing effect on the parliamentary democratic forms introduced in Portugal, Spain, and Greece in the mid-1970s. This is a pitfall of ignoring the possibility of noninstitutionalized political macrointegration. It would be possible to compensate for this shortcoming by appropriate consideration of political microintegration, but this the Soviets do not do. Their study of what has been called here political microintegration is subsumed by the "ideological struggle" and takes three forms: (1) studies of the "climate of opinion," including serious contributions to the history of modern political ideas; (2) studies of international organizations, such as the Socialist International; and (3) studies of national politics in individual West European states, often accompanied by tactical prescriptions and informed by policy norms. Micropolitical integrative structures which have macropolitical significance but which remain noninstitutionalized thus fall through the cracks in the Soviet analytical approach. Such transnational infrastructures arise, of course, only under conditions of unrestricted travel and communication by individuals across national boundaries. They were extremely important for the transition from fascism to parliamentary democracy, and for the stabilization of the latter in Portugal and Spain.(78)

The military form of microintegration is, in the Soviet paradigm, a concomitant of economic microintegration generally. Paradoxically, however, the Soviets seem to think that it is not an essential aspect of economic microintegration. The empirical-theoretical reasoning for this assumption is not explicit and may arise more from normative considerations and policy preferences; the same goes for military macrointegration, which is simultaneously portrayed in the Soviet literature as a bourgeois-monopolist conspiracy and as impossible of realization.

One final criticism of the Soviet study of West European integration concerns the scope of its definition. With good reason, Soviet analysts emphasize Britain, France, and Germany (and their mutual relations and their respective relations with the United States) in their study of that integration. Certainly, these three countries are the most significant; Soviet analyses, however, discount not only the role of other Community members but also that of the European peripheries (i.e., Scandinavia, Iberia, and the Balkans) in West European integration. Not that they fail altogether to address the matter; the expansion of the EC has been analyzed with some sophistication, and Soviet commentaries on NATO often directly concern the peripheries' relationship to that organization. But there is nowhere any systematic and sustained consideration of the prospects for West European integration involving the peripheries, or of the relationship of the European Community to them. This shortcoming is most evident in the Soviet study of political and military integration, on both the macrolevel and the microlevel.

Evaluation of Soviet Policies

The USSR has been slow to formulate a coherent policy response to West European integration, in part because of an early predisposition not to take it seriously. Now that the Soviets have recognized its significance at least in the economic sphere, they may be hard put to discover specific policy options which affect it. Meanwhile, a tendency to discount political integration in West Europe may leave the USSR in a similar position in that regard in the future. Economic integration in West Europe, both microlevel and macrolevel, appears irreversible to the Soviets. Indeed, they welcome it to the extent that it provides them (1) a channel for Western technology, (2) a market for their own raw materials and energy supplies, and (3) the opportunity to use EC-COMECON negotiations to consolidate East European integration.

An integral part of the Soviet reply to political integration in West Europe has been to intensify the ideological struggle. This intensification, during the early and mid-1970s, is suggested by table 5.4, the numbers in which are twelve-month moving totals of articles on the ideological struggle appearing in International Affairs, a Soviet journal which combines mainstream political analysis with more hortative purposes. This journal is published not by a research institute but by an agitation-propaganda society, in English and French as well as in Russian, and so the articles in it are designed to be read by both Western and Eastern publics as well as by Soviet policy makers.

The first phase represents rising concern about the effects of the then-projected CSCE for East Europe as well as trepidation over the then-alarming phenomenon of Eurocommunism. The second phase is a continuation of this trend but also represents the legitimation of the ideological struggle as an element in the Soviet world view. It also coincides with the period of conflict within the Politburo during which Shelepin was removed for advocating too "aggressive" and confrontational a foreign policy line, as against the more benign Peace Program announced by Brezhnev in 1971. The continuing importance of the ideological struggle is indicated by the third phase in table 5.4, in the heightened emphasis it receives even after the peak of the second phase. It was, nevertheless, a rude awakening when the Soviets realized in 1977 that President Carter's human rights campaign was considered by the West European publics to be a legitimate weapon in the ideological struggle.

Table 5.4. Twelve-Month Moving Total of Articles on the Ideological
Struggle in International Affairs

End-Month

	Jan	Feb	Mar	Apr	May	Jun	Jul	Aug	Sep	Oct	Nov	Dec
1972	2	2	2	2	2	3	3	3	3	4	4	5
1973	6	6	5	5	6	6	6	6	6	7	6	5
1974	5	6	6	6	5	6	6	6	7	5	5	5
1975	5	4	4	4	3	4	3	4	4	4	4	4

Phase 1: January 1972 through January 1973

Phase 2: February 1973 through September 1974

Phase 3: October 1974 through December 1975

There is relatively little the USSR can do with respect to military integration in West Europe. If the negotiations on Mutual Balanced Force Reduction (MBFR, from which the Soviets insist on omitting the B) get unstuck, the WTO might attempt to contact the EPG in the context of those talks, as a tactic to split the USA's European allies from their transoceanic partner.

For the Soviets, EC trade policies with the Third World, and the Lomé Convention in particular, represent an attempt to impose imperialist solutions on trade and economic problems. Their own prescriptions is that developing countries expand cooperation with the socialist countries and that discriminatory agreements such as Lomé be abrogated in favor of global free trade.(79) As is often the case with such wide-ranging proposals, the Soviets do not suggest means for their realization. The Soviets will continue to have difficulty addressing other forms of political integration in West Europe because of deficiencies in their analysis of it. They will continue to attempt to play on "interimperialist contradictions" to their own advantage, favoring some West European countries as against others in trade, and attempting to reach bilateral political understandings where possible.(80) The USSR will probably continue also to oppose the European Parliament but will have only negligible effect on its deliberations.

The centerpiece of Soviet European policy in the 1970s was CSCE; it is, therefore, appropriate to ask what security in Europe means to the USSR, and specifically what its relationship to European integration is. Robert Legvold has persuasively argued that, in Soviet eyes,

... idealized European security appears to revolve around liberation of Europe's two systems from their embodiment as political-military blocs. Rather than the challenge of structuring security in the absence of blocs, it is the advantages of reducing the present competing political-military blocs to integral systems that seem to occupy Soviet leaders.(81)

The USSR desires integration in Europe to follow three general paths: first, the integration of East Europe should be consolidated if not accelerated; second, the integration of West Europe should increase its independence of the United States; and third, the integration of West Europe should, nevertheless, be hampered by its internal conflicts, particularly among Britain, France, and Germany. These conditions translate into a weakening of Atlanticism in West Europe and the growth there of a semicontinental and stunted Europeanism. The relation of Soviet security in Europe to European integration, as perceived by the Soviets, is twofold: first, the USSR wants West European integration to take place to the exclusion of United States influence, while East European integration continues to be supervised by the USSR; and second, it is desired that West European integration, though it may continue in the economic sphere, not find military or political expression.

Final Remarks

Two projects for further research emerge from this study:

1. The commercial and political relations of the individual West European countries with the USSR should be analyzed to determine the relationship of their collective patterns to the patterns of their collective relationship studied here. A synthesis of these two sets of patterns would yield a more complete understanding of West European relations with the USSR. This project is complicated by the necessity of addressing the relations of individual West European countries with individual East European countries, but a judicious methodology should make that task less imposing.
2. The six-fold typology adopted in this chapter – economic/political/military by macrointegration/microintegration – could be refined and applied to the comparative study of West and East European integration. This, too, is not a small project, but it is also more promising than the first from the standpoint of the theory of regional integration.

NOTES

(1) A good review of international relations research in the USSR through 1967 is William Zimmerman, Soviet Perspectives on International Relations, 1956-1967 (Princeton, N.J.: Princeton University Press, 1969). See also John Goormaghtigh, "International Relations as a Field of Study in the Soviet Union," Yearbook of World Affairs 28 (1974): 250-61.

(2) A.N. Yakovlev [Iakovlev], Fundamentals of Political Science: Textbook for Primary Political Education (Moscow: Progress, 1975). The Russian-language isomorphism of the English "political science" (politicheskaia nauka) is sometimes used in Soviet commentaries on the Western discipline. The word politologiia has, however, been coined for more general use; a practitioner of this art (or science) is thus a "politologist."

(3) "Pravo v ideologicheskoi bor'be sovremennosti" [Law in the Ideological Struggle of Modern Times], Sovetskoe gosudarstvo i pravo, no. 10 (October 1971), p. 18.

(4) See, for instance, Richard Neff, "Soviet Meddling Jolts Dutchmen," Christian Science Monitor, July 10, 1979, p. 11. More generally, see Lothar Ruehl, "Soviet Policy and the Domestic Politics of Western Europe," in Soviet Strategy in Europe edited by Richard Pipes. (New York: Crane, Russak & Co., 1976), pp. 65-104.

(5) R.I. Kosolapov, "International Relations and Social Progress," translated in Soviet Studies in Philosophy 14 (Fall 1975): 29 and 31. Emphasis in the original.

(6) Nauchno-tekhnicheskaia revoliutsiia i mirovoi revoliutsionnyi protsess [The Scientific-Technological Revolution and the World Revolutionary Process], edited by S.V. Aleksandrov et al. (Kiev: Politizdat Ukrainy, 1977), pp. 67-69. With specific reference to the Common Market, see V. Liubimova, "Sotsial'naia politika EES: deklaratsiia i rezul'taty" [EEC Social Policy: Declarations and Results], Mirovaia ekonomika i mezhdunarodnye otnosheniia [hereafter MEMO], no. 4 (April 1976), pp. 62-79.

(7) S. Madzoevskii, "Mezhimperialisticheskie protivorechiia v usloviiakh mirnogo sosushchestvovaniia dvukh sistem" [Interimperialist Contradictions under Conditions of Peaceful Coexistence of the Two Systems], MEMO, no. 5 (May 1974), p. 37.

(8) For a Soviet critique of trilateralism, see A.I. Utkin, Doktriny atlantizma i evropeiskaia integratsiia [Doctrines of Atlanticism and European Integration] (Moscow: Nauka, 1979), pp. 187-202.

(9) Madzoevskii, "Mezhimperialisticheskie protivorechiia v usloviiakh mirnogo sosushchestvovaniia dvukh sistem," p. 39.

(10) V.I. Kuznetsov, Economic Integration: Two Approaches (Moscow: Progress, 1976), p. 11.

(11) L. Afanasiev [Afanas'ev] and V. Kolovnyakov [Kolovniakov], Contradictions of Agrarian Integration in the Common Market (Moscow: Progress, 1976), pp. 7-8.

(12) L. Maier, D. Mel'nikov, and V. Shenaev, "Zapadnoevropeiskii tsentr imperialisticheskogo sopernichestva" [The West European Center of Imperialist Rivalry], MEMO, no. 12 (December 1978), p. 31.

(13) On the origin of the terms "macrointegration" and "microintegration," see Christopher A.P. Binns, "From USE to EEC: The Soviet Analysis of European Integration under Capitalism," Soviet Studies 30 (April 1978): 257-258.

(14) Maier, Mel'nikov, and Shenaev, "Zapadnoevropeiskii tsentr imperialisticheskogo sopernichestva," p. 28.

(15) V. Gromeka, "The United States-Western Europe: Scientific and Technological Competition," International Affairs (Moscow) [hereafter IA], no. 6 (June 1973), p. 33.

(16) S. Madzoevskii, "V 'treugol'nike' London-Parizh-Bonn" [In the London-Paris-Bonn "Triangle"], MEMO, no. 10 (October 1972), p. 39.

(17) M.I. Zakhmatov, "Dva tsentra ekonomicheskogo sopernichestva" [Two Centers of Economic Rivalry], in SShA-Zapadnaia Evropa: partnerstvo i sopernichestvo [USA-West Europe: Partnership and Rivalry], edited by Iu. P. Davydov (Moscow: Nauka, 1978), p. 256.

(18) Abram Mileikovsky [Mileikovskii], "The Scientific-Technological Revolution and Capitalism," New Times, no. 14 (April 1973), p. 18.

(19) M. Maksimova, "Kapitalisticheskaia integratsiia i mirovoe razvitie" [Capitalist Integration and World Development], MEMO, no. 4 (April 1978), pp. 14-24.

(20) An. Khachaturov, "US Capital and the Enlarged Common Market," IA, no. 8 (August 1973), p. 92.

(21) L. Glukharev, "The Euro-Dollar Market and Interimperialist Contradictions," IA, no. 9 (September 1972), pp. 52-53.

(22) Gromeka, "The United States-Western Europe," p. 39.

(23) G. Shakhnazarov, "The Labyrinths of Capitalist Integration," IA, no. 9 (September 1977), p. 36.

(24) R.S. Ovinnikov, Sverkhmonopolii - novoe orudie imperializma [Supermonopolies – Imperialism's New Weapon] (Moscow: Mezhdunarodnye otnosheniia, 1978), pp. 98-104.

(25) A. Rusin, "The Rough Edges of the West European Triangle," IA, no. 11 (November 1977), p. 112.

(26) D. Mel'nikov, "Zapadnoevropeiskii tsentr – aspekt politicheskii" [The West European Center – The Political Aspect], MEMO, no. 5 (May 1978), p. 19.

(27) Rusin, "The Rough Edges of the West European Triangle," p. 107.

(28) Madzoevskii, "V 'treugol'nike' London-Parizh-Bonn," pp. 40-45.

(29) Mel'nikov, "Zapadnoevropeiskii tsentr," pp. 20-21, 23-24, and 27-28.

(30) Cf. S. Madzoevskii, D. Mel'nikov, and Iu. Rubinskii, "O politicheskikh aspektakh zapadnoevropeiskoi integratsii" [On the Political Aspects of West European Integration], MEMO, no. 4 (April 1974), pp. 57-58.

(31) Kuznetsov, Economic Integration, pp. 93 and 101.

(32) S. Sokol'skii, "Mezhnatsional'nye partiinye ob''edineniia v EES" [International Partisan Amalgamations in the EEC], MEMO, no. 5 (May 1977), pp. 121-124, is one of the rare pieces seriously to address this development.

(33) See Pertti Joenniemi, "Political Parties and Foreign Policy in Finland," Cooperation and Conflict (Oslo) 13, no. 1 (1978): 43-60, for a good account of domestic-foreign linkages in the Finnish political system.

(34) Shakhnazarov, "The Labyrinths of Capitalist Integration," pp. 38-39.

(35) Rusin, "The Rough Edges of the West European Triangle," p. 113.

(36) Cf. G.A. Vorontsov, Atlanticheskie otnosheniia i sovremennost' [Atlantic Relations and the Present Day] (Moscow: Mezhdunarodnye otnosheniia, 1977), pp. 28-29, 69, and 78; and A.I. Utkin, "SShA i zapadnoevropeiskaia integratsiia" [The USA and West European Integration], in SShA-Zapadnaia Evropa, pp. 48-52.

(37) V. Shein, "NATO: The Price of 'Mature Partnership'," IA, no. 2 (February 1972), p. 52.

(38) Utkin, "SShA i zapadnoevropeiskaia integratsiia," pp. 42-43.

(39) W. Stankiewicz, "The Contradictions of Military-Industrial Integration in Western Europe," IA, no. 7 (July 1972), p. 28.

(40) G. Kosolov and S. Madzojewski (Madzoevskii), "The Plans for Military Integration of Europe: The British Variant," IA, no. 9 (September 1973), p. 54. Cf. V.S. Shein, "Integratsiia i dezintegratsiia v NATO" [Integration and Disintegration in NATO], in SShA-Zapadnaia Evrope, pp. 163-164. For an interesting commentary on Eurogroup and its "subgroups," see V. Leushkanov, "Atlanticheskii generator vooruzhenii" [The Atlantic Generator of Armaments], MEMO, no. 9 (September 1978), pp. 110-115.

(41) Madzoevskii, "V 'treugol'nike' London-Parizh-Bonn," p. 44.

(42) S. Madzoevskii, "Evoliutsiia global'noi strategii Londona" [The Evolution of London's Global Strategy], MEMO, no. 6 (June 1973), p. 27; Kosolov and Madzojewski, "The Plans for Military Integration of Europe," p. 54.

(43) Madzoevskii, Mel'nikov, and Rubinskii, "O politicheskikh aspektakh zapadnoevropeiskoi integratsii," pp. 58-59.

(44) Ibid., pp. 59-60.

(45) Shein, "Integratsiia i dezintegratsiia v NATO," pp. 163-164 and 166-67.

(46) Kosolov and Madzojewski, "The Plans for Military Integration of Europe," p. 56.

(47) Ovinnikov, Sverkhmonopolii, pp. 98-104.

(48) Leushkanov, "Atlanticheskii generator vooruzhenii," p. 115. Cf. Rusin, "The Rough Edges of the West European Triangle," pp. 111-112; Kosolov and Madzojewski, "The Plans for Military Integration of Europe," p. 54; S. Madzoevskii and S. Sladkevich, "Zapadnoevropeiskii tsentr: tendentsii v razvitii voennykh vzaimosviazei" [The West European Center: Tendencies toward the Development of Military Mutual Relations], MEMO, no. 1 (January 1978), pp. 95-96.

(49) Adam B. Ulam, Expansion and Coexistence: Soviet Foreign Policy, 1917-1973, 2nd ed. (New York: Praeger, 1974), pp. 432-440. For details, see Zbigniew K. Brzezinski, The Soviet Bloc, rev. ed. (Cambridge: Harvard University Press, 1967), chap. 5.

(50) Andrzej Korbonski, "Detente, East-West Trade, and the Future of Economic Integration in Eastern Europe," World Politics 28 (July 1976): 568-589.

(51) James A. Caporaso, "The External Consequences of Regional Integration for Pan-European Relations: Inequality, Dependence, Polarization, and Symmetry," International Studies Quarterly 20 (September 1976): 370 and 379.

(52) Christopher A.P. Binns, "The Development of the Soviet Policy Response to the EEC," Co-existence 14, no. 2 (October 1977): 243-245. Cf. Eberhard Schulz, Moskau und die europaische Integration (Munich: R. Oldenbourg Verlag, 1975), pp. 72-84.

(53) Brzezinski, The Soviet Bloc, p. 174.

(54) Ibid., chap. 6, is a detailed treatment of this issue. Also, see George Modelski, The Communist International System (Princeton, N.J.: Center of International Studies, Woodrow Wilson School of Public and International Affairs, Princeton University, 1961).

(55) The difficulties created by transferable rubles for COMECON integration are discussed by Lawrence J. Brainard, "The CMEA Financial System and Integration," in Eastern European Integration and East-West Trade, edited by Paul Marer and J.M. Montias (New York: Praeger, forthcoming).

(56) C.H. McMillan, "The Bilateral Character of Soviet and Eastern European Foreign Trade," Journal of Common Market Studies 13, no. 1-2 (1975): 17. McMillan provides the best concise discussion of IBEC's functions that I have come across, pp. 14-16 ff.

(57) Cal Clark, "Foreign Trade as an Indicator of Political Integration in the Soviet Bloc," International Studies Quarterly 15 (September 1971): 259-295.

(58) Brzezinski, The Soviet Bloc, chap. 18, esp. pp. 471-481; Richard W. Mansbach, "Bilateralism and Multilateralism in the Soviet Bloc," International Organization 24 (Spring 1970): 371-380. For an attempt to measure foreign policy cohesion and to interpret that as political integration, see Barry Hughes and Thomas Volgy, "Distance in Foreign Policy Behavior: A Comparative Study of Eastern Europe," Midwest Journal of Political Science 14 (August 1970): 459-492; the validity of this approach is debated by Kenneth S. Hempel, "Comparative Research on Eastern Europe: A Critique of Hughes and Volgy's 'Distance in Foreign Policy Behavior'," and by Hughes and Volgy, "On the Difficult Business of Conducting Empirical Research in a Data-Poor Area," American Journal of Political Science 17 (May 1973): 367-393 and 394-406 respectively.

(59) Brzezinski, The Soviet Bloc, pp. 453-454.

(60) Binns, "The Development of the Soviet Policy Response to the EEC," pp. 253-54.

(61) Korbonski, "Detente, East-West Trade, and the Future of Economic Integration in Eastern Europe," pp. 575-582, provides an admirably clear and concise examination of the reforms undertaken. His analysis emphasizes the motivations of the East European national political elites in liberalizing their economic planning systems, stresses the contrasts among the policies they adopted, and discusses the Soviet response to those policies.

(62) Peter Marsh, "The Integration Process in Eastern Europe, 1968 to 1975," Journal of Common Market Studies 14 (June 1976): 322-327; quotation at 326-27. But Frantisek Pindak, "Comecon's Programme of 'S.E.I.'," Jahrbuch der Wirtschaft Osteuropas 5 (1974): 435-453, maintains that the USSR made few real compromises. For a comprehensive review of institutional developments in COMECON in the early 1970s, see Zbigniew M. Fallenbuchl, "East European Integration: COMECON," in United States Congress, Joint Economic Committee, Reorientation and Commercial Relations of the Economies of Eastern Europe (Washington, D.C.: U.S. Government Printing Office, 1974).

(63) Cf. Arpad Abonyi and Ivan J. Sylvain, "CMEA Integration and Policy Options for Eastern Europe: A Development Strategy of Dependent States," Journal of Common Market Studies 16 (December 1977): 148, who make this argument, and Pindak, "Comecon's Programme of 'S.E.I.'," pp. 442-444, upon whom they draw.

(64) In support of this interpretation, see Marsh, "The Integration Process in Eastern Europe, 1968 to 1975," pp. 327-29, esp. p. 328. There were also, undoubtedly, domestic Soviet pressures for reform as a result of the original structure's inefficiency for production.

(65) Korbonski, "Detente, East-West Trade, and the Future of Economic Integration in Eastern Europe," p. 575. The best discussion of the 1973 organizational reforms is Alice C. Gorlin, "Industrial Reorganization: The Associations," in United States Congress, Joint Economic Committee, Soviet Economy in a New Perspective (Washington, D.C.: U.S. Government Printing Office, 1976), pp. 162-188.

(66) Pindak, "Comecon's Programme of 'S.E.I.'," p. 443; cf. Abonyi and Sylvain, "CMEA Integration and Policy Options for Eastern Europe," p. 148.

(67) Marsh, "The Integration Process in Eastern Europe, 1968 to 1975," p. 329.

(68) Paul Marer, "Prospects for Integration in the Council for Mutual Economic Assistance (CMEA)," International Organization 30 (Autumn 1976): 631-648.

(69) Brainard, "The CMEA Financial System and Integration."

(70) See Christopher D. Jones, "Soviet Hegemony in Eastern Europe: The Dynamics of Political Autonomy and Military Intervention," World Politics 29 (January 1977): 216-241; Nish Jamgotch, Jr., "Alliance Management in Eastern Europe (The New Type of International Relations)," World Politics 27 (April 1975): 405-429.

(71) Harvey Starr, "A Collective Goods Analysis of the Warsaw Pact," International Organization 28 (Winter 1974): 521-532.

(72) The relation of these issues to Soviet-East European political integration is discussed in William Zimmerman, "The Energy Crisis, Western 'Stagflation' and the Evolution of Soviet-East European Relations: An Initial Assessment," Discussion Paper No. 130 (Ann Arbor, Mich.: Institute of Public Policy Studies, University of Michigan, 1979).

(73) For details on interbloc institutional contacts, see John Pinder, "Economic Integration and East-West Trade: Conflict of Interests or Comedy of Errors?" Journal of Common Market Studies 16 (September 1977): 1-3.

(74) Pravda, December 21, 1972, p. 1.

(75) John Pinder, "The Community and Comecon: What Could Negotiations Achieve?", World Today 33 (May 1977): 180-181.

(76) See, however, Philip Hanson, "The European Community's Commercial Relations with the CMEA Countries: Problems and Prospects," in Carl H. McMillan, Changing Perspectives on East-West Commerce (Lexington, Mass.: Lexington Books, D.C. Heath and Co., 1974), pp. 31-58.

(77) See Philip Hanson and Michael Kaser, "Soviet Economic Relations with Western Europe," and John Pinder and Pauline Pinder, "West European Economic Relations with the Soviet Union," both in Pipes (ed.), Soviet Strategy in Europe, pp. 213-267 and 269-303 respectively.

(78) See, for instance: Pierre Letamendia, "L'intervention des organisations partisanes transnationales dans le processus de democratisation espagnol," mémoire ronéotypé (Bordeaux: Centre d'étude et de recherche sur l'Espagne et le monde hispanique, Université de Bordeaux-I, 1979), cited in Charles Zorgbibe, "Puissance d'opinion," Le monde diplomatique 26 (December 1979), p. 23.

(79) Z. Kuzina, "Politika EES v 'tret'em mire'" (The EEC's Policy toward the "Third World"), MEMO, no. 4 (April 1977), pp. 63-71. See also Vasily Vakhrushchev, Neocolonialism: Methods and Manoeuvres (Moscow: Progress, 1973), chap. 5.

(80) See, e.g., Trond Gilberg, "Soviet Policies in West Europe," Current History 61 (October 1971): 198-205, on the issue of bilateral ties.

(81) Robert Legvold, "The Problem of European Security," Problems of Communism 23 (January-February 1974): 17.

6 EC and COMECON: Intricate Negotiations Between the Two Integration Systems in Europe

Max Baumer
Hanns-Dieter Jacobsen

In 1973, in a remarkable demarche, COMECON's Secretary General, N. Faddeyev, approached the then presiding member of the EC's Council of Ministers and proposed negotiations on the establishment of formal relations between COMECON and the European Community. Even though some progress has been made it is still unclear, however, if and when an agreement will be reached. It is uncertain whether the existing, rather extensive network of economic relations between Western and Eastern Europe will be secured and given a long-term perspective through the conclusion of such an agreement. Why are these negotiations so difficult and long-lasting? What are the goals and interests of the parties involved? Are there interrelationships between the progress of the EC-COMECON negotiations and that of the CSCE negotiations?(1)

Dealing with these questions, we first try to shed a light on the more general background for the initiatives of the COMECON countries. In the second section, we analyze the politico-economic interests and goals of the countries involved which help to explain their behavior. Next, we point to some questions of status and framework conditions before, in the fourth section, analyzing individual initiatives, proposals, and counterproposals in more detail and putting them into relation. Finally, the present stand of the negotiations is discussed, conclusions are drawn, and some tentative attempts are made to evaluate the chances and impediments for a successful conclusion of a meaningful agreement between the EC and COMECON, and of a closer all-European cooperation in general.

THE POLITICO-ECONOMIC BACKGROUND

In February 1976, COMECON presented to the EC a proposal for an agreement "on the foundations of mutual relations." This initiative becomes understandable when viewed in context with several other issues and developments. Three of these shall be pointed out here: a change in the assessment of the EC integration process, the continuing integration process in COMECON itself, and the progress and outcome of the Conference on Security and Cooperation in Europe (CSCE).

At the end of the 1960s, it became apparent that the assessment of the EC integration process had changed, foremost in the smaller COMECON countries.(2) The Soviet policy of strictly rejecting the "imperialistic integration" was gradually replaced by a more realistic approach in the early 1970s. Thus, M. Maximowa reasoned that "Capitalist integration for all its inherent contradictions increases the economic and scientific and technological potential of the integration countries, helping increase the efficacy of their economies. This must be taken into account when considering the question of economic competition between the two systems."(3) The Soviet author also states that:

> For all its limitations and incompleteness, capitalist integration is a factor exerting considerable influence on the development of centripetal and centrifugal tendencies in the capitalist camp, on the relationship and alignment of the forces there, and on the position of both individual capitalist countries and certain regional groupings. This is of great importance for the foreign policy of the Soviet Union and the countries of the socialist community.(4)

The then progressing integration plans of the EC member countries caused the statement that ". . . the main centers of the imperialist rivalry   are   . . . the USA, Western Europe, and Japan,"(5) and not solely the USA any more.

At the beginning of the 1970s, the "international socialist division of labor" within COMECON was redefined as "socialist integration." This development was reflected in the adoption of the "Comprehensive Program" by the COMECON member countries in 1971.(6) Although based on the least common denominator and incorporating contradictions and inconsistencies as far as the envisaged integration methods are concerned, this long-term integration program was intended to build the basis for closer economic and political cooperation within COMECON, and for coordinating and channeling the external activities of the member countries, particularly with respect to the international economic relations of the smaller East European countries.

The third aspect which should be accounted for when discussing COMECON's proposals for an agreement with the EC lies in the fact that the CSCE was viewed as an instrument to weaken or prevent integrative Western actions, and to confirm and consolidate the political and juridical status quo in Europe.(7) The East European countries and the Soviet Union repeatedly stressed the desire for a close all-European, economic cooperation. This was one of the main goals of the Eastern countries in the CSCE negotiations, together with a renunciation of force and the formulation of principal codes of conduct. Basket III (cooperation in humanitarian and other matters) was accepted only because the Western nations insisted upon it.(8)

This is the point where COMECON's proposal to the EC gains its specific contours. A more "realistic" assessment of the EC on the part of the Soviet Union meant that Soviet leaders came to the conclusion that certain successes of integration in the EC might not be without repercussions on their own interests in Eastern and Western Europe.(9) Furthermore, direct relations with the European Community might open new ways to influence the West European integration process and the development of the Atlantic Community, particularly since integration progress in matters of economic policy became rather slow in 1973-74.

From a Soviet and East European point of view, the CSCE as well as the initiatives toward the EC doubtlessly serve the same purpose. Both aim at the creation of conditions which are thought to suit best the economic and socio-political development of the COMECON countries: to maximize economic gains and to secure the political status quo at the same time. The main difference between the proposals to the EC and the principles of CSCE's Final Act lies in the fact that certain interrelationships between Basket II (economic cooperation) and the other two Baskets of the Final Act play no explicit role in EC-COMECON contacts.

Expanding their intra-European economic relations, the COMECON member countries attempted to relate strategy to tactics. This becomes obvious when examining the progress over time: COMECON's Secretary General approached the presiding member of EC's Council of Ministers (August 27, 1973) shortly after the conclusion of CSCE's first phase in Helsinki (July 3 to 7, 1973); and six months after the signing of the Final Act (August 1, 1975), a COMECON representative submitted a draft agreement to the EC (February 16, 1976). In comparison with the wording and the contents of CSCE's Basket II, the draft agreement goes much further; it is similar to the conceptions with which the Soviet Union and the East European countries went into CSCE preparations in the beginning of the 1970s. Thus, COMECON proposed to the EC formulations and measures in the field of economics which were unattainable at the CSCE level, without having to negotiate on human matters (as in Basket III of the CSCE).

With respect to COMECON's initiatives, the three aspects which we stress here were to fulfill the following functions. The "recognition" of EC integration successes theoretically and ideologically paved the way for establishing contacts with the European Community. Fresh steps to further integration internally strengthened COMECON as an institution and tied the East European countries still closer to the Soviet Union. Finally, the drive for an all-European security conference aimed at getting recognized the political status quo in Europe, thereby reducing the risks and dangers of set-backs. These were the environmental preconditions for COMECON to propose negotiations to the EC on the foundations of mutual relations.

GOALS AND CONSTRAINTS FOR THE EC, COMECON, AND THEIR MEMBER COUNTRIES

The motives causing COMECON and its member countries to take up contacts with the EC are part of the more general reasons which led to a decrease of tensions and to an increase in economic relations between East and West; these were mainly to reach the economic development goals and to reduce and eventually close the "technological gap" with the help of increased imports from the West. In order to balance these imports, a reduction of tariff and nontariff barriers to trade, more credits and better credit conditions, removal of discriminations, co-operation agreements, joint commissions, and other instruments were brought into the discussion.

However, motivations for and expectations from the conclusion of an agreement between the EC and COMECON differ. The position of the Soviet Union cannot be defined clearly. On the one hand, she seems to have great interest in establishing a framework within which her East European partners can formalize their relations with the Community. On the other hand, apart from the fact that an agreement economically is less important for the USSR than for the smaller East European countries, she seems to feel that her own political and economic objectives are better served by bilateral contacts with individual West European states than by negotiations with the EC as such. From a Soviet point of view, closer relations with COMECON may also have an influence on some EC countries' positions as far as the EC integration process and the Atlantic Community are concerned. The East European countries, being much more dependent on foreign trade than the Soviet Union (e.g., endowment with natural resources, size of national markets, etc.), expect to reach more concessions through bilateral contacts with individual EC members than through coordinated EC-COMECON settlements (Romania is a case in point for this type of thinking). Although not stated explicitly, these countries seem to hope that the Soviet hegemony within COMECON will at least not be increased in this way.

Similar considerations may have caused the EC and its member countries to react rather reservedly in this matter. Although the coordination of the national economic policies vis a vis Centrally Planned Economies (CPEs) is an integration goal, this interest is superseded by reservations against supporting Soviet dominance in the COMECON area. Furthermore, some EC member states seem to believe that their economic competitiveness position vis a vis Western rivals for the Eastern markets can be ensured by continued bilateral relations with individual COMECON states.

THE STATE OF THE EC AND COMECON: FRAMEWORK CONDITIONS AND LONGER-TERM TRENDS

The legal basis for the EC's joint trade policy is clear.(10) On January 1, 1973, the competence for the conclusion of trade agreements with third countries switched from individual EC members to the EC Commission; the last bilateral trade agreements expired on December 31, 1974. In the fall of 1974, the EC submitted to each COMECON member a "scheme" for trade agreements with the Community. The main features of this "scheme" – they coincided with the bargaining position of the EC in the CSCE negotiations – were the following:(11)

- EC's readiness to conclude long-term, non-preferential trade agreements which ensure equal mutual benefit;
- creation of conditions for promoting the dynamic development of mutual trade;
- mutual most-favored-nation (MFN) treatment (i.e., EC-MFN in return for reciprocal concessions by the CPEs);
- search for possibilities to liberalize imports;
- payments and financial problems in foreign trade are to be discussed case by case; and
- common agricultural policy is not mentioned as a subject for negotiations.

None of the COMECON countries reacted favorably, nor concluded an agreement with the EC on the basis of this scheme. Hence, since the beginning of 1975, trade between EC and COMECON member countries lacks a contractual basis. In order to bridge the situation, the Community autonomously takes charge of the member countries' import regulations.

The urgency to sign a trade agreement with the EC, however, was not very high for the COMECON states. Most EC countries decided to conclude long-term, bilateral, cooperation agreements with individual CPEs in which the distinction between matters of trade and those of cooperation was not altogether clear-cut. Since the EC competence covers matters of trade but not economic cooperation, this practice could be interpreted as a dodging of EC regulations. In the summer of 1974, the Commission initiated an information and consulting procedure for the conclusion of economic cooperation agreements between EC members and third countries. According to that, the Commission and/or other member countries can now demand information on the terms of a new cooperation agreement, yet they have no direct influence on its formulation.(12)

The basis for COMECON's foreign trade policy is not unequivocally determined. According to its statute, the Council for Mutual Economic Assistance is not a supranational institution and has no supranational powers. Consequently, it cannot issue binding regulations, it can only make recommendations. Moreover, national governments have the option to announce their disinterest in any particular matter under discussion (Art. IV COMECON Statute). This was one of the main reasons for the EC to argue that it would not negotiate with COMECON as such on matters of trade and that trade agreements could only be negotiated and signed by individual COMECON countries. Even though the COMECON statutes had been revised in June 1974 in order to allow for COMECON to sign contracts with other countries and with international organizations, and despite the fact that in June 1976 the COMECON member countries officially instructed COMECON to conduct negotiations with the European Community, the EC's position has not basically changed.(13) Should the two parties agree to leave the present procedure of exchanging visits and draft agreements and start to negotiate seriously, the EC will find that COMECON's internal structures and conditions have substantially changed since the first part of the 1970s. Before discussing the draft agreements and proposals in more detail, it seems useful to elaborate a bit on these changes.

COMECON's "Comprehensive Program" can be interpreted as a compromise between the member countries' diverging interests as far as extent and methods of COMECON integration are concerned. It consists of more "market-oriented" parts (e.g., greater role for prices and exchange rates, convertibility), but also exhibits "central-plan" components (like plan coordination, joint planning in some industrial branches). Apart from considerations of consistency, it is noteworthy that since the adoption of the Comprehensive Program in 1971, substantial progress has only been made in the field of "centralizing" measures. The trend toward an internationalization of production within COMECON, an "integration through plan" is reflected by the subsequent adoption of the "Coordinated Plan of Multilateral Integration Measures" in 1975, and the "Long-Term Target Programs" in 1978 and 1979. These measures and programs, having long been propagated and finally initialed by the Soviet Union, provided the normative background for "joint" investments, the creation of "International Economic Organizations" and some joint enterprises within COMECON.(14) However, they are not truly multilateral; e.g., the investment projects which resulted from the "Coordinated Plan of Multilateral Integration Measures" were not based on multilaterally agreed contracts but, rather, on a system of bilateral contracts between the Soviet Union and individual East European countries. Thus, the repeated references to national sovereignty and freedom of choice in COMECON documents and protocols have to be looked upon in the light of more recent de facto developments which demonstrate a higher stage of the COMECON integration process and indicate supranational tendencies, "through the back door."

The fact that the key role the Soviet Union always has played within the Eastern Bloc has still gained importance in the last five years becomes clear not only by considering the extent of her being able to determine the direction of the integration process but by looking at the development of her economic position within COMECON as well. The dramatic increases in energy and some raw material prices since 1973 have shifted the terms of trade within COMECON in favor of the USSR.

In trade with the West, the exports of the smaller East European countries were much more susceptible to inflation, recession, and import restrictions than the raw material exports of the Soviet Union. The resulting deficits in the balance of payments and the foreign indebtedness decisively limited the chances to become less dependent on the Soviet Union for energy and raw material imports; prices on the world market were (and are) still higher and must be paid in convertible currencies. These are the main economic reasons why the present trend of greater adjustment to Soviet conceptions is likely to continue in the smaller East European COMECON countries.

BARGAINING POSITIONS AND DEVELOPMENT OF CONTACTS BETWEEN COMECON AND THE EC

In this section we will examine whether and to what extent the socialist countries have changed their conceptions in their attempt to promote and achieve a comprehensive economic cooperation between Eastern and Western Europe.

COMECON's Conceptions of Economic Cooperation in Europe and Their Realization in the Final Act of the CSCE

In comparison to the topics of Basket III, the notions of the Soviet Union and the other COMECON countries on the contents of Basket II were less controversial. Agreement without major difficulties was possible on a number of specific issues ranging from industrial coopera- tion, environmental protection and other topics (e.g., transport, tour- ism, training of specialists), to some question of trade. However, since some crucial problem areas were left out (e.g., financing and credits, currency and convertibility problems)(15) and agreement could not be reached in others, it is doubtful whether the text of Basket II provides sufficient guiding principles in order to build the basis for a compre- hensive and long-term economic cooperation between Eastern and Western Europe. This is particularly true for the socialist countries' claim for most-favored-nation treatment which was understood as ". . . the comprehensive application of the Most-Favored-Nation regime on the basis of reciprocity."(16) Thereby, the socialist countries aimed at reducing, and eventually eliminating the tariff, and, by also claiming nondiscrimination, the nontariff barriers to trade which restricted their exports to the industrialized Western economies. However, the MFN clause is very much an instrument of foreign economic policy between market economies and is oriented toward the principle of free trade; it means that country A concedes to country B that its imports from B are only subject to the smallest import restrictions (tariff or otherwise) that country A applied to any other country. As most COMECON countries do not have a meaningful and effective tariff system, reciprocity of concessions can hardly be determined.(17) As far as nontariff barriers to trade are concerned (e.g., quantitative restrictions such as quotas), it is difficult if not impossible to apply the principle of MFN treatment since there is no yardstick for the determination of reciprocity. The COMECON countries argue that they are discriminated against since they do not quantitatively restrict imports from the West, whereas the Western countries resist abolishment of their restrictions. However, this argument does not take into consideration that the key element which determines the volume, structure, and forms of the external economic relations of the socialist countries is the import plan.

Only a few days before the closing of the CSCE, agreement was reached on a formulation for the Final Act which took into account the Western reservations. The advantageous effects on the development of trade which can result from the granting of MFN treatment were generally recognized;(18) in the preamble of Basket II, it is mentioned that agreements between signatory states should ensure that gains and obligations are mutually balanced and of comparable dimensions,(19) i.e., the principle of reciprocity has been stressed in the Final Act.

In this context it is noteworthy that – in contrast to COMECON – the EC actively took part in the second phase of the CSCE negotiations(20) and that the Italian prime minister, then presiding member of the EC Council of Ministers, signed the Final Act not only in the name of his country, but for the European Community as well. Thereby, the EC's role in matters of trade and foreign economic policy vis a vis the Eastern countries has been confirmed.

The COMECON Draft for a Treaty with the EC (February 1976)

About six months after the beginning of the Final Act of the CSCE, COMECON submitted the draft for a treaty with the EC in Luxembourg. In its preamble, the draft explicitly cites the CSCE Final Act, and states that the contracting parties wish to expand and consolidate their economic relations for their mutual benefit on a bilateral as well as a multilateral basis. This means that a framework agreement is proposed which is to be filled out by bilateral agreements between individual countries and groups of countries.

Some of the proposed subjects were not to be very controversial,(21) whereas others will be difficult to settle (e.g., the demands for credits at best possible terms (Art. 10) and for reciprocal granting of MFN treatment (Art. 11)). These latter subjects were already dealt with at the CSCE, but were not settled there. The agricultural sector, which was explicitly excluded from the EC's "model" agreement of 1974, is mentioned in Art. 9 of the draft. The draft does not explicitly exempt the joint trade policy of the EC.(22) However, Art. 11 tends to neglect the Commission's competence in this field by providing for bilateral as well as for multilateral settlements in questions of foreign trade.

The Response of the EC (November 1976)

In November 1976, the EC Commission reacted by submitting its own draft for an agreement with COMECON to the officiating chairman of the COMECON Executive Council in Warsaw. The EC draft agreement is rather restrictive insofar as matters of trade policy, particularly the demand for most-favored-nation treatment and nondiscrimination are not mentioned. The argumentation runs basically along the same lines as during the CSCE: Instruments of foreign trade policy decidedly have diverse functions in CPEs and in market economies; hence, realization of the principle of reciprocity would be very difficult. Additionally, in its letter of advice, the EC refers to its offer of 1974 (to conclude trade agreements with individual COMECON countries) and stresses that its present draft provides for a skeleton agreement which does not exclude agreements between the Commission and individual COMECON members; the content of such an agreement is limited by the existing asymmetry in material competences, as reflected by the EEC Treaty and the COMECON Statute respectively. Finally, the EC rejects the mention of the CSCE Final Act in the COMECON draft as this would tend to give binding force to the CSCE recommendations.(23)

No mention is made in the EC draft of problems of credit availability and credit conditions. Rather, it concentrates on questions where, in the judgment of the Commission, both organizations have equal competences to conclude contracts: economic prognoses, statistics, problems of environmental protection, and standardization. Intensification of information exchange, particularly in these areas, is to provide the basis for improved working relations between the two organizations and their member countries. Since these four areas are mentioned in the COMECON draft as well, it was conceivable that an agreement between the two integration systems in Europe could be reached, even though these are basically problem areas which should be dealt with by the UN Economic Commission for Europe (ECE).

The Situation at the Beginning of the 1980s

The bargaining positions have become less divergent in the last five years. In the course of a number of exchanges of notes and mutual visits, however slowly and minutely, progress has been made. Thus, in the fall of 1979, the EC took up the long-lasting demand of COMECON for dealing with questions of trade in an agreement between the EC and COMECON. In a very general and not very meaningful formulation, it conceded that the expansion of trade and the reduction of restrictions would be desirable. The EC still insists that trade agreements can be concluded only between the EC and individual COMECON member countries, but it no longer refuses for the term "trade" to be mentioned in talks with COMECON. In the fall of 1979, both parties agreed, for the first time, to establish a joint working group which is to draw up the draft for a treaty.

Despite these more encouraging developments, a number of substantial problems remain to be solved. The chief blocking stone seems to be that neither party is really prepared to acknowledge the competences of the other side to accept and, by concluding an agreement, to sanction the internal, politico-economic state-of-affairs in the other camp.(24) In addition to these political questions, the negotiation process is hampered by the fact that the more economically-oriented motivation for the conclusion of a treaty differs substantially among the negotiating countries, i.e., economic pressures and expected gains vary widely. Thus, some EC negotiators claim to be at a loss when asked what economic gains the EC could derive from the conclusion of an agreement, i.e., what they should ask for in return for Western concessions. There are considerable differences in opinion among EC members with respect to the extent to which the Western markets can or should be open to Eastern exports in certain supposedly sensitive sectors. Beyond the consideration that some EC nations might fear national, competitive losses in Eastern markets from a more coordinated EC policy, the distribution of potential, additional gains among the EC countries remains a delicate and unresolved question. As far as the COMECON countries are concerned, the exports of the smaller East European nations are much more affected by EC import restrictions than the, primarily, raw material exports of the Soviet Union. Insofar as their share of foreign trade in GNP is much higher than in the case of the USSR, their interest in an agreement is incomparably higher, as we have already noted.

PERSPECTIVES FOR AN ALL-EUROPEAN COOPERATION IN THE 1980s

The changes and partial reorganizations in the world economy did not eliminate Eastern reservations against a closer integration into the global economic organizations,(25) particularly since the continuing political and military rivalry between the USA and the USSR seems to prevent a closer economic cooperation between the two Super-powers.(26) Viewed against this background, COMECON's initiatives vis a vis the EC, the Eastern proposals for a closer all-European economic cooperation gain new dimensions. The COMECON countries, in particular the Soviet Union, seem to concentrate their international economic efforts and strategies on Western Europe. Emphasis seems to lie on considering such things as the potentials for a long-term economic division of labor in Europe and improvement of the European infrastructure, and not so much on shorter-term economic gains. Thereby, geographical proximity (e.g., transport costs and knowledge of the internal political, social, and economic conditions) plays a role as well as the fact that almost all high technology and credit needs can be covered from West European sources at competitive prices. Furthermore, rarely have West European countries found it useful to link economic concessions explicitly with demands for a certain political conduct.

An agreement between the EC and COMECON can only provide the skeleton for expanding economic relations. Such a skeleton agreement would have to be filled out by concrete projects and regulations between the two institutions and/or their member countries, according to the mutual competences in each case under consideration. The skeleton should be big enough and offer a sufficient number of places of attachment to be able to handle the volume and the branchings of mutual politico-economic relations. From this point of view, a treaty covering only the areas in which a principal understanding has already been achieved (e.g., statistics, standardization) will not suffice. However, a broader, more extensive agreement which could provide the basis for a long-term, diversified foreign economic policy presupposes the political will to put an end to the lasting quarrel over mutual competences; i.e., the underlying resistance to mutual recognition would have to be given up. One of the reasons why the EC has been hesitant in this respect can be seen in the fact that (beyond considerations of contrast of interests within the EC) there is one clearly dominating member within COMECON – The Soviet Union.(27)

A successful conclusion of the negotiations between the EC and COMECON might also be desirable as a counterweight to the slowdown or even stagflation in the detente process. Their postulate of economic growth requires that the COMECON countries continue to open their economies to the West, particularly Western Europe. Giving the expansion of economic relations with the COMECON countries a long-term, politico-economic dimension by concluding an agreement with COMECON, there is a better chance to overcome traditional structures and to create moderating constraints in the COMECON countries. West European decision makers will have to take this into account when – in the light of increased tensions between the Superpowers – reconsidering their policy vis a vis the COMECON countries.

Apart from the EC-COMECON negotiations, a number of other proposals have been made which aim at closer economic ties between Eastern and Western Europe. Linked with the CSCE negotiations and the UN Economic Commission for Europe, these proposals – essentially put forward by the Eastern European countries and the Soviet Union – cover a wide range of macro- as well as microeconomic fields such as the creation of an all-European free trade area, installation of joint facilities for a better financing of East-West economic relations, East-West European cooperation in the fields of energy, transport, and environmental protection.

As far as trade is concerned, the creation of a free-trade zone is the most far-reaching proposal.(28) It entails not only mutual granting of MFN but the gradual abolishment of internal tariff and nontariff barriers to trade altogether. Irrespective of doubtless very serious political problems, the question of reciprocity would still be more difficult to solve than in the case of the EC-COMECON negotiations. Finland has been the first OECD member which tried to find a solution to this problem at the bilateral level. After signing a cooperation agreement with COMECON in 1973,(29) Finland concluded free-trade agreements with most COMECON member countries. The question of reciprocity between countries having differing economic systems has been tackled in article 9 of the treaty with the CSSR (Czechoslovakia) (1974). There it is stipulated that the CSSR use all instruments which are available within the limits of its economic system to assure that its imports from Finland are equally privileged as Finnish imports from the CSSR.(30) This rather imprecise, nonbinding formulation demonstrates that a magic key to the problem of reciprocity could not be found, and that confidence in mutual good will is crucial. However, there are also some safeguard clauses to be found in the agreement which are not customary for free-trade agreements between developed market economies. Only experience can show whether such bilateral compromises are functional and to what extent they are accepted by other Western countries.

The Soviets proposed All-European arrangements in the fields of energy, transport, and environmental protection. This reflects their interest in finding regulations in certain economic sectors with neighboring Western Europe. Though at a varying degree, the sectors chosen are also of interest and importance for the West European countries. The conference on environmental protection, held by the ECE in the fall of 1979, dealt with questions of transborder air pollution, environmentally acceptable technologies, and the protection of water, wildlife, and plants.(31) No spectacular results were to be expected from this first conference. However, the process is to continue and it is conceivable that problems of nuclear technology, e.g., disposal and storage of nuclear waste, will be taken on the agenda.

Preparations for a conference on energy have proceeded far enough that the CSCE follow-up scheduled to be held in the fall of 1980 in Madrid, is likely to convene it. The EC member countries have so far been unable to arrive at a joint energy policy and coordination seems difficult to achieve. However, the economic problems arising from this sector are much felt, and the specific types of energy problems in Eastern and Western Europe seem to differ from each other to such a degree that substantial negotiations are conceivable.(32) The potential for political tensions arising from insufficient energy and power supplies could be reduced by cooperating in the planning and construction of exploitation measures, energy transport systems, and measures for the saving of energy; e.g., connecting the electrical power systems of Western and Eastern Europe could be mutually advantageous.

An all-European conference on questions of transport and traffic – the third of the proposed sectors for negotiations – could usefully strive to find methods of coordination in the expansion of East-West transport ways and systems, including such problems as standardization and common regulations. Controversial issues, such as the Eastern quest for improved East-West transport ways and facilities and the Western demand for economically calculated international transport rates, could be brought in a bargaining context and possibly be solved. The West European countries have reacted rather reservedly to the project of an all-European conference on transport. This may be explained by the lack of a joint or even coordinated transport policy within the EC, and the political and strategic problems involved.

NOTES

(1) This paper is based on the authors' "Integration of COMECON into the World Economy?" Aussenpolitik, 27, no. 1 (1976), pp. 31-45; and "CMEA and the World Economy: Institutional Concepts," in East European Economies Post-Helsinki, A Compendium of Papers Submitted to the Joint Economic Committee, U.S. Congress, 95th Congress, 1st Session (Washington, D.C.: United States Government Printing Office, August 25, 1977), pp. 999-1018.

(2) See E. Schulz, Moskau und die europäische Integration (Munich/Vienna: Oldenbourg, 1975).

(3) M.M. Maximowa, Economic Aspects of Capitalist Integration (Moscow: Progress Publishers, 1973), p. 331

(4) Ibid., pp. 330-31; see also W.I. Kusnezow, "Rechtliche Fragen einer Zusammenarbeit zwischen RGW und EWG," Sowjetwissenschaft, Gesellschaftswissenschaftliche Beiträge, no. 9 (1978), pp. 945-54.

(5) L.I. Breznev, "Rechenschaftsbericht des ZK der KPdSU an den XXIV. Parteitag, March 30, 1971," Parteitag der KPdSU, March 30-April 9, 1971 (Dokumente, Moskau 1971), p. 27.

(6) Comprehensive Program for the Further Extension and Improvement of Cooperation and the Development of Socialist Economic Integration by the CMEA Member Countries (Moscow: CMEA Secretariat, 1971).

(7) The former West German Undersecretary of State W. Frank stated that ". . . according to Soviet conceptions, CSCE's all-European perspectives could be an alternative to West European integration and to cooperation within NATO." [W. Frank, "Zielsetzungen der Bundesrepublik Deutschland im Rahmen europaischer Sicherheitsverhandlungen," Europa-Archiv, 27, no. 5 (1972), p. 155].

(8) In a communiqué of NATO's Council of Ministers it is claimed that a greater international mobility of people, ideas, and information as well as closer cooperation in cultural affairs should be promoted, Europa-Archiv, 25, no. 13 (1970), p. D318.

(9) See Ch. Royen, Das sowjetkommunistische Herrschaftssystem und die "friedliche Koexistenz" in Europe (Ebenhausen: Stiftung Wissenschaft und Politik, July 1976), p. 28.

(10) The EEC-Treaty provided for the introduction of a Common Commercial Policy by the end of 1969. In December 1969, the EC Council of Ministers decided to postpone the introduction in relations with the state trading countries. However, since the beginning of 1973, the COMECON countries have been subjected to the same regulations as all other third countries.

(11) See O.G. Schwerin, "Die Solidarität der EG-Staaten in der KSZE," Europa-Archiv, 30, no. 15 (1975), p. 483.

(12) See K.M. Sachs, EG-Handelspolitik und zwischenstaatliche Kooperationsabkommen (Baden-Baden: Nomos, 1976), p. 99.

(13) COMECON signed international treaties before 1974, e.g., a cooperation agreement with Finland in May 1973. For details of the agreement and possible similarities with an EC-COMECON agreement, see M. Baumer, Zur Multilateralisierung des Aussenhandels der RGW-Mitgliedstaaten (Ebenhausen: Stiftung Wissenschaft und Politik, February 1975).

(14) See H.D. Jacobsen, "Internationale Produktion und Supranationalität im RGW," Deutschland Archiv, 9, no. 6 (1976), pp. 606-613.

(15) The socialist countries did not succeed in calling for credits at preferred rates and for measures which were to solve the foreign exchange and the financing problems of trade between Eastern and Western Europe. Conceptions along these lines were put forward in a joint statement by the GDR and Hungary. See H. Volle and W. Wagner, eds., KSZE in Beiträgen und Dokumenten aus dem Europa-Archiv (Bonn: Verlag für Internationale Politik, 1976), pp. 223 ff.

(16) Joint Statement by the GDR and Hungary, cited in ibid., p. 223.

(17) Problems of granting MFN status and reciprocity played an important role in the GATT accession negotiations of some COMECON countries (Poland, Romania, Hungary).

(18) Final Act of the CSCE, reprinted in KSZE in Beiträgen und Dokumenten, p. 249.

(19) Ibid., p. 248.

(20) Only a few days before publication of this decision taken by secretaries of state of the member countries (Sept. 9, 1973), COMECON's Secretary General approached the president of the EC's Council of Ministers for the first time (Aug. 27, 1973).

(21) In Art. 3 of the draft agreement, a number of areas are listed: conditions for economic and trade cooperation between EC and COMECON member countries should be improved by collaborating in standardization, environmental protection, statistics, and prognoses of production and demand in selected sector. An unofficial translation of the draft agreement is reprinted in J. Bethkenhagen and H. Machowski, Integration im Rat für gegenseitige Wirtschaftshilfe (Berlin: Berlin Verlag, 1976), pp. 125-130.

(22) Art. 13 of the draft agreement stipulates that the proposed agreement may not infringe upon any contracts which the organizations or their member countries have already concluded.

(23) The listing of CSCE principles in the preamble of COMECON's draft does not mention Basket III, thereby neglecting one of the essentials of Helsinki, namely, equality of rank of all three Baskets.

(24) The more legal aspects are dealt with in A. Lebahn, "RGW und EG – Faktoren des Ost-West-Handels," Aussenpolitik, 29, no. 2 (1978), pp. 129 ff.

(25) See M. Baumer and H.D. Jacobsen, "CMEA's Economic 'Westpolitik' Between Global Limitations and European Opportunities," in A Compendium of Papers on Eastern Europe Submitted to the Joint Economic Committee, U.S. Congress, 96th Congress, 2nd Session (Washington, D.C.: United States Government Printing Office, 1980), forthcoming.

(26) For more details see H.D. Jacobsen, Die Ostwirtschaftspolitik der USA - Möglichkeiten und Grenzen einer "linkage" - Politik (Ebenhausen: Stiftung Wissenschaft und Politik, March 1980).

(27) This point has been stressed by J. Pinder in his contribution to the Eleventh World Congress of the International Political Science Association in Moscow, August 12-18, 1979, Integration in Western and Eastern Europe: Relations Between the EC and CMEA, mimeographed.

(28) See R. Lawniczak, "The Free Trade Area Idea and East-West Trade Promotion," EFTA-Bulletin, no. 1 (1975), pp. 11-14. In his contribution to the IPSA Congress in Moscow, M. Schmidt, Director of the GDR Institute for International Politics and Economics (IPW), reactivated the idea of an all-European free trade area, in "Economic Cooperation as a Factor in Giving Substance to Relations of Peaceful Coexistence Between States with Differing Social Systems," mimeographed.

(29) In contrast to the treaty between Finland and the EC (1973), the treaty between Finland and COMECON does not deal with the question of trade (texts are reprinted in Europe-Archiv, 29, no. 5 (1974), pp. D99-D112).

(30) "The Finland-Czechoslovakia Free Trade Agreement," Journal of World Trade Law, 11, no. 5 (Sept./Oct. 1977), pp. 479 ff.

(31) An introduction into related problems is given by J. Fullenbach, Umweltschutz zwischen Ost und West (Bonn: DGAP, 1977).

(32) See F. Muller, "Gesamteuropäische Zusammenarbeit im Energiebereich," Europa-Archiv, 34, no. 11 (1979), pp. 313-22.

7 Eurocommunism and East-West Relations

Steven J. Baker

THE EMERGENCE OF EUROCOMMUNISM

Eurocommunism is the phenomenon of mass-based, Western European communist parties that eschew revolution, vaunt their independence from the Soviet Union, and espouse moderate reformism with considerable electoral success. While this phenomenon has roots which go back to the immediate postwar period, two more recent trends have favored the emergence of Eurocommunism. The attenuation of the Cold War in the late 1960s and early 1970s led to a decline of domestic anticommunism in Western Europe; in the age of detente, domestic communists were no longer pariahs, left and center parties had a new potential ally, and communist parties were less dependent than in the past on the Soviet Union for external support. At the same time, the parties of the center and right appeared unable to satisfactorily manage the high growth, mass consumption, industrial societies which they are largely responsible for creating; communists emerged both as protest parties and, abandoning the rhetoric of revolutionary social and economic change, as a practical political alternative to the parties in power. Detente had made the participation of communist parties in a French, Italian, or Spanish government conceivable, while domestic social and economic problems made it possible.(1)

The Western European communist parties vascillate between identifying themselves as part of a single movement – as the Eurocommunist summit in Madrid in the spring of 1977 – and emphasizing the individuality of their programs.(2) The attempt to stress the common features of communist parties operating in liberal democratic political systems has important theoretical implications for communism, not the least of which is that it provides a modicum of international solidarity to a set of phenomena that otherwise would seem to be divisive. The

*I would like to thank Peter Lange and Gianfranco Pasquino for comments on earlier drafts.

Eurocommunist identity rescues "national roads to socialism" from the heresy of national "deviationism," and helps to buttress the Western communist parties against the charge that they have been coopted by their respective political systems. The charge of cooptation comes from the Soviets within the World Communist Movement and from extreme left critics within each of the West European countries. But this common identity falls far short of a unified political program, beyond the affirmation of loyalty to liberal democratic political practices. In pursuing national roads to socialism, it is the "national road" that is most often stressed by the Eurocommunists and not "socialism"; and, in practice, the major Western communist parties seem to have little in common beyond their labels and their common desire to be recognized as distinct from and independent of the Soviet Union and Eastern bloc.

To establish a distinctive identity, the Eurocommunists stress more the specific national character of each party and its policies than any transnational West European identity, particularly when the policies and/or the shifting political fortunes of other communist parties seem to cause political problems at home. The Italian communists chose to identify with the French communists in 1977 until the French Communist Party (PCF) adopted intransigent positions in favor of programs such as nationalization of industries which were an embarrassment to the Italian Communist Party (PCI). But the fortunes of the Eurocommunists are linked perceptually, whether they like it or not; and the failure of the French left to win the March 1978 elections, even if due to peculiarly French circumstances, was widely believed to make even less likely the immediate entry of the PCI into an Italian cabinet. The electoral setback of the PCI in June 1979 contributed to the perception that Eurocommunism is a phenomenon on the wane.

While it is tempting to generalize in assessing the impact of Eurocommunism on East-West relations, it is prudent to focus on specific Western countries and individual communist parties – Italy and the PCI will be examined in this perspective. But there are a few general observations that serve to frame the discussion of the more specific factors. First, it is a fact that the Eurocommunist phenomenon is confined to Latin Europe – France, Italy, Spain (and arguably, Portugal). Eurocommunism corresponds to one of Europe's most profound cultural and historical divisions, that between the predominately Catholic, less industrialized South, and the predominately Protestant, more industrialized North. This division has been narrowed in the postwar period with the establishment of the European Community and is based on the kinds of considerations that should be less important today than ever before. Indeed, increasingly, secularization and industrialization are two of the major social and economic trends that seem to have contributed to the emergence of Eurocommunism. Nevertheless, the absence of a parallel Eurocommunist phenomenon in West Germany and Great Britain, however explained, serves to strengthen at least the image of a North-South split in Western Europe.

A second general consideration closely related to the first is that the states in which Eurocommunism is strongest are also those farthest from the primary area of military confrontation in Central Europe. There has always been a distinction within NATO between frontline nations (particularly West Germany) and flank countries, and this distinction is formalized in the talks on Mutual Force Reductions in which France is a nonparticipant by choice and Italy is one of the rotating observers not directly involved in the negotiations. Despite the importance of the United States' bases located there, Spain is not, of course, a member of NATO; and, for the present, post-Franco Spain seems little more likely to be integrated into the Alliance than Franco Spain. The reinforcement of this geographical East-West distinction by more profound political divisions, were communists to share power in flank countries, might very well reduce further Alliance cohesion to the extent that objective differences of national interest grounded in geopolitical factors would be reinforced by differences of political perception on the part of the leaders of the countries in question.

A third general consideration is that, while the emergence of communist parties in Western Europe as legitimate contenders for national political power is the result of decades of evolution of social and economic conditions in the nations in question, changes continue to take place and their impact on the political fortunes of communist parties is far from clear. Eurocommunism is an ongoing process as well as a phenomenon. If the position of communist parties (CPs) is relatively stronger in Western Europe today than ever before, the role of political parties in general has never in the postwar period been weaker. Apathy and extra-party social and political movements have reduced the appeal and authority of traditional political parties in all the Western European countries. The CPs have done little better than their political opponents at responding to the kinds of concerns that motivate activists today – ecology, women's liberation, nuclear energy, and the assorted discontents of life in industrial societies.   Party membership and effective participation in communist parties have declined in some countries, even as the electoral strength of communist parties show increases. And the ability of communist parties to "deliver" their constituents is more open to question than in the past.

A final general consideration concerns the framework within which one might expect a change in foreign policy to result from the inclusion of communists and a coalition government in a country such as Italy, France, or Spain. While the relationship of domestic politics to foreign policy is notoriously difficult to express with much precision, there are a few widely-accepted general categories of determinants of foreign policy that can serve as a framework.(3) A nation's foreign policy may be seen as resulting from the interaction of geopolitical and material resource factors, the patterns of dominance and subordination characteristic of the world at the moment, the social and economic needs of the nations, and the perceptions of its leaders. The first three of these sets of determinants are largely fixed for most nations at most times, even though the perception of the constraints they impose may well vary somewhat as a function of the fourth set of determinants. These relatively-fixed kinds of determinants lend a kind of stability and continuity to the foreign policies of nations in spite of changes of government and, often, in spite of changes of regime. The most obvious source of change in foreign policy resulting from the inclusion of communists in a coalition government would be changes in leaders' perceptions that this would presumably entail, and the more that one qualifies the differences between Eurocommunists and those who presently dominate in each of these countries, the more marginal the changes in foreign policy that can be expected. On the face of it, Eurocommunists sharing in power would seem to imply shifts in emphasis rather than dramatic turns in foreign policy.

Since the total impact of these kinds of generalizations on the course of Eurocommunism and its impact on East-West relations is so equivocal, it is essential to understand the specific situations. While the first significant brush with communism in a major European government took place in Portugal in 1974-75, the second and ultimately more significant confrontation came in Italy where it was feared that the electoral gains of the PCI in regional elections in June 1975 might be repeated at the national level in the national elections of June 1976,(4) making the communists part of the governing coalition. Suddenly, there was a shift in emphasis away from Central Europe as the dominant area of concern for East-West relations to the southern flank, and a shift of emphasis away from the external threat to the internal one.

That a portentous shift in the political balance in Western Europe might begin in Italy is something of an anomaly since Italy is geographically peripheral to the major area of postwar confrontation in Germany, and a somewhat marginal member of the European Community. One might have thought that Italy's problems were so particular and its role in the major defense and economic organizations in Europe so qualified, that any political change south of the Alps would have little impact on the rest of Europe. But while the situation in Central Europe is a continuing source of preoccupation, the concern for the political situation in the Mediterranean has increased. The Middle East and oil crises; revolutions in Portugal, Spain, and Greece; the Cyprus conflict which has put Greek and Turkish NATO participation in question; the enlarged Soviet naval presence in the Mediterranean have all served to increase Italy's importance in the European security equation. At the same time, Italy's economic problems(5) are seen by some as but the most extreme variant of difficulties faced by other West European countries. Italy's increasingly important role in European security combined with the growing power of the Italian communist party to make Italy a test case for Eurocommunism.

In the summer of 1976, concern about the international implications of communist participation in an Italian government and the pressures of domestic electoral politics led to concerted action on the part of the American and West German governments to prevent communists from sharing in power. Henry Kissinger emphasized the negative impact on European defense of having communists participate in a NATO member state's government, and he and Helmut Schmidt both threatened to impose economic sanctions on Italy were the communists admitted to a coalition government. This kind of external pressure, the opposition of a large part of the Christian Democrats (DC) to any formal cooperation with the communists, and the refusal of the communists to form a coalition which excluded the Catholics combined to keep the PCI out of the post-June 1976 government, despite its impressive electoral gains. But while the DCs refused to share governmental authority with the PCI, they could not rule without its indirect support; and so, like the Socialist Party (PSI) during the "opening to the left" of the early 1960s, the communists made their entrance into the ranks of governmental parties by abstaining on the vote of confidence on the formation of a minority Christian Democrat government. The result of the interplay of foreign and domestic politics was that the communists increased their political power without direct governmental responsibilities.

From mid-1976 to the spring of 1978, the PCI was in the uncomfortable position of supporting an ineffective Christian Democratic government whose austerity programs, largely imposed at the behest of Italy's international creditors, seemed to fall disproportionately on the shoulders of the PCI's working-class electorate. These circumstances caused divisions within the PCI as to the wisdom of the strategy adopted; and, as the domestic economic situation worsened and an unprecedented wave of violence (political and nonpolitical) gripped the nation, the communists took one step closer to sharing power by voting in support of the DC government's economic austerity and "law and order" platform in October 1977, further alienating left wing extremist groups. This was followed in January 1978 by renewed pressure by the Communists to be given positions in the Italian cabinet along side the DC. An agreement on direct PCI support as part of the government majority without, however, cabinet portfolios was reached in March of 1978 just before the kidnapping of Christian Democrat Aldo Moro, an act widely interpreted as an attempt by the extreme left to break up the DC and PCI coalition. But the two parties went forward with their commitment to deal with the immediate threats of political terrorism and economic chaos, and the PCI moved one step closer to direct participation in a national government. The Andreotti government that was created in the Spring of 1978 presided over a modest economic improvement, but also over continuing political terrorism and, by January 1979, differences between the major coalition partners as well as disagreements within the PCI over the wisdom of cooperation with the DC in the face of eroding support from communist rank and file led the PCI to withdraw their support from Andreotti, causing his government to fall. This set the scene for elections in June 1979, which many saw as a kind of plebescite on communist attempts to realize an "historic compromise" with the Christian Democrats.

The PCI suffered its first major electoral setback in 30 years in the national elections of June 1979. Its share of the vote fell 4 percent to 30 percent of the total, while the Christian Democrats held firm at 39 percent. The center and lay parties were the major beneficiaries of the shift in votes. Analysts of the returns cited the apparent dissatisfaction of some communist voters with the policies followed by the PCI since 1976 as helping to account for communist losses, as well as the apparent attraction for young voters of the social-issue-oriented parties of the center such as the Radicals. Berlinguer explained the losses as resulting from party campaign errors, policy errors while supporting the DC governments – especially support for economic austerity programs – and international events such as the wars among the communist governments in Southeast Asia that were used by demagogues to tarnish the PCI's public image.(6) For the present, the PCI went back into opposition and the "historic compromise" was dead. But no apparent governing alternative emerged from the 1979 elections, and Italy drifted for months without a government that could command a parliamentary majority.

One international change was expected to favor PCI participation in a government with the advent of the Carter administration in January 1977; adamant opposition to communist participation in West European governments changed to a more pragmatic policy of being "not indifferent" to such a course of events. It was widely supposed that the U.S. government would not pose any major obstacle and, indeed, there was reason to believe that many within the new administration might welcome communist participation in an Italian government as a contribution to political stability.(7) It came as a surprise, then, in January 1978, when the Carter administration took a hard-line position against PCI participation in an Italian cabinet; and whereas Kissinger had stressed the impact of such a course of events on the Western Alliance, the Carter administration stressed that while it would not "interfere," in its judgment the PCI did not share the U.S. commitment to "democratic values."(8) Thus, in spite of rhetorical shifts, the substance of the policy of the Carter administration toward Eurocommunism remained the same as Kissinger's, particularly in seeking to block the direct participation of the PCI in an Italian government.(9) But this time, the American government stood without the overt support of the Germans. Schmidt's policy toward the PCI had become markedly more pragmatic since the summer of 1976. With a severely reduced parliamentary majority, continuing domestic economic problems, and the growing problem of political terrorism to cope with, Schmidt chose to remain publicly noncommittal on the possible advent of communists to power in Italy in 1978. With foreign pressures somewhat reduced, eventual participation of communists in an Italian government became less than ever before a function of the international situation and more a function of Italy's chaotic domestic situation.

EUROCOMMUNISM AND THE ATLANTIC COMMUNITY:
THE UNITED STATES, ITALY, AND NATO

In the postwar period, Italy found itself in that part of Europe in which the United States was to exercise predominant influence. Indeed, the wartime occupation of liberated Italy set the precedent for dividing

Europe between the major allies instead of sharing responsibilities and influence. Those political forces whose rebirth after 20 years of fascism was promoted by American occupation authorities cemented Italy's position in the American-led Western bloc in 1949 by adherence to NATO. The Christian Democrats' decision to join the Alliance in the face of strong neutralist and/or leftist opposition was a fundamental choice, a so-called "choice of civilizations"(10) which helped to fix the postwar orientation of Italian political life toward the United States and the Western European countries allied with the U.S.; it also helped to establish a permanence of U.S. intervention in Italian political life.(11) Making this irreversible choice in the face of fundamental opposition from the left reduced the discussion of foreign and defense policy questions in postwar Italy to highly symbolic exchanges which are a function of domestic political competition.(12) The direct linkage between the domestic distribution of political power in Italy and the nation's foreign policy orientation has persisted up to the present. And while Alliance relations are by no means the most substantial ties between Italy and the United States – ethnic, cultural, and economic relations all are very important – positions on NATO have a symbolic importance for both parties that transcends the objective importance of the Alliance. And the impact of Eurocommunism on Alliance relations is a major concern of observers.(13)

Thirty years after the end of World War II, American forces continue to be stationed in Western Europe in part as a function of commitments to the Atlantic Alliance. The coincidence of the existence of NATO and the absence of war in Europe, despite the history of two wars earlier in this century and high levels of political tension and military preparedness since 1945, are the most potent obstacles to any change in the military status quo. Many in the West equate the existence of NATO with the maintenance of European peace and security.

From the beginning, the Alliance has been both anti-Soviet and anticommunist. In Central Europe, NATO was designed to contain the possible military expansion of the Soviet Union. In the rest of Europe, particularly in France, Italy, and Greece, the Alliance served as an external guarantee against an internal communist threat. In the political climate of the postwar period, the direct linkage between the external and internal threats was unquestioned by dominant political groups in Europe and America. Many of NATO's problems today stem from a declining perception of Soviet military or domestic communist political threats, and the even greater willingness to deny any linkage between the two.

If the only measure of the Soviet military threat were the level of Soviet forces deployed in Eastern Europe, one might conclude that the threat today to Western European security is greater than any time since the immediate postwar years. Of course, this is the proposition being advanced in NATO circles. The Soviet military build-up in Central Europe of the past few years is interpreted by some as a sign of Soviet aggressive intent or as a tool for potential Soviet political leverage over the West. But NATO, too, is better manned, equipped, and trained than in the past, and the 1978 agreement of NATO countries to increase defense spending 3 percent in each of the next several years is a measure of growing concern about the military balance in Central Europe. The popularity of a book such as General Hackett's The Third World War is evidence of some public interest in the problem.(14)

While defense planners emphasize the growing Soviet military threat, the changes in the political climate in Western Europe are such that the generally perceived feeling of threat is lower than in the immediate postwar years, even if it is slightly more than it was four or five years ago. Relatively high material prosperity and short-term economic difficulties combine to diminish the European public's preoccupation with external threats. The threat of war plays a very marginal part in peoples' perceptions in the kind of postindustrial societies that are emerging in the Atlantic Community. While, objectively, the Soviet military threat may be described accurately as rising, the Soviet threat is not a major problem in the public consciousness in Western Europe. Under the best of circumstances, gaining parliamentary approval for NATO defense spending increases, manpower increases, and acceptance of controversial new weapons or doctrines has been difficult. Present political and economic circumstances in Western Europe are far from the best as the neutron bomb controversy suggests.

The relevance of NATO in an era in which the Soviet military threat is not widely perceived is questionable. That NATO's continued existence is a necessary precondition to the diminution of the Soviet threat is a proposition that is widely accepted in defense circles but less among the general public, and is a proposition that can only be tested after the fact. The counterarguments that NATO was never necessary because the Soviet Union has not had aggressive designs on Western Europe, and/or that the Soviet Union has become a prosperous, status quo power unlikely to risk war in Europe are increasingly plausible to many people. When statesmen such as Germany's Willy Brandt and Henry Kissinger argued in the early 1970s that a strong Western Alliance is necessary to pursue Ostpolitik and detente, they had to justify the results of their policies as having reduced international tensions and diminished the likelihood of war. To the extent that they were successful, they made a strong Western Alliance appear to be less necessary than in the past, even though this was clearly not their intent. Given a choice, many people in America and Europe preferred to believe that the Soviet threat has declined. The implications − psychological, political and economic − of the opposite view are very unappealing.

The Alliance's second ostensible purpose, anticommunism, is the one which is of growing relevance to the problem of allied relations since it is possible that communists may participate in major NATO governments. Belief in a monolithic world communist movement has disappeared. Few argue today that West European communist parties are dominated by the Soviet Union or that they are intent on creating Soviet-style "peoples democracies" in the West. Rather, the arguments center on the degree of influence that the Soviet Union might exercise over the West European communist parties on those issues of direct relevance to foreign policy and security, and this is an important distinction.

Then Secretary of State Kissinger took the lead in 1976 in opposing the inclusion of communists in an Italian government coalition. Kissinger did not argue in 1976 that the PCI would make Italy into a Mediterranean Bulgaria nor that the PCI would lead Italy into a reversal of alliances and participation in the Warsaw Pact; rather, the threat as defined by Kissinger was that the PCI in a government would neglect Italy's Alliance commitments, and result in doubts as to whether in times of crisis Italy would carry out NATO obligations, or so compromise NATO defense plans through its informal links to the communist countries that Italy might have to be expelled from the alliance.(15) As important as these considerations are, they are still a somewhat limited definition of the threat posed by communist participation in an Italian government consistent with the view that the foreign policy shifts to be expected were circumscribed by largely fixed parameters. To assess even these limited fears, it is necessary to understand something of Italy's role in NATO as well as NATO's impact on Italy.

Italy's role in NATO has, until recently, been rather limited, even though NATO's impact on Italian politics and defense policy has been massive. Geographically outside the area of major East-West tension in Central Europe, Italy's role within the alliance has been largely passive, accepting the policies and priorities of the Alliance without a major independent policy contribution.(16) This pattern of participation is consistent with Italy's role as a subordinate part of a region dominated by the United States,(17) but this characterization should not minimize the impact of adherence to NATO on Italian domestic politics which has been very important. Choosing to align itself with the United States in the face of opposition of the left parties, the Christian Democrats guaranteed that the debate over foreign policy would be highly polemic. But, in practice, the very fact that the differences in foreign policy have been fundamental rather than instrumental has resulted in an almost total lack of substance in foreign policy and a lack of substantial parliamentary control over foreign and defense policy.(18) The resulting defense posture, weapons acquisition policies, and force deployments reflect NATO postwar priorities – emphasis on a large, standing army concentrated in the North-East area near the Yugoslav border with naval commands in the Naples-Gaeta area. There is a general feeling that the air force and navy have been neglected and that overall military effectiveness is low. Only in the last few years have serious questions been raised as to whether or not these policies correspond to Italian defense needs as distinct from Alliance priorities.(19)

In the postwar period, foreign policy has been preempted as a substantive issue; and for ideological and practical reasons, the PCI has been even less concerned with substantive questions of foreign policy than other parties. As a matter of dogma, the PCI has seen Italian foreign policy conditioned by domestic economic and social circumstances which, in turn, they have seen as greatly influenced by regional and global factors. They share the general perception of Italy as a subordinate actor within a regional and international system, and opposition to the United States has been a function of the American role in these systems that perpetuates Italian subordination. Within the general context of opposition to American hegemony, the PCI's attitude has varied over time on specific American foreign policy initiatives and on Italy's role in NATO,(20) according to whether such positions contribute to a more positive evolution of the international situation or a less positive one. Of course, a more positive situation has been identified with circumstances in which the realization of the PCI's interests and goals seems more rather than less likely. As a practical matter, however, while the party has helped to facilitate Italian governmental and commercial relations with the communist countries of Eastern Europe, the PCI has had little prospect of affecting Italian foreign policy and, therefore, has been more concerned with relations with "fraternal communist parties" of the international communist movement than conventional foreign policy.

It is striking that the PCI should have so few foreign or defense policy experts as usually defined.(21) This could be critical to estimating the impact of PCI participation in a coalition government on foreign and defense policies because it could give rise to two divergent possibilities. One possibility is that having an unconventional approach to foreign policy, the PCI in power would seek to radically redefine Italian national interests and push for policies based on very different premises from past Italian governments – e.g., neutralism, the dissolution of the blocs. This possibility has been specifically disavowed.(22) Alternatively and more probably, the result of PCI participation in a coalition would be to leave foreign policy questions to other parties of the coalition and to the bureaucracy which are both more interested in and have more experience with these questions. The result of this second possibility would be little immediate change in Italian foreign policy as a consequence of PCI participation in a government; only over time, as the communists' presence in the relevant ministries grew and higher priority problems were dealt with might one expect major changes of foreign policy.

The tendency to treat substantive foreign and defense policy as a low priority question was evident during the crucial 1976 parliamentary elections. The PCI succeeded in persuading prominent noncommunists to present themselves as independents in the communist list of candidates for the parliament. Two of these who were subsequently elected (retired Air Force General Nino Pasti and European Communities Commissioner Altiero Spinelli) were temporarily coopted as spokesmen for the party on defense and European questions respectively. Of course, this was an example of the PCI's political opportunism and part of its bid for greater respectability. But it is also a sign of lack of interest in or substantive experience with many of the concrete problems that a governing party would have to cope with.

General Pasti's appearance on the communist lists came as something of a shock outside of Italy. As Deputy Supreme Allied Commander in Europe for Nuclear Affairs from 1966 to 1968, Pasti had been the highest ranking Italian in NATO and one with an intimate knowledge of the Alliance's nuclear defenses. His candidacy caused consternation at NATO headquarters in Brussels where communist access to nuclear secrets is frequently raised as a major objection to having a government with communist participation part of the Alliance. Since his retirement in 1969, Pasti has criticized NATO's tactical nuclear weapons policy,(23) stated that he thinks Soviet military capabilities have been overestimated, and cautioned against higher levels of defense effort to offset these "inflated" estimates of Soviet capabilities.(24) At the same time, Pasti suggested that NATO continues to perform a necessary defensive role and that its defensive capabilities should be strengthened.(25) There is nothing in such views that could be characterized as radical or even specifically leftist, let alone communist. These are views which are widely held among Western defense intellectuals. To the extent that such views, in part, challenge the U.S.-led consensus within the Alliance and depart from past Italian passivity, they could be construed as validating some of the U.S. government's fears about having communists in a NATO government, but hardly as representing a fundamental threat to NATO. The real question is the extent to which these moderate views are representative of the views of the PCI, either in its leadership cadres or within the ranks of party militants and its mass electorate.

Without abandoning the long-term vision of ending Europe's division into hostile blocs, the PCI has come to accept the existence of NATO and Italy's participation in the Alliance as an integral part of the present international "balance of forces" which makes it possible for them to pursue their domestic political ambitions. Unilateral Italian withdrawal from NATO would upset the balance and compromise the achievement of domestic reforms. It is in this sense that the PCI abandoned its position of "NATO out of Italy, Italy out of NATO," in 1970 in favor of its present, more pragmatic acceptance of an Italian contribution to an Alliance which it defines as properly having a purely "defensive" function.(26) Berlinguer has even gone so far as to recognize that NATO membership could constitute a kind of guarantee against Soviet interference in an Italy governed by a coalition including the PCI.(27)

While fundamentally important in terms of the theoretical evolution of the PCI, the shift in favor of continued participation in NATO was facilitated by the fact that communist opposition to NATO had been largely rhetorical since the early 1950s. Since then, the PCI has not posed substantial opposition to Italian defense policy, nor has it tried to cripple the national defense effort nor posed serious obstacles to the location of NATO bases in Italy. This kind of pragmatic, instrumental approach to NATO membership is not qualitatively different from that of many members of the Christian Democrats. In the immediate postwar period, many in the DC supported NATO membership because it served to guarantee the liberal democratic political system in Italy and helped to preserve the DC's own political predominance within the system.(28) The PCI's acceptance of membership in NATO also serves to guarantee the domestic political system but, in changed international political circumstances, also allows the PCI to challenge the DC for political predominance within the system.

Of course, Americans and others would prefer a more positive kind of commitment to the Alliance. Kissinger observed that, as great as the differences were between General De Gaulle and the United States, De Gaulle could always be relied on to support the West in times of crisis, and he questioned whether the PCI could likewise be relied upon. The refusal of PCI leaders to admit to the existence of a "threat" from the Soviet Union while acknowledging the need to provide a defensive capability (against whom or what?) is not encouraging to NATO supporters. But in a period in which the general belief in a Soviet military threat is low, the difference between the PCI and other Italian parties is one of degree rather than kind.

The one security crisis which would most directly involve Italy centers on Yugoslavia, not an invasion of Italy by the Yugoslavs but an invasion of Yugoslavia by the Soviet Union/Warsaw Pact countries in some kind of post-Tito power play. Such an event is believed by many to be highly unlikely. While the reaction of any Italian government to such an eventuality would be problematic and contingent on the specific situation, there is no reason to believe that the reaction of an Italian government with PCI participation would necessarily be less militant than that of any other Italian government. This scenario would pose an objective security problem for Italy, but any Italian government would hesitate to take strong action short of an actual violation of its national territory. No matter which government would be in power at the time, Italy's allies must be mindful of Italy's tradition of sacro egoismo that has led to ambivalent fidelity to alliance commitments.

On the other hand, this kind of Soviet move would confirm the worst suspicions of Soviet intentions and could constitute a major domestic political embarrassment for the Italian communists as well as a potential security threat for the nation. Defensive action might very well be taken, all the more because the political future of the PCI would be threatened. The Communists might feel even more compelled to demonstrate their commitment to national defense in these circumstances than noncommunist parties. The Soviets' anticipation that intervention in Yugoslavia might either provoke a strong reaction from a government with PCI participation or alternatively lead to the ouster of the PCI from the government by anticommunist elements could condition Soviet behavior, arguably restraining them or inclining them toward intervention depending on what outcome they might favor. Certainly, these possibilities are as plausible as the fear that, if faced with this kind of dramatic external security and domestic political crisis, the PCI in a coalition is more likely than other Italian parties to remain immobile and seek to impose a policy of neutrality on the nation.

The major problem for NATO resulting from PCI participation in a government would probably be on the less dramatic questions of Alliance policy, especially regarding manpower levels and deployment and defense expenditures. It is here that Kissinger's concern for the communists' "neglect" of defense commitments is most relevant. It seems highly unlikely that a government with PCI participation would automatically respond positively to directives from Brussels to increase their defense effort, and the PCI might be more inclined to favor reforms of the Italian armed forces than governments to date have been, with uncertain impact on the Italian contribution to the Alliance. The deployment of new tactical nuclear weapons in Italy such as the neutron bomb or Pershing II missile would almost certainly be opposed by the PCI. But in contemplating the impact of communist participation in an Italian government on NATO, there may be a tendency to exaggerate Italy's past contribution to the Alliance and, thereby, provide an unrealistic standard for judging the impact of future contingencies. Italy has consistently lagged in defense modernization and like other Alliance members, unilaterally cut manpower levels. Italy's most valuable contribution to the Alliance has been and remains as a naval base and location of the principal Alliance Mediterranean commands.(29) But the use of these bases in times of crisis has always been subject to political conditions imposed by the Italian government. Like other European governments, the Italian government refused official permission for use of these bases by the United States in its resupply effort during the 1973 Middle East War. In any future conflict in the Mediterranean, Alliance commitments to the contrary notwithstanding, it cannot automatically be assumed that the United States and the Italian governments would necessarily agree on the kind of threat posed and act in unison to meet that threat. That the Italian government in question might have communist participants may provide additional complications, but does not categorically change the situation, since Italian positions on the Middle East have often differed from those of the United States.

While it is probable that the sophisticated, intellectual leadership of the PCI can see many benefits to be obtained by continued Italian membership in NATO, it is equally likely that the less sophisticated, mass base of the party is more prone to question the compatibility of communist participation in an Italian government and Italian participation in an anticommunist Alliance. An implicit recognition of this gap between the leadership and the mass following is found in the failure of the party press to report Berlinguer's observation that NATO would guarantee Italy against interference from the Soviet Union.(30) One of the questions most often asked is whether the present moderate leadership will be able to impose on other leadership factions and the masses political action to which there is substantial internal opposition. This is the problem Berlinguer faced from March 1978 to January 1979, and the decision to withdraw support for the Andreotti government was, in part, the result of the growing criticism within the party of the leadership's line as well as PCI losses in local elections that seemed to repudiate the party policy. Public opinion data suggest that rank-and-file communists still oppose Italy's integration into an American-led military alliance more than other Italians.(31)

The question is not whether the PCI can be "trusted" to keep its word but, rather, whether it continues to be in the interest of the PCI to keep its word. The crucial factor in the PCI leadership's considerations is that NATO membership must be seen as a sort of political guarantee to people within and without Italy who would otherwise be violently opposed to PCI participation in an Italian government. At the same time, NATO must not be seen as a means of American interference in Italian political life as it has been in the past, with the aim of either keeping the communists out of power or, failing that, of making it as difficult as possible for them to govern the nation.

It is at this point that the intersection between domestic policy and foreign policy alignment occurs. As long as a government with PCI participation is successful in coping with high priority issues such as the economy, unemployment, reform of the administrative bureaucracy, and improvements in social services, its electoral following is unlikely to press for a break with NATO or for any other foreign policy change. However, if for any reason the PCI in government should prove to be incapable of dealing with these kinds of issues, there may be a temptation to turn to lower priority issues such as foreign policy to seek compensatory gains and, in particular, highly symbolic issues such as NATO. The real threat to continued Italian participation in NATO is not the PCI's taking part in a government, but in that government's failure to markedly improve the domestic economic and political situation.

The PCI's record of positive administrative experience in Bologna and the so-called Red Belt across central Italy – Emilia-Romagna, Tuscany, and Umbria – is evidence that a government with PCI participation might be more effective than past Italian governments. But governing alone in Bologna and governing the country in coalition with other parties in Rome are very different circumstances, and the PCI's local effectiveness may well be dissipated at the national level. A government with PCI participation cannot be expected to resolve deep-rooted, structural problems automatically. External American efforts at destabilization a la Chile might only provide the PCI with a convenient scapegoat for what may well be their own political shortcomings. The most unfortunate aspect of American pressures against PCI participation in an Italian government to date has been to provide an American scapegoat for the failure of the PCI to win a share in the government without encouraging American friends in the DC to mend their ways. The impact of communist participation in an Italian government on relations with the United States would be more a function of U.S. responses than of PCI initiatives.

American objections in 1976 to PCI participation in an Italian government were based on a mixture of foreign policy and American domestic political considerations. Kissinger apparently did not want to lend credence to the objection that, in essence, detente with the Soviet

Union meant that "what is theirs is theirs while what is ours is negotiable." Rather he sought to implement the principle that detente, in effect, means freezing the political division of Europe between the United States and Soviet Union, the ideas most clearly expressed in the so-called Sonnenfeld Doctrine. American interference in the 1976 Italian election campaign came to be called the American counterpart to Soviet interference in the domestic affairs of the countries of Eastern Europe, a hegemonial "Brezhfeld Doctrine."(32) But equally important, communist gains in Italy would have weakened Ford vis a vis challenger Ronald Reagan in the primaries and against vociferous, antidetente, Democrat opponents such as Senator Jackson.

There is no evidence that Kissinger's policy was based on any in-depth analysis or understanding of the political situation in Italy, although he was undoubtedly encouraged to take a public hard-line stand against the PCI by some Christian Democrats. The threats of Kissinger and other administration spokesmen are widely felt to have been counterproductive, serving to make many legitimate anticom-munists appear to be the tools of American policy, while allowing the PCI to appear even more autonomous and nationalist than its opponents. But the kind of international pressures which Kissinger mobilized probably did help to keep the PCI out of the government for a year or so.

Kissinger's policy could not be successful ultimately because it failed to comprehend the nature of the problem: voters were turning to the PCI because of the domestic situation irrespective of possible foreign policy implications. Increases in PCI strength reflect a wide range of long-term changes in Italian society(33) as well as a response to the corruption and ineptitude of the Christian Democrats. To insist that the communist alternative to domestic problems be rejected because of possible international implications was largely irrelevant to many Italian voters. To prop up a Christian Democratic party which has proven itself incapable of internal reform was to perpetuate the source of many of the nation's problems. And to threaten economic sanctions in concert with Germany and other Western countries if Italian voters freely opted for the communist alternative was unseemly behavior for friends, particularly friends who base their opposition to communism, in part, on their supposed dedication to democratic practices such as free elections.

To the extent that Kissinger's policies were predicated on the international political implications of PCI participation in a govern-ment, his policy was mistaken. Reducing American policy toward Italy to a subordinate function of Soviet-American relations was to revert to the earliest days of the Cold War, a refusal to acknowledge the kinds of changes which had taken place since then and which Kissinger out of office was perceptive in analysing. Refusal to acknowledge changes in the Italian situation and to alter American policies accordingly risked creating a self-fulfilling prophecy. Emphasizing that communist partic-ipation in an Italian coalition was incompatible with participation in the Alliance reinforced NATO's image as being aimed at the domestic communist threat at a time when such a threat was least credible to Italians. In doing so, the U.S. government would assume the onus of driving an Italy governed in part by the PCI out of the Alliance. Insofar as the Alliance's anti-Soviet aims are concerned, it is difficult to see how no Italian participation in the Alliance could be preferable to politically qualified Italian participation. And insofar as there might be any domestic political costs incurred in Italy's leaving NATO, it is difficult to see why the United States should be willing to assume the burden of those costs instead of letting them rest on the PCI.

Emphasizing the growing Soviet military threat since the early 1970s and the need for an increased NATO military capability to deal with it, the United States has served to sharpen the growing gap in perceptions between the U.S. government and public opinion in Western Europe; the higher NATO's visibility, the more politically contentious NATO and associated defense policies become. Demands for defense-spending increases and debates over weapons such as the neutron bomb and cruise missiles seem highly likely to have a negative political impact on European public opinion, whatever the intent of the Alliance's proponents. This policy was intensified by demands during the Senate debate on SALT II that a major portion of defense expenditure increases be earmarked for NATO. An Italy governed in part by the communists could live within a NATO whose demands are limited and whose intrusions into domestic life are not excessive. Continuing to accept that Italy and other European NATO partners exercise some latitude in changes in domestic political alignments, in defense expenditures, and in levels of manpower is the price the United States must pay for the continued existence of the Alliance. But if the United States uses NATO commitments to block these kinds of domestically determined policy changes, then the continued viability of some Europeans' NATO participation may well be challenged, even by future Italian governments without communist participation.

Eurocommunism raises, in a dramatic way, the question of the proper role of the United States in Western Europe; in this sense, it is the "Gaullism" of the 1970s. The American refusal to compromise with Eurocommunism, persisting through two otherwise significantly different administrations, is a sign of the American reluctance to abandon the leadership role assumed in the conditions of post-World War II. Thus, Eurocommunism in general and the PCI in particular do pose a real problem for U.S. policy. In a period of detente, the linkage between Western European domestic communism and the Soviet-led world communist movement declined considerably in the eyes of many; thus, Kissinger's attempt to make an electoral victory of Italian communists appear to be an advantage to the Soviet Union struck a hollow cord for many. Carter's shift to opposition based on the PCI's supposed lack of commitment to democracy is a measure of the U.S. government's realization that Eurocommunism is a domestic political phenomenon. But even if the success of Western communist parties is not a clear advantage for the Soviet Union, it is a loss for the United States, nonetheless, for being largely symbolic. Parties inspired, however vaguely, by alternative political and economic systems implicitly reject the American model. And more substantially, an Italian government including the PCI might well be less inclined to ritualistic lip service for America's NATO policies than past governments.

The question that remains unanswered is whether Eurocommunism can survive the end of detente. There is no question but that expectations for continued improvements in East-West relations have ended, and the major differences are now between those who think relations will deteriorate no further as opposed to those who argue that relations could return to a renewed Cold War atmosphere. On the surface, one might argue that precisely the predominance of domestic over international concerns that underlies the rise of Eurocommunism should insulate it from deteriorating East-West relations. But the PCI's own analysis seems to suggest that the continued success of their policies does depend on the continuation of detente; the domestic political situation is inextricably linked to the regional and international situation. While neither the United States nor the Soviet Union is likely to cause a worsening of their relations with one another in order to reassert their respective positions as bloc leaders, neither is likely to fail to attempt such a reassertion as a consequence of deterioration of detente. That the conditions for such a reassertion are not propitious does not exclude the possibility of such an attempt by the superpowers, with all the tensions that are likely to flow from it.

In assessing the impact of Eurocommunism on alliance relations, an additional dimension of the Alliance's purposes should be borne in mind: like all alliances, NATO not only provides for common action against an external threat but also serves to regulate relations among its members. The overemphasis on the purely military aspects of the Alliance should not be allowed to obscure its function as one dimension of a kind of "security community" within which there is no expectation of nor preparation for armed conflict among its members.(34) This is perhaps the greatest contribution of the Alliance to European security. While the first preference of the PCI may be for the dissolution of the military blocs, it is unlikely to favor such dissolution if the result is a Europe dominated by a West Germany unrestrained by collective defense ties to other European countries. Like many in Europe, from the Gaullist right to the extreme left, the PCI remains suspicious of West Germany, less because of fears of military aggression than because of concerns about the growing economic and political strength of Germany in Western Europe. To the extent that NATO is seen as a political check on German preponderance and not a vehicle for it, the Alliance will continue to have a pragmatic appeal even to the PCI, an appeal no less important for being rarely publicly stated.

This kind of broader political question makes all the more unfortunate the collaboration of Kissinger and Schmidt to block PCI participation in a government in 1976, a policy which tended to discredit the possibility that NATO could function without being a means of American interference in Italian domestic affairs and without reinforcing German predominance in Europe; rather, the 1976 policy tended to confirm the most negative expectations of NATO's potential for institutionalizing an undesirable German-American hegemony in Western Europe. If such policies continue to be pursued in the future, the question will not be whether communist participation in Alliance governments is compatible with Alliance goals, but whether the continued existence of the Alliance is compatible with the future well-being, singly and collectively, of the nations of Western Europe. The security of Western Europe depends primarily on the relations among the nations of Western Europe and the United States, and only secondarily on the relations between East and West. An American policy which is inflexible toward Western allies cannot contribute positively to East-West relations. The Eurocommunist phenomenon raises, once again, the problem of the proper role of the United States in Western Europe in a period very different from that of 30 years ago.

EUROCOMMUNISM AND THE EUROPEAN COMMUNITY: ITALY, GERMANY, AND THE EC

The European Community emerged as part of the American-sponsored, postwar order in Western Europe. This does not mean that the initiatives leading to the EC and their success or failure are not predominantly European, nor does it ignore a certain tension within the Community as to the purposes of cooperation, one of which was clearly to lessen dependence on the United States. But it does mean that political and economic cooperation in Western Europe has been generally favored by the dominant external power in postwar Europe, the United States,(35) as strengthening Europe against possible pressures from the Soviet bloc and consolidating the liberal-democratic political systems and market economies of the region. The initial opposition of Western European communist parties to European integration was the mirror image of these American hopes for the process of integration.

The achievements of the European Community to date are far short of the expectations of many that a federal union of European states was being constructed, but the accomplishments of the EC are impressive all the same. Like NATO, the EC's emergence has coincided with a period of declining international hostility among West European countries and growing prosperity within each nation. While evidence of a causal link between the operation of the European Common Market and these two trends is ambiguous,(36) the continued existence and viability of the EC is largely due to the politically important perception that institutionalized cooperation has contributed to both peace and prosperity in Western Europe. Any major negative change in the status of the EC may be perceived to threaten both of these accomplishments.

Different standards for judging the EC's performance produce different results. If the standard adopted is the capacity of EC institutions to act independently of the member governments on issues of direct concern to national sovereignty, such as defense and foreign policy – the "high politics" standard – then the role of the EC must be seen as being very limited in fact and potential. Even though foreign policy coordination through the Davignon Political Committee and the European summits has been facilitated on questions such as external relations, the Conference on Security and Cooperation in Europe, and policy toward Portugal in 1975, the overall record of the EC on high politics issues is not impressive and shows little short-term prospect of improvement.

If, on the other hand, the standard for judging the EC's performance is its role as a locus of decision making and implementation for policies on a wide range of economic and social questions – the "low politics" standard – then the performance of the EC must be judged much more positively. None of the EC members can pretend to exercise full national sovereignty in economic questions. Decisions made in Brussels must be taken into account by national policymakers at many levels. One need not go so far as to proclaim the "victory of economics over politics"(37) and the subordination of high politics to low politics to recognize that economic issues have a higher salience today than ever before, and the EC's role in determining economic policies makes it an increasingly important set of institutions. The direct election of the European Parliament in June 1979 increased the EC's viability and legitimacy.

If one of the implicit motives behind international economic cooperation as promoted by the founders of the Common Market was anticommunism, then Eurocommunism might logically be seen to be fundamentally incompatible with European institutions. Only those political forces committed to liberal democracy and some variant of free market economics would be fit participants in Community politics. While no European politician would endorse this proposition today, this premise was implicit in Schmidt's 1976 threats to impose economic sanctions on Italy if the PCI were admitted to the cabinet,(38) as well as in President Carter's 1978 objections to PCI participation in an Italian government. In effect, Schmidt and Carter were saying that the changes resulting from PCI participation in an Italian government would be difficult for Italy's political allies and economic partners to tolerate.

That West Germany should have been the European state to take the lead in opposition to the PCI in 1976 symbolizes an important political evolution within the EC, one with implications for the future of Europe more important than the emergence of Eurocommunism; not only is Germany economically dominant within the EC, but it is also increasingly politically assertive and willing to impose its political priorities.(39) With the most productive and stable European economy, it is not surprising that Germany should set the pace within the EC.(40) In particular, West Germany was in a good position to threaten economic sanctions on Italy because it is Italy's largest individual creditor and Italy's access to EC lending funds depends on German support.(41) Increasingly, "European solutions" to economic and political problems are German solutions.

The expectation that Germany would, indeed, play such a dominant role in the EC probably influenced the 1969 French decision to welcome

Britain into the EC in order to serve as a political counterweight to Germany. But Britain has proved to be a drag on the entire EC, and under President Giscard d'Estaing, France has moved back to a position of close cooperation with Germany on Community affairs, often forming a kind of bloc against the other major EC nations.(42) In 1974, Willy Brandt began to talk about a "two-tier" or "two-speed" Europe – one in which those countries willing and able would take further steps towards economic union, leaving the others to catch up if they could. Among the second-speed countries were, clearly, Britain and Italy.(43) This concept became embodied in the blueprint for the European Community's evolution prepared by Belgium's Leo Tindemanns in 1976; the report was shelved because of the profound political objections it encountered. But this has not prevented the EC from evolving along these lines, as the agreement on currency union from January 1976 suggests: this was a German initiative supported by France, opposed – but of necessity acquiesced in – by Great Britain and Italy.

An EC dominated by its strongest member is incompatible with the hopes and expectations of "Europeans." The trend toward the predominance of Germany within the EC and a pattern of future integration which favors the economically stronger at the expense of the weaker are as undesirable as a completely fragmented Western Europe of autonomous, competing nations. If the EC is to have a positive future it will require charting a middle course between these two extremes. Eurocommunism has emerged at a time and in a manner which sharpens awareness of the present evolution of the EC and could contribute to charting this middle course.

The present structure of the EC is perfectly suited to a high degree of political pluralism among its members. Precisely because it is less than a federally integrated political system, the EC can tolerate a range of types of governments and political coalitions among its members. The uniformity of "background conditions"(44) which was assumed to facilitate the process of integration has never succeeded. Domestic political, social, and economic diversity has, from the beginning, imposed real limits on the kind of commonality of interests necessary to make economic integration proceed and "spill over" into political integration as well. To the extent that the focus of EC activity is short-run economics rather than long-run politics, the EC can accommodate regimes such as those of Greece, Portugal, and Spain whose economies are weak, whose historical experiences are diverse, and whose credentials as liberal democracies are far from well established. PCI participation in an Italian government poses fewer political problems for the EC as presently constituted than the admission of any disparate candidate members to the Community.

PCI policies toward the EC give little cause for concern to those who favor the limited kind of EC which has evolved. While regional integration was recognized as potentially a positive historical trend, the PCI initially opposed the European Common Market in 1958(45) as being part of an attempt to consolidate capitalism and to facilitate the penetration of Europe by American and German capital. This characterization of the EC has, in large part, proven to be accurate, but, from the mid-1960s on, the PCI has accepted Italy's integration at the regional level as an objective fact with important theoretical and practical political implications. While the consequences for Italy of this integration have not always been positively perceived – e.g., the PCI feels, along with many others, that the Community's agricultural policies have aggravated North/South disparities in Italy – the PCI has argued that purely national responses to Italy's problems are no longer adequate and Europe-wide action by popular political forces is necessary.(46) From the early 1960s on, the Italian communists have plunged into the practical work of the Community, especially in labor affairs, and have made a positive contribution, in the process lending legitimacy to Community institutions in the eyes of the PCI's electorate. The PCI has consistently pressed for the democratization of the EC institutions as a means of imparting a positive direction to the process of regional integration. Communist participation in the various EC bodies – e.g., labor union groups, the Italian delegation to the European Parliament – has been positive and nonobstructionist. So long as the EC continues to perform useful, positive functions, there is no reason to expect PCI behavior toward the EC to change. As is the case with their commitment to NATO, the question is not whether the PCI can be trusted to keep to their commitments to Europe but, rather, whether it is in their interest to do so. Is continued participation in the EC likely to be perceived as an aid to resolving Italy's problems, as perceived by the PCI, or an obstacle?

The principal problems in the compatibility of the PCI's brand of Eurocommunism and European integration lie in two interrelated areas: the evolution of the PCI's policy toward Europe, and the evolution of the EC itself. The PCI is on record as being firmly committed to continued fidelity to obligations assumed under the EC, and is seen by others as one of the most pro-European parties in Italy.(47) Certainly, the identification of Alterio Spinelli, one of the leaders of the European integration movement, with the PCI policy on the EC reinforces the communists' image as "Good Europeans." As a member of the European Commission, Spinelli was a vocal and convinced advocate of Community policy initiatives in scientific cooperation, industrial policy, and other areas(48) that often went beyond the policies of governments in Rome. The problem with Spinelli, as with Pasti, is whether or not his views are representative of the PCI views. If the PCI in power proved to be considerably less pro-European than Spinelli, that would put them more in line with Italian governments to date which have often been very nationalistic in their policies in the EC.   More than most European governments, Italy has cited special circumstances for excepting itself from Community commercial and financial regulations.

Without questioning the importance of the PCI's theoretical shift to a European perspective, practical problems could result in rather different PCI policy toward the EC than has been followed up to now. It is understandable that a party with scant prospects for sharing power in Rome should transpose the search for solutions to Italy's problems to the European level. But once admitted to the Italian government, the PCI might come to different conclusions about the potential for dealing with Italian problems on a national basis; such a government might be even more prone than past Italian governments to cite exceptional circumstances for relieving Italy of obligations imposed by the Community. This is particularly likely when politically unpopular, economic austerity measures are perceived as being imposed by Italy's foreign lenders, the EC in general and West Germany in particular. It would also be true if further steps toward economic union were perceived to be damaging to Italian national economic interests. One of the major issues that promoted the PCI withdrawal of support from the Andreotti government in January 1979 was opposition to the Christian Democrats' decision in favor of participation in the European Monetary Union. The PCI felt that more concessions should have been allowed Italy, in particular that Italy should have been given more time to prepare for the negative impact of the agreement on the Italian economy.(49) Such policies stem not from any lack of commitment to the hazy goals of European unity but to the PCI's estimation of concrete national economic interests. And the resort to more and more nationalistic kinds of solutions to Italy's economic problems could be rationalized by communist theoreticians. If the creation of a European Economic Community became a salient fact of the late 1950s and early 1960s requiring a shift in the focus of policy to the European level, the advent of the communist party to power in a coalition government in the 1980s would equally be a new "objective condition" of far-reaching theoretical and practical implications.

The second, related source of potential problems concerns the evolution of the EC and, in particular, the role of Germany within it. It is comprehensible that any West German government should prefer not to see communists, even reformists, emerge as participants in the governments of its major European partners. Eurocommunists are ritually suspicious of West Germany as the heir to Nazism. The Western communist parties maintain fraternal relations with the government in the Democratic Republic of Germany (East Germany); and, while West Germany seeks to normalize its own relations with East Germany as much as possible and has long since abandoned the "Hallstein doctrine" by which governments could have relations with only one or the other Germany, it is still reluctant to see the process of normalization proceed to the point where relations between governments in France and Italy might conceivably be friendlier with Pankow than with Bonn. Certainly, the political acceptability in Europe of West German economic power would decline if Germany were to become politically isolated within the EC. While such isolation is not a necessary consequence of communist participation in governments in Italy or France, it is more likely with such participation than without. This is the kind of concern that Kissinger was able to play on in gaining Schmidt's support for his anti-PCI policies in 1976. And this kind of cooperation lends political substance to the kind of "bigemonic" German-American relationship that some have advocated(50) but others distrust.

German preference for not having communists in a coalition in Italy is understandable, but outright opposition from the German government came as a surprise. The PCI cultivated good relations with the Social Democratic Party in Germany (SPD) and had reason to expect a more understanding attitude from a German government.(51) But the German Social Democrats are a part of the anticommunist left in Europe that Americans sometimes overlook,(52) and Schmidt is identified with the right-wing faction of the SPD. The challenge of the Christian Democrats in the elections of October 1976 led Schmidt to take a stronger anticommunist stand at that time than he might have otherwise done. Indeed, subsequent to the elections he assumed a position more consistent with past German policies: demands for economic austerity but pragmatic acceptance of the course of political events in Italy on the premise that the Italian economy must be supported because it is an important market for Germany. The emergence in 1979 of Franz Joseph Strauss as the Christian Democrat's choice for Chancellor may have symbolic and practical importance. Strauss' acceptability as a candidate is a significant shift to the right, since he is identified with Cold War themes and policies. His eventual election as Chancellor would seem to make German cooperation with Eurocommunists almost impossible.

Past German pressures on Italy, especially the identity of German pressures with EC positions, raises the problem of the future evolution of the EC. The communist party participating in an Italian government will clearly have domestic economic and social priorities, not foreign and defense policy priorities. But the EC is precisely less a foreign policy organization than an economic policy organization. Any major reforms which the PCI may want to institute in the Italian economy will be influenced by and have an impact on the EC. In terms of the policy priorities of the PCI, the EC is a much more intrusive organization than NATO and, therefore, participation in the EC could be a greater source of political tensions than continued participation in the Atlantic Alliance for the PCI in a coalition government. If EC policies were to be perceived as being increasingly restrictive and intrusive, as they will necessarily be if the EC is to make major progress toward the goal of Economic Union (which was originally slated for 1980 but then postponed), then the problems between the EC and an Italy governed in part by the PCI could grow. To the extent that Germany may continue to assume a role of force moteur in the economic integration process, the difficulties which would arise between Italy and the EC would involve Germany as well. Like NATO, a low profile EC seems best able to provide the kind of ongoing, positively perceived functions that allow for international cooperation among European governments while allowing for domestic policy divergencies of various kinds. Increased integration of a supranational sort can only exacerbate the economic differences between the most dynamic economies, e.g., Germany, and the weakest economies, e.g., Italy. If these economic difficulties are compounded by political differences, the likelihood of confrontation is high and disintegration possible.

A willingness to accept the present level and pattern of integration in Europe might be one of the costs of accepting the PCI in an Italian government, whatever lip service communist spokesmen may pay to the goal of European integration. In practice, the PCI might be even less likely than other Italian parties to subordinate national economic interests to the goal of regional integration. But given the implications of further steps toward economic or political union, the present level of integration may be the best obtainable. If the purpose of integration is economic satisfaction, the process may have reached the tolerable limits imposed by the fundamental economic disparities of the participants. At present there is an amorphous balance of interdependent costs and benefits, and political mechanisms exist for adjusting the balance as new demands are articulated. These mechanisms should improve with the new, directly elected European Parliament. Further steps toward economic integration at this time seem likely to be at the expense of the weaker parties to the process, increasing national and regional disparities rather than redressing them, creating greater political strains within the Community.

The most valuable contribution of the debate over Eurocommunism's impact on the EC may be to raise some fundamental questions on the purposes of the Community 20 years after the Treaties of Rome. If the purpose of the integration effort is political union, especially that kind of political union intended to give Europe an independent role in world politics, the desirability and feasibility of that purpose are more open to question today than ever before. Practically, a European military superpower seems as far away as ever. And, in principle, it is not clear that the contribution of such a superpower to international peace and stability would be positive; there is no reason to suppose that a European superpower would be any wiser, more humane, or more responsible than the United States and the Soviet Union have proven to be. Nor is it clear that a genuine "multipolar" international system including a European "third force" would be more stable or desirable than the more complex "bi-multipolar" world which has emerged. It is even arguable in the age of deterrence whether a European nuclear force and/or an integrated European defense community would necessarily be more effective than the national forces now existing. The idea of a European Third force is less compelling in a period in which East-West relations are substantially multilateral, and the role of military force in relations among industrial countries, communist and noncommunist, seems to be more ambiguous than in the past. Nor, finally, would a united Europe be any less a part of the metaphorical North in the North/South economic and political issues which may be replacing the communist/anticommunist split as the dominant conflict in international politics. In other words, at best, a united Europe would simply reinforce that international division which is the major source of emerging tension.

But of most direct concern to Europeans, it is not clear that an independent, united Europe is necessary to preserve European freedom of action on questions of direct importance to Europe. In an age in which economic preoccupations predominate, politically motivated economic organizations such as OPEC are perhaps a more appropriate model than the two superpowers for regions wishing to foster cooperation to realize common goals. Cooperation on a limited range of economic and political questions short of the creation of a European superstate may well be sufficient to the needs of Europe. In a period in which the centralized nation-state is besieged by transnational economic forces from without and from within by subnational separatist tendencies, the desirability and feasibility of seeking to recreate an anlogous form of state at the regional level deserves to be challenged. The strains resulting from efforts to go beyond the present level of economic cooperation could easily erode the political consensus on which the European Community rests.

Along with NATO, the EC is one of the institutional embodiments of a pattern of European political cooperation which can continue only so long as its evolution is consistent with satisfaction of the political and economic needs of all its members. The emergence of Eurocommunism is one facet of trends which reinforce a certain conception of the European Community — one which stresses continued political pluralism among the members of the Community while, at the same time, maintaining the overarching framework of economic cooperation. The real importance of possible PCI participation in an Italian government may be to sharpen awareness of the present state of the European integration movement and its future evolution, so that a reasoned choice among possibilities may be made. As was the case with NATO, the overall impact of Eurocommunism on the EC will be less a result of initiatives of individual communist parties than of responses from Germany and the EC institutions.

EUROCOMMUNISM AND THE EASTERN BLOC: THE SOVIET UNION, ITALY AND NATIONAL AUTONOMY

If the impact of Eurocommunism on the Western side of the East-West equation is more a function of the policies of the United States and West Germany than of the Eurocommunists, then the impact on the Eastern side of the equation will also be largely a result of Soviet and other communist nations' responses. The analysis of their responses is best left to students of communism and Soviet politics, but a few general observations seem relevant to the task of putting this analysis in perspective.

The Soviets must view the Eurocommunist phenomenon with considerable ambivalence. The Soviets occupy a position in the international system similar to that of the United States in that they are both the leaders of a major European military bloc as well as the principal force in a worldwide political movement. The emergence of politically successful communist parties in Western Europe should be welcomed on the face of it by the Soviet Union, given the divisive potential of such a phenomenon on the Western bloc and the reinforcement that the international communist movement would receive thereby. If the Soviet leaders shared Kissinger's estimation of the impact of Eurocommunism, they should be ready to support the Western communist parties. In fact, however, the Soviets have been very unsupportive; they openly slighted the PCF during the 1974 presidential elections in France, have expressed with moderation their differences with the policies of the PCI's Enrico Berlinguer, and have castigated the PCE's Santiago Carrillo for the anti-Soviet positions expressed in Eurocommunism and the State.(53) The Soviets' differences with the Eurocommunists are both ideological and practical, and it is not too much to say that Eurocommunism poses even more problems for the Soviet Union than it does for the United States.

Ideologically, the CPSU has one major difference with the Eurocommunists, as well as many minor differences. For the Soviets, the principles and practice of bourgeois democracy are a means to an end, a temporary if necessary expedient in the conquest of power by representatives of the working class. The Soviets continue to argue that it is not possible to achieve socialism through bourgeois democratic means. The Eurocommunists have accepted in principle and follow in practice the proposition that bourgeois democracy is an end in itself, the necessary process for the gradual introduction of elements of socialism into society.(54) Those in the United States who question the Eurocommunists' commitment to democratic values do no more than echo the position of the CPSU, implicitly affirming the premise that the CPSU would like the Eurocommunists to recognize: there is really only one road to socialism, and that is the road already traveled by the Soviet Union. One of the reasons that Kissinger and the leaders in the Kremlin got along so well is the evident similarity of their views on so many questions.

The second source of Soviet concern regarding the Eurocommunist phenomenon is more pragmatic, and relates to the spread of these kinds of ideas to Eastern Europe. The widening breach in the world communist movement has already been exploited by some East European governments to gain a little more freedom to maneuvre.(55) The Eurocommunists' support for the "Prague Spring" and the condemnation of Soviet military intervention in Czechoslovakia pose genuine threats to continued Soviet-imposed controls. The principle of "proletarian internationalism" has been used by the Soviets to subordinate the Eastern bloc countries, and "national roads to socialism" provides a corrosive alternative. At the 1976 communist summit in Berlin, the Soviets were compelled to delete all references to "proletarian internationalism" from the final communique at the insistence of the Eurocommunists.(56) Having confronted the Chinese schism in the 1960s, the Soviets now find their control over the communist movement challenged by even more serious centrifugal tendencies.

With specific reference to the Italian situation, the Soviet Union has never provided a model for postwar Italian communists, less so today than ever before. The Soviets' rigid ideology has little appeal, their economy serves neither as a model of development nor as a plausible source of potential external support for the Italian economy, and their society and culture are very unsophisticated by Italian standards. These factors, combined with Italy's relative geographic isolation from the Soviet Union and the Soviet bloc, would severely limit the kind of influence that the Soviets might hope to exercise over an Italian government in which the PCI participated directly, even if relations between the CPSU and the PCI were tolerably good. The most direct impact the Soviets have and will continue to exercise on Italy, whatever the makeup of its government, will be as a function of Soviet relations with the United States and other major regional actors such as West Germany and the EC.

If the continued success of the Eurocommunist parties in general and the PCI in particular rests on the continuation of detente, then the Soviets have a very real influence over the evolution of these parties' fortunes. The deterioration of detente is, in large part, the result of American reactions to the Soviet military build-up in Central Europe, their strategic nuclear build-up, adventurism in Africa, and human rights questions. These are all policies that the Soviets could modify in order to preserve some measure of good relations with the United States and the Western bloc if they chose to do so, and in the process, they could remove a major question mark in the future of Eurocommunism. But the benefits of detente to the Soviet Union must seem equivocal, especially if it challenges their leadership in the world communist movement; their willingness to modify their policies in order to preserve detente is open to question. That the collapse of detente would prejudice the future of Eurocommunism would probably be seen as at least a "silver lining" to the Soviet leadership partially offsetting whatever gains they had hoped to achieve through detente. Eurocommunism in general and the future of the PCI in particular would, thereby, be confirmed as functions of relations between the superpowers.

CONCLUSIONS

Italy's domestic diversity − regional, historical, social, economic, and political − has kept Italy relatively weak and dependent upon external forces to resolve Italian domestic problems. The major political parties − the Christian Democrats and the Communists − have each sought support from abroad in the past, from the United States and the Soviet Union; and both now look to the European Community to help solve Italy's problems. This lack of autonomy is deplorable because it has reduced Italy's capacity to cope with problems which are essentially Italian in origin, rooted in the nation's history and culture, while at the same time reducing the effectiveness of Italy's contribution to its military and economic alliances. International ties have not resolved Italy's problems; Italy's problems have limited Italy's capacity to benefit from international ties.

The Western countries' strength depends on the successful satisfaction of the rapidly changing and growing needs and desires of their peoples. Satisfaction of these needs is the precondition for domestic political stability, for the maintenance of those military capabilities judged to be essential to meet the legitmate needs of national defense, as well as for sustaining a high level of international cooperation on a wide range of problems. The rise of the PCI as a protest party is one piece of evidence of the failure of the Italian political system as it is presently operating to provide this kind of satisfaction. However, the PCI is not merely a protest phenomenon but a party that offers a practical political alternative, with considerable experience to substantiate its moderate programmatic appeal; if the PCI is a sign of the problem it may also be part of the solution. The Kissinger-Schmidt-Carter policy opposing the PCI's participation in a government must be judged negatively because it rejects a possible solution while ignoring the problem; the resulting perpetuation of the stalemate in Italian political life can only further reduce Italy's ability to contribute positively to East-West relations.

The promise of the PCI is that it is different from the Christian Democrats, but not too different. By circumstances and inclination, a government with PCI participation might tend to be more inclined to develop multiple international ties which would reduce the influence of any single patron – the United States or a European Community increasingly dominated by West Germany or, alternatively, the Soviet Union – in a more complex pattern which could increase the government's capacity to deal with Italian problems. This is the kind of policy which the Christian Democrats could not carry out even if they wished to because the party is deeply divided internally with a half a dozen institutionalized factions which cannot agree among themselves nor implement a coherent policy. The PCI is relatively free of internal factionalism because the principle of democratic centralism is used to impose rigid discipline. Anticommunists point to the lack of internal freedom within the PCI as an example of communist intolerance of dissent and lack of commitment to genuine democracy. But in a parliamentary system such as Italy's, a lack of internal party discipline is less a measure of democracy than an excuse for irresponsibility. Unlike the DC, the PCI is better able to deliver on the promises it makes, a quintessentially democratic attribute, and an essential precondition to any progress in resolving deep-rooted Italian problems.

The accession of communists to power in a coalition government in Italy would seem to result in, at best, marginal changes in policy toward NATO or the European Community unless the United States and/or the Soviet Union should choose to provoke more serious and far-reaching implications. And while there are many uncertainties, it might well be that an Italian government marginally less dominated by the United States in foreign and defense policy, marginally less dominated in international economic and trade affairs by West Germany and the EC, and marginally more competent in implementing domestic reforms could, over time, effect major improvements in Italy. More generally,

Eurocommunism as a phenomenon seems rather less interesting intrinsically than the questions raised by its emergence; indeed, the debate over Eurocommunism distracts attention from more serious questions such as the future of energy-intensive industrial societies, questions for which the ideologies of liberal democracy and communism seem equally unable to produce answers. If these questions are not new – What is the proper United States role in Western Europe? Whither the European Community? What are the prospects for national autonomy? – the need for new answers is more pressing than ever before.

NOTES

(1) The electoral strength of the communist parties in these countries varies from 30 percent in Italy (1979), to 19 percent in France (1978), to 10 percent in Spain (1979).

(2) James O. Goldsborough, "Eurocommunism After Madrid," Foreign Affairs 55, no. 4 (July 1977).

(3) These categories are adapted from J.K. Holsti, International Politics: A Framework for Analysis (Englewood Cliffs, N.J.: Prentice-Hall, 1977), chap. 4.

(4) In the 1975 local and regional elections, the PCI increased its share of the vote 4.9 percent over the 1972 national returns, for a total of 32.4 percent. The Christian Democrats' (DCs) share of the vote fell from 38.7 percent in 1972 to 35.6 percent in 1975. As a result of these elections, the PCI emerged as the dominant party in all the major cities north of Naples. In the June 1976 national elections, the PCI increased its share of the vote to 34 percent, up 7 percent from the 1972 national election returns. The DC maintained its 1972 share at 39 percent, improving somewhat over its 1975 local and regional returns. Communist gains were largely at the expense of left and center parties. In local elections in May 1978, the DC gained 5 percent over its 1976 returns, while the PCI lost 9 percent. While the basis of comparison is of questionable validity, many conclude from these returns that, were elections called in the near future, the PCI would lose much of the ground gained in 1976.

(5) See, for example, Guido Caril, "Italy's Malaise," Foreign Affairs 54, no. 4 (July 1976): 708-718.

(6) Corriere della Sera, July 4, 1979.

(7) See, for example, Robert Leonardi, "The United States and the Historic Compromise: An End to the Cold War?" paper prepared for delivery at the annual meetings of the American Political Science Association, September 1-4, 1977, pp. 13-19.

(8) For the text of the Carter statement see The New York Times, January 13, 1978, p. 2.

(9) Peter Lange and Maurizio Vannicelli, "Carter in the Italian Maze," Foreign Policy, no. 23 (Winter 1978-79), p. 161.

(10) Primo Vannicelli, Italy, NATO, and the European Community (Cambridge, Mass.: Center for International Affairs, Harvard University, 1974), pp. 5-9.

(11) Robert Leonardi and Alan Platt, "Stati Uniti e Sinistra Italiana," in Il Mulino 26, no. 252 (July-August 1977).

(12) See Stanley Hoffman's Introduction in Vanicelli, Italy, NATO, and the European Community.

(13) See, for example, Peter Lange, "What is to Be Done – About Italian Communism?" Foreign Policy, no. 21 (Winter 1975-76), pp. 224-40; Peter Nichols, "On the Italian Crisis," Foreign Affairs 54, no. 4 (April 1976); Richard Pipes, "Liberal Communism in Western Europe?" Orbis 20, no. 3 (Fall 1976); James K. Dougherty and Diane K. Pfaltzgraff, Eurocommunism and the Atlantic Alliance (Cambridge, Mass.: Institute for Foreign Policy Analysis, 1977); Arrigo Levi, "Italy's New Communism," Foreign Policy, no. 26 (Spring 1977); Fabio Basagni and Gregory Flynn, "Italy, Europe, and Western Security," Survival 20, no. 3 (May-June 1977); Giorgio Napoletano, "The Italian Crisis: A Communist Perspective," Foreign Affairs 56, no. 4 (July 1978).

(14) John Hackett, John Barradough, Bernard Burrow, Kenneth Hunt, Ian McGeoch, Norman MacRae, and John Strawson, The Third World War: August, 1985 (New York: Macmillan, 1978).

(15) The New York Times, April 14, 1976, p. 1; April 22, 1976, p. 12; April 28, 1976, p. 4. See also Kissinger's statement on June 9, 1977, reprinted by Circolo Stato e Liberta, Rome, 1977.

(16) See, for example, Alan Posner, "Italy: Dependence and Political Fragmentation," International Organization 31, no. 4 (Autumn 1977): 809-38.

(17) Angelo Panebianco, "La Politica Italiana: Un Modello Interpretative," Il Mulino 26, no. 254 (November-December 1977).

(18) Fabrizio DeBenedetti, "Il Ministro Degli Affari Esteri," in La Politica Estera Della Republica Italiana (Rome: Istituto Affari Internazionali, 1967), pp. 821-53.

(19) Fabrizio DeBenedetti, "Studio Critico Sulle Forze Armate," in Fabrizio DeBenedetti, Il Potere Militaire in Italia (Bari: Editori Laterza, 1971) pp. 272-73.

(20) Luciano Bardi, "The Italian Communist Party and Italy's Foreign Policy," 1978, unpublished manuscript.

(21) For the views of the PCI's official foreign policy spokesman, see Sergio Segre, "The 'Communist Question' in Italy," Foreign Affairs 54, no. 4 (July 1976): 691-707.

(22) Ibid., p. 699.

(23) For Pasti's views, see Il Belfagor 24 (Summer 1969); and The New York Times, May 21, 1976.

(24) Remarks made at the ISODARCO Vith Course, Nemi, Italy, June 22-July 3, 1976.

(25) Ibid.

(26) The New York Times, March 21, 1976.

(27) See the interview with Berlinguer in Corriere Della Sera, June 15, 1976.

(28) Vannicelli, Italy, NATO, and the European Community, p. 26.

(29) American bases in Italy have three different statuses — NATO facilities, American bases under a bilateral agreement with the Italian government, and bases which have a mixed NATO-American status. The existence of these three different statuses could cause ambiguities in a crisis situation: American use of these bases could be variously interpreted as implementaiton of Alliance commitment, as pursuant to the bilateral agreements, or even American unilateral action. Multiple statuses also leave open the possibility that, for example, if Italy were to leave NATO it would not automatically mean the departure of all American forces from Italy. See, for example, "United States Military Installations and Objectives in the Mediterranean," Report prepared for the Subcommittee on Europe and the Middle East, Committee on International Relations, US House of Representatives, March 27, 1977; and Antonio Gambino, "NATO e PCI," in Panorama 14, no. 527 (May 25, 1976): 26-28.

(30) Compare the interview in Corriere della Sera, fn. 27 above, with the version in Unita, June 25, 1976. My thanks to Dr. Bona Pozzoli for bringing this to my attention.

(31) John F. Leich, "The European Policy of the Italian Communist Party: Leaders and Followers," April 1979, unpublished, p. 10.

(32) Robert J. Lieber, "The Pendulum Swings to Europe," Foreign Policy, no. 26 (Spring 1977), pp. 44-46.

(33) Lange, "What is to be Done?" pp. 228-32; Gianfranco Pasquino, Ed., Continuita e Mutamento Elettorale in Italia (Bologna: Il Mulino, 1977); and Bernard E. Brown "The European Left Confronts Modernity," in Eurocommunism and Eurosocialism, edited by Bernard E. Brown (New York: Cyrco, 1979).

(34) The concept is Karl Deutsch's. See Deutsch, et al., Political Community and the North Atlantic Area (Princeton: Princeton University Press, 1957).

(35) See for example, Max Beloff, The United States and the Unity of Europe (New York: Vintage, 1963).

(36) See for example, Charles G. Nelson, "European Integration: Trade Data and Measurement Problems," International Organization 23, no. 3 (Summer 1974).

(37) Ernst Haas, "Technocracy, Pluralism, and the New Europe," in A New Europe? edited by Stephen Graubard (Boston: Beacon Press, 1963), p. 71.

(38) Schmidt announced during a visit to Washington that the leaders of the Western countries had decided at the June 1976 economic summit in Puerto Rico to block further economic aid to Italy if communists were allowed in the cabinet. The British and French governments publically denied any such agreement. The New York Times July 17, 1976, p. 5; July 18, 1976, p. 3; July 20, 1976, p. 9; July 24, 1976, p. 6; July 29, 1976, p. 31; August 5, 1976, p. 7.

(39) Robert Gerald Livingston, "Germany Steps Up," Foreign Policy, no. 22 (Spring 1976).

(40) C. Fred Bergsten, "US Foreign Economic Policy and Europe: The Ascendence of Germany and the Stagnation of the Common Market," in Toward a New Economic Order edited by C. Fred Bergsten (Lexington, Mass.: Lexington Books, 1975), pp. 325-32.

(41) Italy's foreign debt reached a high of $19 billion in 1977, with major loans from West Germany, the U.S., the EC, and the IMF. Most loans were conditional on the Italian government's taking antiinflationary measures or other moves aimed at restoring the nation's economy and, in the case of at least one major German loan, were backed by Italy's substantial gold reserves as collateral. Carli, "Italy's Malaise," p. 716.

(42) James O. Goldsborough, "The Franco-German Entente," Foreign Affairs 54, no. 3 (April 1976).

(43) L'Espresso 22, no. 5 (February 1, 1976): 32-33.

(44) See for example, Ernst Haas and Phillippe Schmitter, "Economic and Differential Patterns of Political Integration: Projections about Unity in Latin America," in an anthology entitled International Political Communities (New York: Anchor Doubleday, 1966), pp. 266-73.

(45) Donald M. Blackmer, "The International Strategy of the Italian Communist Party," in The International Role of the Communist Parties of Italy and France, edited by Donald M. Blackmer and Annie Kriegel (Cambridge, Mass.: Center for International Affairs, Harvard University, 1975).

(46) Donald Sassoon, "The Italian Communist Party's European Strategy," Political Quarterly 47, no. 3 (July-September 1976).

(47) Pierre Hassner, "Eurocommunism and Western Europe," Atlantic Community Quarterly 16, no. 3 (Fall 1978), 273; and Leich, "The European Policy of the Italian Communist Party."

(48) See for example Altiero Spinelli, The European Adventure (London: C. Knight, 1972).

(49) Corriere della Sera, December 13, 1978, p. 1; December 14, 1978, p. 1.

(50) C. Fred Bergsten, "The United States and Germany: The Imperative of Economic Bigemony," in Toward a New Economic Order, pp. 333-44.

(51) Blackmer, "The International Strategy of the Italian Communist Party," pp. 22 and 24.

(52) J.F. Revel, "The Myths of Eurocommunism," Foreign Affairs 56, no. 2 (January 1978): 296.

(53) Santiago Carrillo, Eurocommunism and the State (New York: Lawrence Hill, 1978).

(54) Claudio Terzi, "L'URSS e Eurocommunismo," Il Mulino 27, no. 257 (May-June 1978): 396. See also Robert Leguold, "The Soviet Union and West European Communism" in Eurocommunism and Detente, edited by Rudolf L. Tokes (New York: New York University Press, 1978).

(55) Heinz Timmermann, "Eurocommunism and Eastern Europe," Atlantic Community Quarterly 16, no. 3 (Fall 1978).

(56) Fernando Claudin, Eurocommunism and Socialism (London: NLB, 1978), chap. 2.

8 The European Community and China: Economic and Political Implications of a New Relationship

R. Gavin Boyd

Within the framework of a common commercial policy, which is being slowly extended to cover monetary affairs, members of the European Community, particularly the larger capital exporters, trade technology for primary products and low technology manufactures with China. For the Community, this commerce is small, but it is a large part of China's foreign trade. The exchanges are growing at a significant pace, but this cannot be increased substantially because economic backwardness limits China's capacity to finance imports and to utilize advanced plants and machinery. Over the long term, the West European contribution to China's industrialization will probably be large, but it may not be as great as Japan's, and, as at present, will be affected by a smaller congruence of interests.

Each of the larger West European technology exporting countries manages its trade with China under constraints deriving from much larger commercial relationships with the USSR and the other COMECON states, and from perceived requirements to maintain detente in Europe. Such factors are highly significant for the present West German administraiton, but are somewhat less important for Britain. In varying degrees, these two states, together with France, see some political and strategic benefits in economic cooperation with China, because this amounts to a form of pressure against the USSR, and helps to sustain Chinese hostility to the Soviet Union; but each of these members of the Community is reluctant to antagonize the USSR by greatly enlarging its collaboration with Peking. In several cases, this collaboration has a strategic dimension, because modest quantities of military equipment are being sold to China, principally by Britain and France, with the apparent approval of the United States. Most of the West European administrations consider that they derive security benefits from China's hostility to the Soviet Union, as this causes the USSR to deploy roughly one third of its armed strength along the border with China and in Mongolia.

The relationships between European Community members and China constitute an important secondary pattern in the configuration of East-West interactions. In that configuraiton, the most significant economic component is the relatively large flow of West European technology to the COMECON members, which is increasing interdependencies that may influence Soviet policy. Western economic cooperation with China, however, especially because of its modest military component, tends to cause resentment in the USSR, thus affecting Soviet receptivity to the "bourgeois" cultural influences introduced through economic contacts. Chinese receptivity to such influences may be somewhat higher, because of a fairly positive orientation toward the West European states, as adversaries of the USSR, and a new recognition of the crucial importance of Western technology for modernization. However, the encouragement of political change in the USSR is more significant for Western Europe than the development of such change in China.

The major West European countries trading with China are primarily competitors, and evidently see few incentives to coordinate their economic policies toward Peking. Their diverging strategic perspectives, moreover, preclude the development of a common Asian security policy. Of course, if there is significant progress toward structural integration within the European Community, the development of a common policy toward China may be feasible, as part of a broader design for engagement with the communist states. For the immediate future, however, the Community's development is likely to remain limited to disjointed incremental policy coordination on the present confederal basis, and the principal challenges to move toward structural integration will continue to be posed not by China but by major trading partners, principally the United States, the OPEC states, and Japan.

For China, the European Community's major technology exporters rank after Japan as important sources of advanced technology; and, politically, trade with that country has much higher utility, partly because on the Japanese side it is less influenced by desires for coexistence with the USSR. Trade with the United States also has higher political utility for Peking, notwithstanding the reluctance of the present U.S. administration to sell the Chinese military equipment. Peking's commerce with members of the European Community appears to be managed largely on the basis of economic considerations; and, in this trade, frustrations are more likely to be experienced than in commercial dealings with Japan and the United States, because of the Community's strong protectionist measures relating to agricultural products and low technology manufactures.

ANALYSIS

The external relations of the European Community members, managed individually but with some degree of coordination and collectivity within restricted economic issue areas, can be studied on the basis of insights drawn from research on comparative foreign policies and international organizations. The extensive literature on these subjects helps understanding of the attachments of West European executives and legislators to national values and personal political interests, and also assists appreciation of the executive, bureaucratic, and legislative processes through which Community members cope with issues in the management of their interdependencies, within and outside their association.

China's external policy has to be examined with reference to the literature on modernizing revolutionary states. Guidance has to be taken from research on the behavior of closed authoritarian leaderships with strong ideological beliefs, whose psychological environments tend to lack congruence with their operational environments. The modernization process which the Chinese ruling elite is attempting to push forward is, in some respects, contributing to deradicalization, but this elite is endeavoring to restrict the penetration of "bourgeois" culture while importing advanced foreign technology.

Interactions between the European Community's major technology exporters and China are primarily bilateral, as between those capital exporters and the USSR. In the Chinese case, the trade exhibits features that are characteristic of the foreign economic relations of command economies, particularly with respect to currency and commodity convertibility. For the West European trading partners this commerce has to be managed across long social distances, on the basis of moderate to low levels of understanding, and with uncertainties about the Peking leadership's stability and evolving policy orientations.

The complex dependency relationships which China is developing with Community members have asymmetries with considerable potential for change. There are incentives to become more pragmatic in domestic and external policy, so as to maximize the benefits from West European technology transfers. There are also incentives to evolve a more useful strategic dimension in the relationships with Community members, for improved security against the USSR. Those West European states have strong economic incentives to strengthen ties with the USSR, but their strategic interests in China have potentially even greater significance. The U.S. interest in China entails some economic competition against the West Europeans, thus stimulating their trade promotion, but does not diminish Chinese security concerns in dealing with the major Community members, since for the present U.S. policy envisages that they will be Peking's main source of military technology.

Game theoretical insights can be utilized in studying the economic and strategic aspects of West European interaction with China, but rational actor assumptions must be heavily qualified in studying each side's behavior. The major West European states are relatively strong polyarchies whose executive and bureaucratic decision makers in varying degrees tend to favor sectoral and organizational demands rather than societal needs, and who cope with policy issues by disaggregating them, in order to function incrementally. Transnational enterprises in these states seek profit apolitically on a basis of comparative advantage, with varying degrees of state direction and support. In China the ruling elite's political psychology is strongly ideological and is influenced by the nation's distinctive traditional culture. There is a heavy concentration of authority in this elite, moreover, and the processing of information of significance for policy issues is negatively affected by the political discipline imposed on officials.

ACTOR ATTRIBUTES

The principal West European technology exporting states are West Germany, France, and Britain. West Germany represents a highly functional combination of political and economic structures and processes; because of the size and dynamism of its industrial establishment it dominates the European Community. The somewhat smaller and slower growing French political economy ranks next; it has major structural deficiencies, which are being remedied only at a slow pace although under strong governmental direction. The British political economy, severely affected by stagnation and under weak political direction, is less active in technology exports. The acquisition of equipment for the Chinese military establishment from Britain, however, is easier, for political reasons, than it is from West Germany, because of the importance of Ostpolitik in Bonn's external relations.

West Germany is the most coherent actor in the European Community. The leaderships of the two major political parties, the bureaucratic and business elites, and most of the top trade union officials are united in a consensus supporting a highly successful export-oriented growth strategy that has been in effect since the 1950s. This consensus, together with a moderately low level of popular demand for social overhead and welfare allocations, facilitates executive direction of foreign economic policy, chiefly to the advantage of the major industrial enterprises. The strongly mercantilist quality of this policy necessitates maximum freedom of action, and thus makes for reluctance to endorse moves toward structural integration within the Community, yet there are incentives to accept greater policy integration in order to manage more effectively, on a collective basis, the difficult trade and monetary issues in the Community's relations with the United States.(1)

West Germany leads the Community in trade with the COMECON states, and this trade is promoted by the administration to expand interdependencies with those states, for the strengthening of detente in Europe, and, thus, for the political benefit of the ruling Social Democratic Party, the initiator of the Ostpolitik, as well as for very fundamental strategic reasons. On this account, West Germany's foreign economic policy in the East-West context is significantly constrained with respect to China.

Politically, France is a deeply divided actor, under a strong executive with weak societal support. The French economy is smaller and less industrialized than West Germany's, but under firm central direction its growth record is approaching that state's, although at the cost of significant inflation. French behavior within the Community has a strongly nationalist quality, deriving from a Gaullist tradition which has been moderated by President Giscard d'Estaing, and is basically opposed to structural integration, yet favors achieving greater policy integration in order to cope more effectively with U.S. bargaining on trade and monetary issues. French trade with the COMECON states is substantial, and is managed in part with some hopes of evolving a distinctive role as mediator between the superpowers. The size of this trade, and the pro-Soviet orientation of the country's large communist party, impose some limitations on the development of ties with China.(2)

Britain is more politically integrated than France but more poly-archic than West Germany, and its economy is in a state of chronic stagflation. Leaders of both major political parties are reluctant to support structural integration in the Community, or any closer policy coordination. There is a tendency to favor the United States on issues between it and the Community, in order to compensate for a lack of bargaining power within the association. In East-West trade, Britain is a weak rival of West Germany, but is less constrained politically in the development of trade with China.(3)

West Germany, France, and Britain provide somewhat divergent forms of leadership in the European Community in shifting coalitions. There is some Anglo-French collaboraiton to offset West Germany's strong bargaining power, but France seeks to cooperate with West Germany on economic issues between the Community and the USA. The differences in alignment and behavior, and their effects on other members, limit the possibilities for common Community policies toward outside states.

The Community is a confederal actor, with competence restricted to commercial policy, principally for control of the terms of access to its market. While this policy is shaped through careful negotiation between all the members, each tends to adopt restrictive interpretations of the Community's powers in that area of external relations. The need to establish a monetary union, however, in order to reduce dependence on the U.S. dollar for international exchange, is necessitating an extension of the Community's external competence.(4)

Increased cohesion and cooperation within the Community are advocated by China, in the hope that greater unity will enable the West Europeans to cope with the Soviet military threat. Such exhortations however have little effect, partly because the language of Chinese political communications does not facilitate rapport. China is a revolutionary state under a leadership which, while divided by personality conflicts and diverging policy orientations, appears to be determined to prevent Soviet type "embourgeoisement" and deradicalization in its drive to modernize with the use of material incentives and an accelerated absorption of Western science and technology. Ideological fervor continues to be maintained with the use of revolutionary rhetoric, and this precludes innovative political communications which would be meaningful for audiences in Western states with instrumental political cultures.(5)

China is a strongly hierarchical actor, and maintains a high degree of closure to the outside world. The ruling elite's strong ideological beliefs and dependence on information processing by strictly subordinated government and party organizations affect its capacity to understand and relate to other societies. There is a concern to maintain the belief system because of fears that ideological sophistication, if permitted, would lead to "revisionism" and deradicalization, and would weaken the regime's social controls, while causing the secondary elite and the middle echelons to view leadership policies more critically. The resultant preservation of cognitive simplicity, together with the heavy concentration of power at the top, of course, allow scope for the expression of idiosyncratic factors in the ruling elite's direction of foreign policy. The members of this elite appear to have very authoritarian personalities; clashes between them are much more intense and destructive than differences within the Soviet ruling group.(6)

POLICIES

The policies of the major Community technology exporters toward China are shaped by commonly recognized incentives, which activate their transnational enterprises and their administrations; by strategic considerations, some in the form of constraints, which mainly influence executive and bureaucratic thinking; and by political factors that in some cases relate to the domestic interests of governmental leaderships. The effectiveness of these types of influences varies considerably, within and between the technology exporting states.

The main political considerations for the West German, French, and British administrations appear to be concerned with the development of economic cooperation with China, and of relatively cordial overall relationships. Such cooperation could help to sustain Peking's determination not to accommodate with the USSR, could be a useful form of pressure against the Soviet Union to accept a genuine detente in Europe, could help to divide and undercut the appeal of the extreme left in Western Europe, and may facilitate competition against the United States for influence on Chinese policies, as well as for access to the expanding Chinese market. Of these factors, the importance of weakening the domestic left is much greater for the French administration than it is for West Germany's, which is more anxious to promote detente with the USSR and is, thus, unwilling to exert pressure that may have provocative effects on the Soviet leadership.(7)

The major economic considerations, for each of the principal West European states, are that widening access to the Chinese market is desirable not only because of its future potential but also because trade promotion in established markets is becoming more difficult. Some strains are developing in relations between Western Europe and the new state associated with the Community under the Lomé Convention, and it may be possible to obtain from China raw materials at cheap prices that normally are bought from the Lomé associates. This might prompt the Chinese regime to avoid excessive agitation in support of Third World demands for a New International Economic Order. There is also the possibility that China, like some of the East European states, can be induced to purchase basically dated technology. All these aspects of the commercial relationship have varying degrees of significance for West German, French, and British enterprises, commercial groups, and bureaucracies, as well as executives.(8)

The most significant strategic considerations are that China's opposition to the USSR results in the deployment of large Soviet forces along the Sino-Soviet border and in Mongolia, thus limiting the availability of Soviet units for the European theatre; and that moderate direct or indirect contributions to China's military development help to perpetuate the Sino-Soviet confrontation, while increasing the risks that the USSR would have to accept if it launched an attack against Western Europe. The Soviet Union has a very substantial capability for rapid conventional warfare against Western Europe, and this could well be used without escalation into a nuclear conflict if the initial penetrations into West Germany and France were very swift. There is an unevenly shared consensus, however, that the scale of assistance to China's military development should not give serious provocation to the USSR, or jeopardize the large West European economic exchanges with the COMECON states, which are giving the Soviet authorities inducements to accept detente on a long-term basis.(9)

For the West German administration, political, security, and economic factors in the relationship with the USSR obligate caution in the development of links with China. The relative success of the Ostpolitik, although now of lower domestic political utility than it was a half decade ago, is an important element in the electoral appeal of the SPD. Hence, it is necessary to continue the strategy of economic interdependence with the Soviet Union and the COMECON states, in order to have a favorable influence on Moscow's policy. West Germany's exports to the USSR in 1977, valued at $2,790 million were more than five times higher than they were in 1971, and roughly five times higher than exports to China. Moreover, these sales to the USSR were increasing much faster than exports to China, and were being accompanied by significant growth in total exports to the COMECON states, especially Czechoslovakia, Poland, and Hungary, each of which were more important trading partners than China.

The West German administration considers that the Chinese lack understanding of international politics, and are less open to constructive diplomacy than the Soviet leadership. Helmut Schmidt visited China in 1975 and commented rather frankly on the very subjective quality of Chinese thinking on international questions. Following the Carter administration's formal recognition of Peking in late 1978, Chancellor Schmidt announced that his administration would not sell arms to the Chinese.(10)

West Germany's foreign economic policy is managed by high-level bureaucrats, principally from the Ministry of Economics, in close cooperation with a vast network of industrial, trading, and banking organizations that aggregate their interests in a highly coherent fashion. A large proportion of these groups have very active interests in trade with the USSR, which they have been expanding since 1973 with the use of government-subsidized, long-term export credits. Strong pressures from these groups could be expected to prevent any major increase in economic cooperation with China if it were clear that this would incur Soviet displeasure; their confidence in their capacity to maintain their dominant role in Western trade with the COMECON states, moreover, evidently restrains their interest in trade with China, and reduces their concern about possible gains in that trade by France and Britain, who have been lagging well behind West Germany in sales to China over the past half decade.(11)

French policy is more complex, more ambivalent, and is managed from a weaker economic position. French exports to the USSR and to the COMECON group as a whole are less than half of West Germany's; and for the Chinese, France clearly ranks well below West Germany as a source of capital goods. The French capacity for competition in international trade is significantly limited by the moderate size and inadequate diversification of the nation's industrial establishment and Paris has not evolved any political methods of compensating for these economic constraints in the context of West-East trade.

The foreign policy that has evolved under Giscard d'Estaing is a form of modified Gaullism, less assertive and less nationalist, more adaptive, and with fewer elements of design. The main feature of this policy is a more constructive orientation toward policy integration in the Community and toward cooperation with West Germany for that purpose. There is relatively little concern with the expansion of exports to the COMECON states. Strategically, France is less constrained than West Germany on the question of selling military technology to China, although there is still a Gaullist tendency to seek an independent role between the two superpowers and, therefore, to develop better relations with the USSR. The promotion of links with China seems to have a relatively low priority, and this appears to be attributable in part to discomfort at the importance which the Chinese are giving to their new relationship with the United States and to Peking's antagonism toward Vietnam.(12)

The French administration is well placed to manage commercial relations with China; it gives strong direction to all enterprises engaged in external trade, and undertakes direct involvement in such trade. Hence, it can bargain very effectively with the state enterprises of communist regimes, while preventing them from exploiting competition between French firms, and can apply pressures to ensure that trading partners comply with the terms of their agreements. Yet the high degree of administrative strength in French external trade relations probably tends to discourage Chinese interest, especially because there is greater scope for Peking to take advantage of rivalries between West German firms, whose technology is more in demand. The Chinese may also be influenced by awareness that executive direction of French foreign economic policy is more susceptible to idiosyncratic factors than West Germany's, because of the strong powers vested in the President.(13)

British policy is severely affected by problems of governability that hold down performance in domestic policy and in foreign economic relations, and restrict options on external security and political issues, while creating imperatives for the use of political methods to offset the effects of economic weakness in foreign policy. Within limits, Britain can extract benefits from tacit alignment with the United States against partners in the European Community on trade and monetary issues, and from the withholding of support for integrative activity within the Community. Politically, however, in the context of East-West trade, Britain has no advantages to compensate for the technological backwardness that hinders competition with West Germany and France in capital goods exports to the COMECON countries. Nevertheless, Britain is less constrained than France and West Germany on the question of selling military technology to China. The local communist movement is relatively small, and Britain is less exposed than West Germany to the Soviet military threat. Indeed, to gain advantages over West Germany in trade with China, Britain has incentives to sell arms to the Peking regime as a means of earning goodwill. While the volume of this trade is not likely to grow very much, because of China's more substantial interest in Japan and the United States technology exporters, it could contribute to a moderate improvement in Britain's balance of payments.(14)

British external policy, in part because of Commonwealth links, tends to have a broader international perspective than France's, but is similarly lacking in design, except for an emphasis on maintaining what is felt to be a "special relationship" with the United States. There is a secondary interest in China, associated with that "special relationship," which is linked with the special position of Hong Kong in British commercial and investment policies. China is a potentially significant source of raw materials outside the Group of 77, and there is an important incentive to meet Chinese technology requirements on reasonable terms in order to ensure that Peking will continue to respect the status quo in Hong Kong. Almost 25 percent of China's foreign exchange is earned by exports to Hong Kong, but the economic vitality of this small territory is heavily dependent on Peking's willingness to refrain from exerting leverage for control of the colony. British considerations of comparative advantage cannot be divorced from the position of Hong Kong, but there may well be expectations that Chinese goodwill could ease the difficulties of competing against West Germany for Peking's technology orders and, perhaps, make possible higher profits than could be earned in the more competitive context of trade with the COMECON states. British leaders visiting China over the past decade have tended to express stronger anti-Soviet views than prominent French figures, apparently persuading the Chinese that their intense denunciations of the USSR have been having significant effects, and that the way is open to encourage Britain to adopt firmer anti-Soviet policies.(15)

Chinese policy toward the three major West European states and the European Community is formulated in the context of a strategic design against the USSR and a drive for accelerated modernization. From the relevant theoretical and official statements, and from Chinese behavior, it is clear that West Germany, France, and Britain rank after Japan as sources of advanced technology; although there is no question of importing Japanese military equipment, as Tokyo is acutely sensitive to the large Soviet military presence in adjacent parts of East Asia. It is also clear that, strategically, the Chinese see a significant identity of interests with West Germany, France, and Britain as major adversaries of the USSR; and may well appreciate that, if the Soviet Union were able to secure major gains in Western Europe, militarily or through political methods, it would then be inclined to resort to coercive diplomacy against their regime. The West Europeans are exhorted to strengthen their armed forces, increase their opposition to Soviet expansionism, strengthen cohesion within their Community, and co-operate more with the United States – although this latter point is made obliquely.(16)

The quest for West European technology is linked with the endeavor to promote greater opposition to the Soviet Union within the Community, and both lines of activity are attributable mainly to the presently dominant military-technocratic faction in the Chinese elite, headed by Deng Xiaoping. The future of this group's control, however, appears to be very uncertain, because most of its members are aged revolutionaries, and there is a cleavage between it and a younger segment of the leadership that had moved upwards during the Cultural Revolution. These currently disadvantaged elements may well be able to challenge the emphasis on importing Western technology, at a later stage, by calling for greater self-reliance and denouncing the "bourgeois" cultural penetration that is incidental to the increased contacts with capitalist states.   A change of policy, in reaction to the somewhat pragmatic dependence on the West, would probably be accompanied by increases in the presently muted struggle against "U.S. Imperialism," and a reduction of interest in high-level contacts with the major West European states.(17)

Perceptions of the technological benefits of the current policy toward the principal Community members, of course, may secure wider support for it among the Chinese elite. It must be stressed, however, that this policy, although it represents a modification of doctrine, is being implemented by a ruling group with an outlook that is still quite subjective, because of the influence of deeply internalized ideological beliefs that are given little exposure to cognitive challenges. On the basis of this outlook, there may well be undue optimism about the regime's capacity to influence West European policies, and about the strategic and economic benefits to be gained from dealings with the Community and its principal members. Setbacks in attempts to obtain greater access to Community markets for agricultural products and light manufactures could be felt very keenly.

The criteria which appear to influence Chinese dealings with the Community's major capital goods exporters are technological levels, credit terms, opportunities for competition, the scope for political leverage through trade, and the potential for pressure against the USSR. The relative importance of each of these is difficult to estimate, and may not be based on any clearly defined principles; but, in various configurations, they seem to explain the fairly stable ranking of West Germany ahead of France and Britain, but behind Japan, in sales of plants and equipment to China. West German technology is more advanced and more diversified than that of France or Britain because high rates of capital investment have been encouraged in support of the export-oriented growth strategy since the early 1950s. West German credit terms may not be more advantageous than those of the two rival Community trading nations, but tax and other incentives given to West German exporters are very substantial, and enable them to offer their technology at very competitive prices. Chinese opportunities to exploit competition between exporting firms are restricted in France by the strong role of the administration in the direction of the private sector; and, in West Germany, by the close partnership between industrial groups, and between them and the federal government. It seems that more advantage can be taken of rivalries between British firms, but their technology is less in demand. Nevertheless, Britain is inclined to identify more positively with China on the military threat posed by the USSR. There is more open recognition of the gravity of the danger to Western Europe, and, therefore, of the need for a strong U.S. military presence to deter a Soviet attack. Significant increases in Soviet hostility appear to be acceptable for Britain, as costs incurred through association with China's hostility and through arms sales to the Chinese. The acceptability of these costs, within limits, could be increased if it were evident that Soviet behavior was strengthening the U.S. resolve to maintain forces in Western Europe, and was causing difficulties for the left in France and Italy.(18)

INTERACTION

West Germany, France, and Britain interact bilaterally with China, mainly on economic issues and on the basis of a 1978 general trade agreement between the Community and China which accorded each side most-favored-nation status. This agreement has a five year term, and the effect is to give China less advantageous access to the Community market than the developing states covered by the Lomé Agreement. Chinese exports of agricultural products and low-technology manufactures face strong protection under the Community's common agricultural and commercial policies, but for the present there can be no question of negotiating better access. General Community interest in the China market is active but not strong, Peking is not well placed to bargain with the members of the Community as a group, and the Community's collective decision-making processes are so slow and so disjointed, that the question of a special commercial relationship with China, if raised, would be difficult to settle. The Chinese have evinced no desire to be given associate status under an extension of that agreement, and most members of the Community would probably not wish China to be a party to such a convention, because Peking would add greatly to the bargaining power of the present group of associated states.

The three major members of the Community interact with China as competitors, responding mainly to interchanges between their trans-national enterprises and Chinese trade organizations. They also act as lesser rivals of Japan and of the United States, but are not inclined to coordinate their policies on that account, and, if they were to attempt such collaboration, would almost certainly find it difficult, especially because of their divergent interests. For each administration, the management of trade and other relations with China, moreover, has to take into account problems in the context of policies toward the superpowers.

The USSR is a powerful factor in the interactive context. While the principal effect of its presence is to inhibit West German contributions to Chinese military development, there is an unused capacity for leverage to restrain each state's initiatives for the promotion of economic cooperation with China, and this leverage could be strengthened if the USSR were to make some impressive gestures to facilitate force reductions in Europe. The USSR, however, is not likely to reduce its very substantial imports of Western technology; indeed, it will almost certainly continue its attempts to increase these, while endeavoring to overcome its balance of payments problems by exporting more primary products.(19)

The United States is potentially a more influential factor in the setting of Community-China relations, but its orientation is more complex and ambivalent, and its influence is more diffuse. The U.S. connection with China appears to have a significant influence on Britain's policy of selling military equipment to the Chinese, and it seems probable that this policy would be modified if Washington's relations with Peking were seriously strained. U.S. foreign economic policy has no direct effects on the nonstrategic commercial dealings of the major West European states with China, except by providing competition. The highly pluralistic processes which generate this external economic policy give it considerable incoherence, however, and, in the implementation of this policy, U.S. firms do not operate in the kind of partnership with government that is usual in West Germany, or under the degree of government direction that is normal in France.(20)

The identities and differences of interests and incentives in the relations between the major Community members and China form asymmetric patterns. In the economic relationship, the leading West European states have significant interests in exporting the technology that China needs; but their demands for Chinese raw materials, foods, and low-technology manufactures are relatively small and are not likely to grow appreciably, despite the advantage of utilizing China as a source of primary exports outside the associated states covered by the Lomé Convention. In the Community's trade with the Third World, India and Singapore are larger markets, for the present, and Malaysia and India are much more important sources of raw materials.(21)

In the political-strategic relationships between major Community members and China, interests on each side are seen very differently, are given little clarification, and give rise to only intermittent discussion and negotiations. The Chinese would like to see increased levels of military strength and preparedness in Western Europe to deter the USSR; but the European NATO members see themselves operating under budgetary constraints and are anxious to maintain detente by not provoking Soviet decision makers and by strengthening economic ties with the USSR. Peking's arguments that detente is based on false hopes are generally not accepted, and related warnings against assisting Soviet industrial development are discounted. On the West European side, there is no coherent and sustained effort to communicate a strategic view to the Chinese; varying degrees of empathy are expressed with their opposition to the USSR, mainly by British officials, but there is no question of developing exchanges for the purpose of reaching common understandings regarding the Soviet Union and the likely contingencies in Europe and Asia which could produce new common strategic interests between the major Community members and China.(22)

Because of the orientation of West European security policies, and the configuration of external economic interests which influence the major Community members, as well as China's military weaknesses and backwardness, there are major differences in bargaining strength which affect Sino-West European interaction. China's capabilities for economic bargaining are low since the West Europeans have more than adequate alternative sources of raw materials, and the Chinese ability to absorb foreign technology is modest and is increasing no faster than that of other relatively more developed Third World states. No significant leverage can be exerted by Peking on economic issues by linking them with security matters, since the West Europeans seek no military cooperation with China and can continue to disappoint Chinese strategic hopes without facing any retaliatory pressures. If Peking improved relations with Moscow, West European strategic interests would be adversely affected, but the leading Community states clearly do not envisage that the Chinese will opt for detente with the USSR.(23)

For the major West European capital goods exporting states, the principal economic issues in their relations with China concern the tariffs and quotas applied to Chinese primary products and low-technology manufactures. China, however, is only one of the minor sources of agricultural products of interest to West Germany and Britain in the context of their dissatisfactions with the Community's Common Agricultural Policy, which is mainly of benefit to France, and this state's satisfaction with that policy makes it disinclined to consider modifications in favor of Third World exporters. For Britain, West

Germany, and France, moreover, Chinese low-technology manufactures do not merit more considerate treatment than that given to those of other developing countries not covered by the Lomé Convention, and are a small factor in the large and difficult problem of trade in these commodities, which is tending to become more acute with general economic slowdowns and heavy drains of reserves to the OPEC states.(24)

For China, questions of comparative advantage in trade with the major West European states are highly important and are linked with political/strategic issues. Access to advanced West European technology, which is necessary in order to avoid undue dependence on Japan and the United States, must be maintained with substantial purchases that must grow at a significant rate in order to ensure continued West German, French, and British interest in competition for Chinese orders. In general, however, purchases of technology from Japan yield greater political advantages and increase the important strategic benefit of limiting Japanese economic cooperation with the USSR, which could lead to a large Japanese role in the development of the Soviet Far East. Substantial reductions of Chinese trade with Japan and large increases in Chinese acquisitions of West European technology would probably lead to a considerable expansion of Japanese trade with the USSR, although Tokyo's interest in the Chinese market would remain strong. Yet, for the West Europeans, the higher level of trade with China would have little significance in the contexts of trade with the communist states as a whole, and of trade with the nonassociated developing states.(25)

On questions of comparative advantage and immediatley related political considerations, the Chinese attitude appears to be relatively pragmatic, but there seems to be a strongly subjective factor in Peking's strategic thinking on the links with Western Europe. There appear to be strong tendencies to overestimate the potency of Chinese strategic advice to the West Europeans, and the professed commitments of the West Europeans to attain higher levels of integration, and to strengthen their defenses. The Chinese evidently wish to believe that the major European powers can do much to deter the USSR from aggression, but if there were dramatic evidence to the contrary, the effects on Chinese elite political psychology could well be disruptive.

OUTCOMES

The modest and gradually increasing commerce between Community members and China is the principal outcome of their exchanges. This trade has a bilateral character attributable to Chinese policy, and is affected by problems associated with features of Peking's command economy. Community restrictions also affect the trade, and these, together with limited Community demand and competition from other Third World countries, tend to hold down Chinese exports of foodstuffs, raw materials, and manufactured items, causing deficits which make West European credits more important for Peking.

Under the Sino-European Community Trade Agreement of 1978, China's desire to achieve a balance of trade each year was given formal recognition, with a stipulation that a Joint Committee would study ways of remedying any obvious imbalance; but West European interests were covered by protection and price clauses which permit unilateral measures to prevent any disturbance of the Community market and which specify that the commerce shall be arranged at "market-related prices." The Community will "endeavor" to liberalize restrictions on imports from China, in return for "favorable consideration" of its exports by the Chinese.(26)

The Chinese appear to seek balanced trade with each Community member, especially the larger ones, because of currency and commodity inconvertibility problems typical of command economies; but such balances are not easy to attain because, in most of the West European states, Peking has to deal with autonomous enterprises that have diverging interests. Chinese purchases of machinery from one West German firm do not give any other West German firm an interest in importing Chinese textiles unless these offer comparative advantages with respect to numerous other external sources of textiles, although the high degree of organization attained by West German business firms may facilitate cross sectoral cooperation in order to meet Chinese expectations, especially with the help of West German government departments. West Germany tends to maintain a substantial favorable balance in trade with China, and so also does France.(27)

In order to balance trade with the Community as a whole and with each major member, China can reduce imports. This was done on a significant scale in 1977, while the Trade Agreement with the Community was being negotiated and, of course, may have been a form of pressure designed to influence the negotiations. Decreases in purchases, however, tend to reduce West European willingness to grant credits, which the Chinese will need on a considerable scale unless their industrialization is to be geared to the slow pace at which their primary and light industrial exports can expand. Such sales, in addition to encountering serious protective barriers in the Community and other advanced markets, are also limited by the discouraging effects of Chinese business methods, which are slow and which restrict the contacts of foreign firms to Peking's trading corporations, thus preventing access to user enterprises.(28)

The outcomes of the intermittent Sino-West European exchanges on political and security matters are increases in each side's familiarity with the other's strategic perspectives, but with little adjustment of views, sharing of doctrines, or evolution of common thinking on contingencies. Only Britain and France appear to seek continuing exchanges with the Chinese, but the interaction is intermittent, and for both the British and the French is hindered by uncertainties about the stability and future orientation of the Peking regime, by its total hostility to detente, and by its strongly ideological language, which still evidences fundamental antagonism to "capitalist" states. The Chinese show no disposition to recognize any justification for deterrence as a basis for Western strategy, and their behavior indicates that they are not prepared to accept anything less than total West European endorsement of their anti-Soviet strategic outlook, although this expectation is inconsistent with their ideological beliefs concerning the inevitable expression of each West European state's class structure in its foreign policy.(29)

Chinese purchases of military equipment and defense-related technology from Western Europe are basically economic transactions sanctioned by relatively ad hoc considerations for the suppliers with respect to the foreign exchange earned, the possible advantages regarding access to the Chinese market, and the utility of added leverage against the USSR. The Chinese appear to be concerned mainly with acquiring small quantities of sophisticated equipment which will help the development of their own industries, despite their evident need for relatively large quantities of weapons to modernize their armed forces as quickly as possible. They are clearly reluctant to accept heavy dependence on Western suppliers of military equipment, and their strategic planning seems to be based on assumptions that their large armed forces, despite serious equipment deficiencies, would be capable of waging a long war of attrition against Soviet invaders.(30)

At the transnational level, China has acquired no significant capabilities to influence West European policies through favored enterprises, as is possible in dealings with Japan. The volume of trade is substantial only in the relationship with West Germany, and in that context it is very much smaller than West German commerce with the USSR. Moreover, although each major West European state maintains a very cordial relationship with Peking, China has little scope for cultural penetration of their societies. Information activities and educational, scientific, literary, and other exchanges are arranged; but efforts to project the Chinese regime as a model for social and economic development are rather ineffective, because Peking's interest in learning from the West is so much in evidence, the ethos of the Chinese regime and its experiences are felt to be remote by many West Europeans, and there are no major leftist parties in Western Europe that are sufficiently influenced by Chinese ideology to be capable of diffusing this effectively within their societies. The principal West European communist parties are in varying degrees pro-Soviet, and the pro-Chinese communist organizations are small splinter groups which have had Maoist orientations and which are in disarray because of intense rivalries and factional strife; none of them seems likely to emerge as a significant national association responsive to Chinese inspiration. For the present, the Chinese leadership appears to be cautious in its dealings with these groups.(31)

There is small-scale West European cultural penetration of China, incidental to trade contacts, routine educational and scientific exchanges, and the involvement of several thousand West European technical personnel in the construction of industrial plants. Firm social controls on the Chinese side appear to impose severe limits on receptivity to Western values. Although Peking encourages a very positive attitude toward the utilization of Western technology and science, officials in Chinese industrial establishments and state trading corporations appear to be somewhat uncertain whether this policy will continue and show cautious attitudes in dealing with Westerners. A vigorous effort to accelerate the introduction of Western technology was drastically modified in 1976 after the death of Chou En-lai, in conjunction with the second purge of Deng Xiaoping, and this is clearly remembered by many of the personnel who are now implementing the current policy.(32)

PROSPECTS

Commerce between the principal members of the Community and China will probably expand at a moderate rate, but may not increase significantly as a proportion of total Community trade with the communist regimes. Trade with the COMECON states will remain much more important for most Community members, especially West Germany, not only because of its economic benefits but also because of its political utility as a means of strengthening detente. The commerce with China, however, will continue to be seen by some Community members as a form of pressure against the USSR, and as a contribution to Chinese development which will reduce the danger of a possible accommodation with Moscow by Peking.

West European, and especially West German, interest in China's technology requirements will continue to be quite active because of the immediate and longer-term possibilities for expanding exports to this market, in exchange for raw materials that may be available at prices below those charged by the ACP members and other developing countries. Difficulties and uncertainties in the now-strained relationships with the ACP members are tending to increase Community interest in trade with other developing states, and China will continue to have special significance among these because it has only generalized political links with the Group of 77 and its strong need for advanced technology gives it incentives to undercut the primary exports of other modernizing states in order to finance its imports.

The development of Community trade with China, however, will continue to be limited by various characteristics of the Chinese command economy. The backwardness of this economy is a severe constraint on the absorption of advanced technology, especially because of the lack of skilled personnel. Pervasive bureaucratic inertia, as in the USSR, slows decisions regarding the acquisition of such technology and the development of exports. Currency inconvertibility and commodity inconvertibility remain difficulties of a permanent character; and, as in the USSR, the operation of the centrally controlled economy makes for a bias against export expansion.(33) Moreover, to the extent that the Chinese regime does increase its foreign trade, there is likely to be a persistent emphasis on the growth of commerce with Japan, because of this state's proximity and the greater political and strategic advantages derived from this connection.

The occasional interaction on political and strategic issues between major West European states and China is unlikely to lead to significant understandings or cooperation. The Chinese cannot be expected to evolve more pragmatic and more persuasive forms of communication; the dominant group in their leadership comprises aged revolutionary figures who have deeply internalized their ideology, and who operate in a relatively closed environment. On the West European side, differences between the strategic perspectives of West Germany, France, and Britain will almost certainly persist, and the evolution of a common orientation at the level of high politics toward China will be very unlikely. British and French inclinations to sell modest quantities of military equipment to the Chinese are likely to remain moderate, sustained by beliefs that gradual increases in Peking's armed strength are desirable, in order to hold down Soviet forces in the Far East, but influenced also by anxieties not to give severe provocation to the USSR. If the United States begins to provide China with substantial quantities of military equipment, however, Britain will almost certainly endeavor to expand its sales of defense items to Peking.

If there are no serious divisions between the major West European states over the question of military sales to China, and if Community exports to that state rise substantially, a closer trading relationship with it may seem desirable to several Community members. China might be offered a preferential trade agreement similar to those which the Community has with most of the Mediterranean rim countries. These, although somewhat less favorable than the Lomé Convention in their wording, give better access to the Community market than the generalized system of preferences applicable to Community imports form nonassociated Third World states. While the Chinese would not wish to let it appear that they were gaining commercial advantages over other developing countries, they would probably be inclined to accept a form of association that would not involve collective bargaining with the Mediterranean rim countries and that would facilitate the maintenance of a separate and relatively advantageous position outside the ACP group.(34)

In the longer term, if the Chinese develop a more substantial economic relationship with the Community, and a somewhat closer political relationship, it may be feasible for them to seek fast breeder reactors from France or possibly West Germany. France and West Germany, with the cooperation of other Community members, are developing fast breeder reactors, which are probably arousing Chinese interest. As the Carter administration is opposing this development, Peking cannot look to the United States as a source of this technology; but the utility of such breeders may well acquire great significance for the Chinese because their modernization program could benefit very much if there were large increases in their electrical output, and if their currently modest oil exports could be expanded through reductions of domestic consumption.(35)

THEORY

The interactions between the Community and China reflect the influence of functional logic, game-theoretic principles, and factors relevant for comparative foreign policy studies. These interactions also reflect aspects of the Community's significance as an emerging confederal actor.

With the growth of Sino-West European commerce, there is increasing awareness among the major Community exporters of some identity of secondary economic interests; but these are perceived differently by the Chinese, who show intense consciousness of what they believe are the vital political and strategic dimensions of the relationship. For the West Europeans, there are only moderate incentives to seek larger and more comprehensive economic bonds with Peking. The possible benefits have to be compared with opportunities in the much more substantial trading partnerships with the OPEC states and the more advanced developing countries.

Sino-West European commerce is growing, and this cooperation is extending into some production-sharing arrangements related to technology imports; it is also resulting in some small-scale monetary cooperation, which makes it easier for Chinese banks to deal in hard currencies. All this, however, is of minor importance in the total context of the Community's external economic relations. For each side, moreover, the political aspects of this modest cooperation are assuming more importance, instead of diminishing with the growth of mutual economic advantages that might push political factors into the background. Professional inputs by experts on each side do not make the interactions less political because they are necessarily linked with allocative decisions. On the other hand, there is no neofunctional logic working for the development of a Sino-Community "system," for institutionalized joint decision making. A continuing interactive process like that in the Community-Arab dialogue is not developing.

Elements of functional and neofunctional logic are more operative in the Community's trade and investment relations with the USSR and in Sino-Japanese commercial relations. In these contexts, relatively high levels of economic exchange motivate endeavors to institutionalize interaction for the management of interdependencies, while increasing the political significance of those interdependencies. Systemic development, however, is significantly hindered by strongly autarkic tendencies in the policies of the Communist partners and by their conflictual value orientations.

Simple game theoretic principles help to explain the active Chinese strategic interest in the encouragement of stronger West European opposition to the USSR, and the differing degrees of support for China as an adversary of the Soviet Union that are forthcoming from major Community members. Full explanation of these forms of behavior requires reference to West European notions of deterrence and Chinese interests in pitting secondary adversaries against the main enemy. West European perceptions of the conflict structure in the central balance differ from Peking's perceptions of that confrontation and of China's own conflict with the USSR, and the contrasts give rise to diverging strategic orientations. But the interaction is inconclusive. On the West European side, there is no coherent design regarding the utilization of China's adversary relationship with the USSR; and, for the Chinese, West European responses to warnings about the USSR are unsatisfactory. West European behavior toward China on the strategic issue is influenced by long-established habits of pragmatic incremental-ism, while Chinese behavior discourages West European engagement at the strategic level by the use of conflictual ideological language which precludes identification of basic common interests. What results is a situation which challenges the USSR to increase its deployments, while no significant West European-Chinese military cooperation develops.

In the perspective of comparative foreign policy studies, the behav-ior of the major West European states toward China is significant as an expression of the constraints of geography and limited power on regional actors. There are some incentives to overcome these con-straints, but they remain effective enough to prevent significant involvement in the affairs of East Asia. If collectively managed, the involvement could be very substantial, but such collective management of secondary matters in a distant area is not likely except as a consequence of structural integration within the Community. This, if it occurs, will probably be due to the development of a common political will to manage major external interdependencies more effectively than is possible on the present confederal basis.

Chinese policy reflects weak bargaining strength of a developing state interacting with a group of industrialized democracies whose principal external economic ties are with other industrialized democ-racies. In addition, Chinese policy illustrates how a socialist state's domestic ideological concerns, with respect to its political culture, can hamper communication with open states that are desired as allies but that are open to dialogue only in terms of their instrumental political values.

Contributions to international theory from the study of Chinese policy are considerably less important than those from work on the development of the European Community; and if this Community attains a significant degree of structural integration it will, of course, have a much greater potential than China for constructive international activity. The Community's evolution is being shaped principally by the effects of long-established common practices of "cybernetic" decision making, and by the challenges of neofunctional logic. The various national patterns of "cybernetic" decision making favor sectoral and organizational demands, but in a disaggregated fashion, incrementally, and disjointedly. They reflect the failures of national executives to attain high-order-value integrations in policy, at cost to national, and even more to Community, interests. But, while this is the general tendency of domestic influences on the foreign policies of Community members, the international and especially extra-Community influences on those policies set increasing requirements for the common management of interdependencies, and, thus, for the recognition of neofunctional logic. Whether the cybernetic orientations can be moderated and integrative motivations aroused depends very much on elite socialization processes, relative levels of institutional development, overall performance in public policy, and leadership capabilities; but it also depends on the magnitude of the challenges to manage interdependencies. These challenges are growing, and may be increased significantly over the next decade, not by China's actions, but by the behavior of the United States responding to Community commercial and monetary policies, and influenced, in part, by the perceived potential of its own connection with China.

NOTES

(1) See Wilhelm Hankel, "West Germany," in Economic Foreign Policies of Industrial States, edited by Wilfrid L. Kohl (Lexington, Mass.: D.C. Heath, 1977), pp. 105-24; and Michael Kreile, "West Germany: The Dynamics of Expansion," International Organization 31, no. 4 (Autumn 1977): 775-808.

(2) See Edward L. Morse, "France," in Economic Foreign Policies, pp. 69-104; and John Zysman, "The French State in the International Economy," International Organization 31, no. 4 (Autumn 1977): 839-78; and Direction of Trade Annual 1971-1977, International Monetary Fund.

(3) See discussion of British interest in Robert Boardman, Britain and the People's Republic of China, 1949-74 (London: Macmillan, 1976); and references to the importance of Ostpolitik for the West German administration in Peter Pulzer, "Responsible Party Government and Stable Coalition: The Case of the German Federal Republic," Political Studies, 26, no. 2 (June 1978): 181-208.

(4) See comments on the Community's external powers in Werner J. Feld, "The Foreign Policy of the European Community: Its Impact on the International System," in The European Community and the Outsiders, edited by Peter Stingelin (Don Mills, Ontario: Longmans, 1973), pp. 1-22; and Michael B. Dolan and James A. Caporaso, "The External Relations of the European Community," The Annals of the American Academy of Political and Social Science 440 (Nov. 1978): 135-55.

(5) See comments on the internal use of communications in China by Lucian W. Pye, "Communications and Chinese Political Culture," Asian Survey 18, no. 3 (March 1978): 221-46.

(6) See Parris H. Chang, Power and Policy in China, 2nd ed. (University Park, Pa.: Pennsylvania State University Press, 1978); and Andrew Nathan, "A Factionalism Model of CCP Politics," China Quarterly 53 (Jan.-Mar. 1973): 34-66.

(7) See discussions of the strength of the left in France in Howard Machin and Vincent Wright, "The French Left Under the Fifth Republic: The Search for Identity in Unity," Comparative Politics 10, no. 1 (October 1977): 35-68; and Victor Leduc, "The French Communist Party: Between Stalinism and Eurocommunism," The Political Quarterly 49, no. 4 (October-December 1978): 400-10. See also Pulzer, "Responsible Party Government," on Ostpolitik.

(8) See discussion of relations with states covered by the Lomé Agreement in Carol Cosgrove Twitchett, "Towards a New ACP-EC Convention," The World Today 34, no. 12 (Dec. 1978): 472-83; and Geoffrey L. Goodwin and James B. Mayall, "The European Alternatives: International Commodity Policy: EEC Policies and Options," Government and Opposition 13, no. 1 (Winter 1978): 3-20. See also Michael Kreile, "West Germany"; John Zysman, "The French State"; and Stephen Blank, "Britain: The Politics of Foreign Economic Policy, the Domestic Economy, and the Problem of Pluralistic Stagnation," International Organization 31, no. 4 (Autumn 1977): 673-722.

(9) See John Pinder and Pauline Pinder, "West European Economic Relations with the Soviet Union," in Soviet Strategy in Europe, edited by Richard Pipes (New York: Crane Russak, 1976), pp. 269-304.

(10) See comments on the Chinese by Helmut Schmidt in German International 19, no. 12 (Dec. 1975): 9-15.

(11) See Direction of Trade.

(12) See discussions of main direction of French foreign policy in Marie Claude Smouts, "French Foreign Policy: The Domestic Debate," International Affairs 53, no. 1 (Jan. 1977): 36-50.

(13) See comments on French foreign economic policy by Zysman, "The French State."

(14) See Lawrence Freedman, "Britain and the Arms Trade," International Affairs 54, no. 1 (July 1978): 377-92.

(15) See references to statements by British visitors in Reinhard Rummel, "China's Fixation on Western Europe," Aussenpolitik, English ed. 29, no. 3 (1978): 275-88.

(16) Ibid., and see Michael B. Yahuda, China's Role in World Affairs (New York: St. Martin's Press, 1978), pp. 269-85.

(17) See Kenneth Lieberthal, "The Politics of Modernization in the PRC," Problems of Communism 28, no. 3 (May-June 1978): 1-17.

(18) For a British view of the Soviet threat, see D.M.O. Miller, "Strategic Factors Affecting a Soviet Conventional Attack in Western Europe," International Defence Review 11, no. 6 (1978): 853-59.

(19) See Philip Hanson and Michael Kaser, "Soviet Economic Relations with Western Europe," in Soviet Strategy in Europe, pp. 213-68.

(20) See Stephen D. Krasner, "U.S. Commercial and Monetary Policy: Unravelling the Paradox of External Strength and Internal Weakness," International Organization 31, no. 4 (Autumn 1977): 635-72.

(21) See Direction of Trade.

(22) See Philip Windsor, "A Watershed for NATO," The World Today 33, no. 11 (Nov. 1977): 409-16; and Sir Bernard Burrows, "European Security," in A Nation Writ Large?, edited by Max Kohnstamm and Wolfgang Hager (New York: John Wiley, 1973), pp. 128-51.

(23) For discussions of West European security perspectives see Andrew Shonfield, "Britain's Future in the International System," Suzanne Berger, "France: Autonomy in Alliance," and Alfred Grosser, "Germany: A European and World Power," in Western Europe: The Trials of Partnership, edited by David S. Landes (Lexington, Mass.: D.C. Heath, 1977).

(24) See Goodwin and Mayall, "The European Alternatives"; Lewis J. Edinger, "West Germany: Problems and Prospects," Political Science Quarterly 93, no. 1 (Spring 1978): 27-34; and Twitchett, "Towards a New ACP-EC Convention."

(25) See Direction of Trade; and Pinder and Pinder, "West European Economic Relations."

(26) See text of agreement, Europe Information, 13/78, Commission of the European Communities, and Working Document 76/77, May 5, 1977, European Parliament.

(27) For a discussion of the bilateral trade preferences of command economies, see C.H. McMillan, "The Bilateral Character of Soviet and Eastern European Foreign Trade," Journal of Common Market Studies 13, nos. 1 and 2 (January 1974): 1-20.

(28) See comments on Chinese methods by Rummel, "China's Fixation"; Gene T. Hai Hsiao, The Foreign Trade of China (Berkeley: University of California Press, 1977); and Alexander Eckstein, China's Economic Revolution (Cambridge, England: Cambridge University Press, 1977), chap. 7.

(29) See Yahuda, China's Role; and Samuel S. Kim, China, The United Nations, and World Order (Princeton, N.J.: Princeton University Press, 1979), chap. 2.

(30) See Gavin Boyd, China's Strategic Perspective (Ottawa: Defence Department, forthcoming).

(31) See Leduc, "The French Communist Party"; and Eric Shaw, "The Italian Historical Compromise," The Political Quarterly 49, no. 4 (Oct.-Dec. 1978): 411-24.

(32) Chinese orders from and interest in the communist slackened in 1976 after the purge of Teng. See Working Document 76/77. The cautious attitudes of Chinese officials have been noted by Western businessmen visiting China, according to Western commercial representatives in Hong Kong.

(33) See McMillan, "Bilateral Character of Soviet and East European Trade."

(34) The Community's relations with the Mediterranean rim countries are reviewed in Loukas Tsoukalis, "The EEC and the Mediterranean," International Affairs 53, no. 3 (July 1977): 422-38.

(35) See Werner J. Feld, "West European Foreign Policies: The Impact of the Oil Crisis," Orbis 22, no. 1 (Spring 1978): 63-88; and Pierre Lellouche, "France in the International Nuclear Energy Controversy: A New Policy Under Giscard d'Estaing," Orbis 22, no. 4 (Winter 1979): 951-66.

9 Trade Between the European Community and the United States: The Diminishing Asymmetry

Hanns-Dieter Jacobsen

INTRODUCTION

The recent growth of the U.S. trade balance deficit and the decline of the value of the dollar in the international monetary system highlight some developments which have raised analytical questions of considerable political and economic significance. What is the meaning of transatlantic relations for both the European Community and the United States? In which direction have the economic asymmetries, which for a long time favored the United States, developed? The economic relevance is immediately evident from the unceasing debate about economic interdependencies in the world economy and growing sensitivities and vulnerabilities among industrialized countries. In particular, the recent discussions on international transmissions of economic disturbances and about locomotive functions of some economies to fight world recession are stressing this point.(1) The political dimension is obvious, too. Transatlantic economic and political relations have been the most important pillars for the coherence of the Western world; any structural changes could lead to altered responsibilities and different political strategies which affect the bilateral relationship as well as the respective position in the international system.(2)

Traditional discussions on international economic interdependencies mostly focused on the question of the consequences of increasing economic relations for the interacting economic units.(3) Since the economic relevance of different countries in the world system is a function not only of their size, stage of development, and resource endowment(4) but of the interaction flows as well, the following analysis concentrates on the evaluation of relevant economic interaction indicators. This will allow us to draw some conclusions about the relative importance of EC and U.S. relations with the rest of the world and, in particular, with each other. This analysis of the width of the channels which influence the impact of external economic disturbances (stemming from political actions of other countries as well as from simple economic interconnectedness) will help to prove some hypotheses about the possibilities for governments to control their national economy and to achieve their respective national economic goals, such as high employment, fair economic growth, and low inflation. Open economies are more susceptible to the pressure of external events than closed ones; their capacities to control foreign influences are more limited; their "talent for independence" is smaller. The term "talent for independence" is supposed to characterize the fact that interacting countries in the world economy have a different range of means at their disposal to respond to the challenges in and between economic issue areas; and they have to pay different costs in order to minimize the consequences of reducing or even breaking off trade relationships with their partners.(5)

The comparison of these sensitivities and vulnerabilities might lead to conclusions about a country's relative talent for independence, about its ability to control its economic policy instruments and, finally, even about the possibilities to influence the economic courses of other countries.(6) The limits to a country's ability to act autonomously and independently in economic affairs, and even to influence its trading partners to act in a certain direction, is, therefore, largely determined by the extent of the asymmetries in their respective foreign economic dependencies.(7)

The subsequent analysis of the foreign trade relations between the EC and the United States will proceed in the following way. First we will analyze the overall export- and import-dependencies of the EC and the United States as well as those in the bilateral relationship.   In a second step, we will prove the asymmetries of these dependencies by interaction coefficients weighted with GDP and total trade figures. These coefficients, complemented by trade-intensity, trade-balance, and terms-of-trade measures, will serve as indicators for the asymmetries of the respective controlability of the considered economies, their talent for independence, and those potential losses which could arise when the relationship is reduced or broken off. These coefficients could be interpreted as indicators of the asymmetries in mutual dependencies (= interdependencies) in the economic sphere as well, since the analysis of channels such as foreign trade, through which foreign events can impinge on an economy, makes it possible to draw further conclusions on the relative ranges of choice of the EC and the United States in their bilateral relationship.

The results presented in this study do not claim to explain the complex subject of transatlantic economic interdependencies. The asymmetry coefficients calculated for the relationship between the EC and the United States, for instance, do not calculate the numerical amount of losses which arises from disturbing events; rather, they have to be interpreted as a first step which should be complemented by further research, in particular on the generation of external events which could affect other economies, their transformation by the considered country's own economic systems and policies into domestic effects and, finally, on their responses in order to reduce the undesired effects of external events.

RESULTS OF THE ANALYSIS

Some Explanatory Remarks

The time frame of this study is the period between 1962 and 1977. This time period was chosen mainly for pragmatic reasons, since the data available were incomplete for the previous years.(8) Furthermore, this time period is sufficient to provide some evidence on medium- to long-term changes.

In this study, the data for the European Community include all nine countries which were then the only member states of the EC (Belgium, Denmark, France, the Federal Republic of Germany, Ireland, Italy, Luxembourg, the Netherlands, and the United Kingdom), even for the time before the accession of Denmark, Ireland and the UK to the EC in 1973. For 1962 and 1965, however, the numbers mostly include only the EC of the six and the UK (because of its minor input, the results are only insignificantly impaired by the missing data for Denmark and Ireland).

In contrast to the United States, the European Community has not been acting as a political unit. Its relatively advanced stage of integration, however, legitimizes the treatment of the EC as an economic unit. For the analysis, this means that the foreign economic relations of the EC exclude the economic interactions of the EC members with each other. Therefore, the foreign trade data of the EC presented in this study does not include intra-EC exports and imports.

It has to be pointed out that the trade figures used in this study are those published by the United Nations (UN) in their Monthly Bulletin of Statistics and their Statistical Yearbook. As those figures include only "free on board" (f.o.b.) data on exports, the import data derived from those sources are f.o.b. figures as well. They do not include – as some other sources do – cost, insurance, freight (c.i.f.) and tend, therefore, to be lower than c.i.f. data by about 5 percent.

A particular problem arose when trying to make the national figures of foreign trade developments (in national currency units) comparable to each other. When figures on the Gross Domestic Product (GDP) and on foreign trade (see tables 9.1-9.5) were not available in U.S. dollars, the data in national currency units were transformed to U.S. dollars on the basis of annual averages in exchange rate changes.(9) The remarkable devaluations of the U.S. dollar since 1973/74 vis a vis other important currencies, however, reduce the meaningfulness of the figures to a certain extent for they tend to be too high when countries other than the U.S. are concerned.(10)

Table 9.1. Gross Domestic Product (GDP) of the United States, the EC, and the EC Member States (current prices, billions of U.S. dollars)(1) 1962-1978

Year	USA	European Community	FRG	France	Italy	Nether-lands	Belgium/ Luxembg.	Denmark	UK	Ireland
	1	2	3	4	5	6	7	8	9	10
1962	565.9	322.8	89.8	74.3	43.5	13.3	12.9	7.4	35.7	2.1
1965	692.1	417.5	115.4	99.1	58.6	19.0	16.8	10.2	45.9	2.7
1969	942.6	556.1	154.7	140.5	82.7	28.6	23.0	14.2	69.3	3.5
1970	999.5	622.8	287.7	145.5	92.7	32.0	25.7	15.7	77.3	3.9
1971	1078.2	703.0	217.3	161.8	101.3	37.2	28.8	17.4	88.0	4.6
1972	1178.2	835.3	260.0	198.6	117.7	46.2	35.6	21.0	108.3	5.5
1973	1302.0	1048.0	346.7	256.4	137.8	59.5	45.6	27.7	139.3	6.5
1974	1399.8	1157.4	380.8	264.4	156.4	70.8	55.9	30.2	163.7	6.8
1975	1518.3	1342.1	409.8	335.3	176.3	82.9	64.9	35.5	191.3	8.0
1976	1685.7	1396.5	447.0	349.3	172.8	90.0	70.1	38.5	206.6	8.0
1977	1869.9	1576.9	516.2	380.7	196.0	106.4	81.5	43.0	240.2	9.2
1978	2107.0	1982.2	641.3	471.6	260.1	130.8	100.3	55.9	310.2	12.0

(1) The dollar figures in this table have been calculated on the basis of data in national currency units.

Sources: IBRD, World Tables 1976; IMF, International Financial Statistics.

Table 9.2. Commodity Composition of EC Exports (X) and Imports (M) (Without IntraEC Exports and Imports), 1962-1977(1) (in millions of U.S. dollars)

Commodity groups according to the Standard International Trade Classification (SITC) of which:

Year	Total Exports (X) and Imports (M) (SITC 0 - 9)		Food, Live Animals, Beverages and Tobacco (SITC 0 + 1)		Crude Materials, Oils, Fats (SITC 2 + 4)		Mineral Fuels (SITC 3)		Chemicals (SITC 5)		Manufactures (SITC 6 + 8)		Machinery (SITC 7)	
	X	M	X	M	X	M	X	M	X	M	X	M	X	M
1962	27,600	27,850	1,965	7,845	945	7,105	1,140	3,580	2,810	1,100	9,520	4,940	10,750	2,330
1965	35,410	34,930	2,500	9,160	1,150	8,325	1,170	4,885	3,855	1,495	12,150	7,150	13,950	3,390
1969	48,600	46,880	3,360	8,680	1,370	9,300	1,350	7,530	5,530	2,310	16,010	12,080	20,240	6,000
1970	55,910	53,310	3,980	9,646	1,500	9,918	1,640	8,218	6,220	2,738	18,180	13,801	23,190	7,954
1971	63,270	56,456	4,590	9,871	1,620	9,643	1,940	10,625	6,810	2,793	20,140	13,584	26,920	8,819
1972	73,956	66,624	5,401	11,884	1,933	10,934	2,098	12,576	8,126	3,223	23,359	16,465	31,616	10,031
1973	99,713	95,195	7,685	15,953	2,784	16,504	3,079	19,195	11,431	4,296	32,136	23,372	40,962	14,676
1974	135,557	150,120	9,197	17,193	3,704	21,805	5,849	53,396	18,399	6,653	44,048	30,705	52,354	17,901
1975	149,839	138,520	9,878	18,160	3,371	18,510	5,889	45,660	16,960	6,310	45,005	29,000	66,035	20,030
1976	157,158	164,320	10,006	21,130	3,665	21,570	6,410	54,770	18,687	7,370	45,908	34,420	69,663	23,000
1977	187,284	177,804	11,921	24,190	4,714	22,980	7,999	55,340	21,809	8,080	56,127	39,370	80,951	26,310
1978	221,597	277,140	---	---	---	---	---	---	---	---	---	---	---	---

(1) 1962 and 1965 EC and the UK; 1969-1977 EC includes UK, Denmark and Ireland

Key: Standard International Trade Classification (SITC):

SITC 0 = Food and Live Animals
SITC 1 = Beverages and Tobacco
SITC 2 = Crude Materials except Fuels
SITC 3 = Mineral Fuels and Related Materials
SITC 4 = Animal and Vegetable Oils and Fats
SITC 5 = Chemicals
SITC 6 = Manufactures
SITC 7 = Machinery
SITC 8 = Miscellaneous Manufactured Goods
SITC 9 = Other Commodities and Transactions

Sources: UN, Monthly Bulletin of Statistics 3/68, 4/75, 2/80, Special Tables; UN, Yearbook of Trade Statistics 1974-1975, Special Table B; and IMF, Directions of Trade, 1970-1977.

Table 9.3. Commodity Composition of U.S. Exports (X) and Imports (M), 1962-1977 (in millions of U.S. dollars)

Commodity groups according to the Standard International Trade Classification (SITC) of which:

	Total Exports (X) and Imports (M) (SITC 0 - 9)		Food, Live Animals, Beverages and Tobacco (SITC 0 + 1)		Crude Materials, Oils, Fats (SITC 2 + 4)		Mineral Fuels (SITC 3)		Chemicals (SITC 5)		Manufactures (SITC 6 + 8)		Machinery (SITC 7)	
	X	M	X	M	X	M	X	M	X	M	X	M	X	M
1962	21,450	16,317	3,680	3,530	2,520	2,960	800	1,770	1,880	485	3,990	5,200	8,060	1,860
1965	27,190	21,348	4,520	3,880	3,330	3,140	950	2,100	2,400	680	4,920	7,650	10,020	3,290
1969	37,460	35,210	4,450	5,070	3,880	3,450	1,130	2,730	3,380	1,140	7,020	12,240	16,400	10,260
1970	42,590	39,135	5,060	5,776	5,100	3,430	1,590	3,248	3,830	1,225	7,660	13,462	17,880	11,610
1971	43,490	46,064	5,080	6,212	4,960	3,568	1,500	4,666	3,840	1,390	7,160	15,056	19,460	14,711
1972	48,979	55,063	6,569	7,117	5,538	4,259	1,552	6,007	4,133	1,830	8,103	17,618	21,533	17,754
1973	70,246	69,348	12,938	8,924	9,064	5,159	1,671	9,890	5,749	2,325	11,121	20,691	27,869	21,817
1974	97,144	100,026	15,233	10,094	12,358	6,448	3,444	26,509	8,819	4,106	16,532	26,641	38,188	25,379
1975	106,157	93,280	16,796	9,280	10,728	5,620	4,465	26,860	8,705	3,650	16,609	22,940	45,710	24,330
1976	113,323	117,110	17,233	11,070	11,869	7,160	4,226	32,880	9,958	4,450	17,828	28,620	49,510	31,340
1977	117,963	141,746	15,950	13,040	14,156	8,120	4,179	43,010	10,827	5,350	18,652	35,440	51,037	37,680
1978	142,532	172,011	---	---	---	---	---	---	---	---	---	---	---	---

Sources: UN, Monthly Bulletin of Statistics 3/68, 4/75, 2/80, Special Tables; UN, Yearbook of Trade Statistics 1974-1975, Special Table B; and IMF, Directions of Trade, 1970-1977.

Table 9.4. Commodity Composition of EC(1) Exports to and Imports from the U.S. 1962-1977 (in millions of U.S. dollars)

Commodity groups according to the Standard International Trade Classification (SITC) of which:

Year	Total Exports (X) and Imports (M) (SITC 0 - 9)		Food, Live Animals, Beverages and Tobacco (SITC 0 + 1)		Crude Materials, Oils, Fats (SITC 2 + 4)		Mineral Fuels (SITC 3)		Chemicals (SITC 5)		Manufactures (SITC 6 + 8)		Machinery (SITC 7)	
	X	M	X	M	X	M	X	M	X	M	X	M	X	M
1962	3,470	5,640	325	1,145	150	800	9	232	197	518	1,610	740	1,090	1,205
1965	4,820	6,820	395	1,384	170	985	12	289	257	710	2,300	1,195	1,610	1,895
1969	8,380	9,500	730	1,270	170	1,240	120	235	405	1,030	3,480	1,900	3,370	3,240
1970	9,150	11,140	880	1,480	165	1,510	130	355	450	1,200	3,770	2,200	3,680	4,080
1971	10,740	10,980	980	1,600	170	1,520	145	340	490	1,150	4,410	1,830	4,450	4,090
1972	12,567	11,690	1,077	1,800	203	1,659	165	374	691	1,203	5,062	2,042	5,259	4,306
1973	15,666	16,378	1,373	2,551	254	2,661	326	367	911	1,556	5,848	2,730	6,823	5,770
1974	18,914	21,586	1,457	3,373	277	3,678	644	722	1,688	2,207	6,951	3,843	7,682	7,180
1975	16,267	22,394	1,350	3,951	233	3,146	401	962	1,415	2,229	5,468	3,738	7,216	7,658
1976	18,126	24,930	1,495	4,499	283	3,722	518	1,028	2,016	2,899	6,141	4,160	7,339	8,078
1977	23,400	25,864	1,706	4,026	379	4,386	1,131	883	2,350	2,926	8,290	4,307	9,090	8,771
1978	29,573	31,253	---	---	---	---	---	---	---	---	---	---	---	---

(1) 1962 and 1965 EC and the UK; 1969-1977, EC includes UK, Denmark and Ireland.

Sources: UN, Monthly Bulletin of Statistics 3/68, 4/75, 2/80, Special Tables; UN, Yearbook of Trade Statistics 1974-1975, Special Table B; and IMF, Directions of Trade, 1970-1977.

Table 9.5. Commodity Composition of the U.S. Exports to and Imports from the EC(1), 1962-1977 (in millions of U.S. dollars)

Commodity groups according to the Standard International Trade Classification (SITC) of which:

Year	Total Exports (X) and Imports (M) (SITC 0 - 9)		Food, Live Animals, Beverages and Tobacco (SITC 0 + 1)		Crude Materials, Oils, Fats (SITC 2 + 4)		Mineral Fuels (SITC 3)		Chemicals (SITC 5)		Manufactures (SITC 6 + 8)		Machinery (SITC 7)	
	X	M	X	M	X	M	X	M	X	M	X	M	X	M
1962	5,640	3,470	1,145	325	800	150	232	9	518	197	740	1,610	1,205	1,090
1965	6,820	4,820	1,384	395	985	170	289	12	710	257	1,195	2,300	1,895	1,610
1969	9,500	8,380	1,270	730	1,240	170	235	120	1,030	405	1,900	3,480	3,240	3,370
1970	11,140	9,150	1,480	880	1,510	165	355	130	1,200	450	2,200	3,770	4,080	3,680
1971	10,980	10,740	1,600	980	1,520	170	340	145	1,150	490	1,830	4,410	4,090	4,450
1972	11,690	12,567	1,800	1,077	1,659	203	374	165	1,203	691	2,042	5,062	4,306	5,259
1973	16,378	15,666	2,551	1,373	2,661	254	367	326	1,556	911	2,730	5,848	5,770	6,823
1974	21,586	18,914	3,373	1,457	3,678	277	722	644	2,207	1,688	3,843	6,951	7,180	7,682
1975	22,394	16,267	3,951	1,350	3,146	233	962	401	2,229	1,415	3,738	5,468	7,658	7,216
1976	24,930	18,126	4,499	1,495	3,722	283	1,028	518	2,899	2,016	4,160	6,141	8,078	7,339
1977	25,864	23,400	4,026	1,706	4,386	379	883	1,131	2,926	2,350	4,307	8,290	8,771	9,090
1978	31,253	29,573	--	--	--	--	--	--	--	--	--	--	--	--

(1) 1962 and 1965 EC (6) and the UK; 1969-1977, EC includes UK, Denmark, and Ireland.

Sources: UN, Monthly Bulletin of Statistics 3/68, 4/75, 2/80, Special Tables; UN, Yearbook of Trade Statistics 1974-1975, Special Table B; and IMF, Directions of Trade, 1970-1977.

The Relevance of Foreign Trade for the EC and the US

The EC is an economic region which currently engages in about one-third of total world trade. Even when subtracting the intra-EC trade, the Community remains the world's largest trade power; in 1977, its share of world trade amounted to about one-fifth. In contrast, the respective export and import volumes of the United States are reaching 12.4 and 13.2 percent, about one-eighth of total world trade.

These differences between the EC and the United States become even more evident when one looks at the relevance of their foreign trade to their economic performances. Since the GDP of the EC is smaller than that of the United States (table 9.1), the EC's overall dependence (exports and imports as a share of GDP) on foreign trade is higher than that of the United States. Within the time period from 1962 to 1977, however, there have been remarkable changes. Compared with the U.S. GDP, the aggregated GDP of the EC countries increased from 54 to 84 percent of the U.S. figure.(11) The comparison of the overall trade dependencies shows an improvement for the EC as well. Certainly, the export and import dependencies rose in the case of both regions; their growth rates, however, have been much higher when compared to those of the United States. This means that the asymmetries in the overall trade dependencies have changed in favor of the EC. The ratio dropped from 2.26 (1962) to 1.88 (1977) in the case of exports; and in imports, there was a ratio reduction of more than one-half, from 3.02 (1962) to 1.49 (1977).(12) Trade sensitivity of the United States is increasing more rapidly than it is for the EC; at present, however, the EC is still more dependent on foreign trade than the U.S.(13) (table 9.6, columns 1 and 2). The trend which can be drawn from these figures shows that the existing differences are likely to diminish in the future.

The Relevance of Bilateral Foreign Trade for
the EC and the United States

These results become even clearer when one relates the bilateral trade of the EC and the U.S. to their GDPs. In 1962, the foreign trade dependency of the EC toward the U.S. was higher than vice versa (in particular, this is true when one looks at the import sector). Although the following period indicates an increasing trend of trade dependencies on each other (when weighing with GDP figures), the development favored the EC to a remarkable extent. The asymmetry analysis indicates that the imbalance of the late 1960s and early 1970s has been replaced by a more balanced situation where bilateral exports have approximately the same significance to both countries. This change was accompanied by an even more impressive development: the initial asymmetry in the relevance of bilateral imports has been diminished continuously from 2.85 in 1962 to 1.31 in 1977 (table 9.6., columns 3 and 4).

Table 9.6. Asymmetries of Dependencies from Total and Bilateral Trade Between the European Community and the United States(1)

| Year | I. Ratio of dependencies from total trade (as weighted with GDP) | | II. Ratio of dependencies from bilateral trade (as weighted with GDP) | | III. Ratio of dependencies from bilateral trade (as weighted with total trade) | |
| | Exports | Imports | Exports | Imports | Exports | Imports |
	1	2	3	4	5	6
1962	2.26	3.02	1.07	2.85	0.48	0.95
1965	2.16	2.69	1.16	2.33	0.54	0.86
1969	2.20	2.25	1.50	1.92	0.68	0.85
1970	2.11	2.18	1.32	1.95	0.63	0.89
1971	2.23	1.88	1.50	1.56	0.67	0.83
1972	2.13	1.61	1.52	1.31	0.71	0.77
1973	1.76	1.70	1.18	1.30	0.67	0.76
1974	1.69	1.80	1.06	1.24	0.63	0.76
1975	1.60	1.52	0.82	1.56	0.51	0.93
1976	1.67	1.54	0.88	1.66	0.52	0.98
1977	1.88	1.49	1.06	1.31	0.57	0.88

(1) Ratios between (I) total exports (imports) of the EC and the U.S. as a share of their GDP, (II) bilateral exports (imports) of the EC and the U.S. as a share of their GDP, (III) bilateral exports (imports) of the EC and the U.S. as a share of their total exports (imports).

Sources: UN, Monthly Bulletin of Statistics, 3/68, 4/75, 2/78, Special Tables; UN, Yearbook of Trade Statistics 1974-1975, Special Table B; and IMF, Directions of Trade, 1970-1977.

In contrast, the estimation of bilateral export and import dependencies based on total trade (and not GDP) figures provides a decreasing trend, in the import even more than in the export sector (table 9.6, columns 5 and 6). The share of EC exports to the United States as related to total EC exports is half as high as the share of the respective U.S. exports to the EC (12.49 percent for the EC; 21.93 percent for the U.S.; figures for 1977). The import sector remained approximately in balance. This contrast between the results of columns 3 and 4 and columns 5 and 6 is due to the use of different weighting measures (GDP versus total exports and imports) and can be disentangled easily. On the basis of GDP developments, total as well as bilateral foreign trade has acquired greater significance for both the EC and the U.S. Growth rates in bilateral trade, however, have not been as high as those in total trade, so that bilateral trade as a share of total trade of the EC and the U.S. has decreased. This means that the relevance of bilateral trade between the EC and the U.S. has increased for both regions. In 1977, the EC and the U.S. traded more with each other than they did 15 years before; but they traded even more with the rest of the world.

Intensity of Bilateral Trade

The asymmetry aspect usually gets lost in analyses of interaction intensities between countries. Nonetheless, such an analysis can help to evaluate the entanglement of both regions under consideration. On the basis of interaction coefficients which relate bilateral trade in different commodity groups to the sum of total exports or imports of the United States and the EC in the same commodity groups, (table 9.7), one discovers that the interaction intensity of total bilateral exports is only a little higher than the interaction intensity of the respective imports (exports: 16.14 percent; imports: 15.42 percent; figures for 1977).

The differences, however, are high when one looks into the different commodity groups. The share of bilateral exports of primary products (SITC 0-4) is nearly three times as high as the share of bilateral imports (21.62 percent vs. 7.77 percent; figures for 1976). This means that within the primary product groups the interaction intensity of the United States and the EC is of much greater relevance in the case of exports than in imports. The responsibility for this lies, of course, with the high agricultural exports of the United States.

This picture changes when one looks at manufactures (SITC 5-8). The data for 1976 indicate that bilateral manufactured imports play a role nearly twice as high as that of the respective bilateral exports (23.71 percent vs. 14.48 percent) when they are related to total trade within the groups. In particular, the figures for chemicals (SITC 5) are striking. The bilateral market shares amount to 41.48 percent (1976) whereas the respective export share within this group only amounts to 17.16 percent. As a general result, in 1976, bilateral interaction as a percentage of total interaction was high in primary product exports

Table 9.7. Interaction Intensity in Bilateral Trade Between the EC and the U.S., 1962-1977 (in %)

Ratio of bilateral exports or imports of the EC and the U.S. to their total exports or imports in SITC (Standard International Trade Classification) – commodity groups.(1)

Year	SITC 0 - 9 X	M	SITC 0 + 1 X	M	SITC 2 + 4 X	M	SITC 3 X	M	SITC 0 - 4 X	M	SITC 5 X	M	SITC 6 + 8 X	M	SITC 7 X	M	SITC 5 - 8 X	M
	1		2		3		4		5		6		7		8		9	
1962	18.57	20.63	26.04	12.92	27.42	9.44	12.42	4.50	24.08	9.93	15.25	45.11	17.39	23.18	12.20	54.77	14.48	35.04
1965	18.59	20.68	25.34	13.64	25.78	10.07	14.20	4.31	23.75	10.27	15.46	44.46	20.47	23.61	14.62	52.47	16.83	33.68
1969	20.78	21.78	25.61	14.55	26.86	11.06	14.31	3.46	24.23	10.24	16.11	58.57	23.36	22.12	18.04	40.65	19.58	30.49
1970	20.60	21.95	26.11	15.30	31.90	12.55	15.02	4.23	23.95	11.23	16.42	41.64	23.10	21.90	18.89	39.66	19.98	30.28
1971	20.34	21.10	26.68	16.04	25.76	12.79	14.10	3.17	24.17	10.67	15.40	39.21	22.86	21.79	18.41	36.29	19.47	29.14
1972	19.73	19.93	24.04	15.14	24.92	12.26	14.77	2.90	22.86	10.00	15.45	37.48	22.58	20.84	18.00	33.70	19.16	27.49
1973	18.85	19.47	19.03	15.77	24.60	13.46	14.59	2.38	20.24	9.96	14.36	37.26	19.83	19.47	18.30	34.51	18.29	27.11
1974	17.40	16.19	19.77	17.70	24.62	14.00	14.70	1.71	20.39	7.49	14.31	36.20	17.82	18.82	16.41	34.34	16.57	26.53
1975	15.10	16.68	19.87	19.32	23.97	14.00	13.16	1.88	19.64	8.09	14.20	36.59	14.94	17.72	13.31	33.53	13.93	26.09
1976	15.72	15.30	22.01	25.53	25.78	16.53	14.54	1.76	21.62	7.77	17.16	41.58	16.16	16.34	12.94	28.37	14.48	23.71
1977	16.14	15.42																

(1) See Table 9.2. for SITC key.

Sources: Tables 9.2 - 9.5.

(21.62 percent) and in manufactures imports (23.71 percent). A closer examination of the time period considered, however, shows additionally that this intensity has gone down remarkably, in particular since the early 1970s.

The Development of the Trade Balance,
Intraindustry Trade

Since the end of World War II, the U.S. trade balance has been characterized by a surplus situation. This development showed a reverse trend after 1971 and led to high deficits (nearly $24 billion in 1977). This was mainly due to high expenditures for oil imports since 1973 and to different business cycles than other industrialized countries. However, the United States was (with the exception of 1972) able to yield a positive trade balance with the EC during the time period considered (table 9.8).

Table 9.8. U.S. and EC Balances of Total and Bilateral Trade, 1962-1977
(in millions of U.S. dollars)

Year	U.S. trade balance		EC trade balance		U.S. balance of trade with the EC	
		1		2		3
1962	+	5,313	−	250	+	2,170
1965	+	5,842	+	480	+	2,000
1969	+	2,250	+	1,720	+	1,120
1970	+	3,455	+	2,600	+	1,990
1971	−	2,574	+	6,814	+	240
1972	−	6,084	+	7,332	−	877
1973	+	898	+	4,518	+	712
1974	−	2,882	−	14,563	+	2,672
1975	+	12,877	+	11,319	+	6,127
1976	−	3,787	−	7,162	+	6,804
1977	−	23,783	+	9,480	+	2,464

Sources: Tables 9.2 - 9.5.

Trade deficits or surpluses within the commodity groups are a measure of the level of intraindustry (IIT) or exchange trade between two countries.(14) In general, low imbalances in bilateral trade within the considered commodity groups indicate a high IIT (and vice versa); when these balances are related to the overall trade within these commodity groups, estimates toward zero signify high IIT, estimates toward 100 signify low IIT or even complementary trade (table 9.9).

Table 9.9. Balances of Bilateral Trade Between the EC and the U.S. 1962-1977, Within the Commodity Groups (Intraindustry trade) as a Share of Total Bilateral Trade Within the Commodity Groups (in %)

	SITC 0 - 9	SITC 0 + 1	SITC 2 + 4	SITC 3	SITC 0 - 4	SITC 5	SITC 6 + 8	SITC 7	SITC 5 - 8
	1	2	3	4	5	6	7	8	9
1962	23.81	55.78	68.42	92.53	63.62	44.90	37.02	5.01	8.10
1965	17.18	55.59	70.56	92.03	64.33	46.85	31.62	8.13	4.61
1969	6.26	27.00	75.89	32.39	45.82	43.55	29.37	1.97	8.08
1970	9.81	25.42	80.30	46.39	48.01	45.45	26.30	5.15	2.73
1971	1.10	24.03	79.88	40.21	45.53	40.24	41.35	4.22	13.89
1972	3.62	25.13	78.20	38.78	45.24	27.03	42.51	9.96	18.64
1973	2.22	30.02	82.57	5.92	48.14	26.15	36.35	8.36	14.92
1974	6.60	39.67	85.99	5.71	53.15	13.32	28.79	3.38	10.46
1975	15.85	49.07	86.21	41.16	60.49	22.34	18.79	2.97	1.71
1976	16.00	50.11	85.87	32.95	60.23	17.97	19.23	4.79	1.17
1977	5.00	40.47	84.09	12.31	48.60	10.92	31.62	1.79	10.43

See Table 9.2 for SITC key.

Sources: Tables 9.2 - 9.5.

When one looks at the results so far, it is not surprising to find that IIT is almost nonexistent within the group of primary products (in particular SITC 2+4), whereas IIT seems to be very high within the groups of manufactures. Further disaggregation of commodity groups (down to 4- or 5-digit SITC classes) would indicate that within these classes an entire product differentiation has taken place and that the level of specialization is very high.

Within the considered time period, the intracommodity-group trade has developed in opposite proportions. As far as primary products are concerned, the high imbalance of 1962 (64 percent) decreased until 1972 (45 percent) and then increased to more than 60 percent in 1975 and 1976. Conversely, starting from the small figure of 8 percent (1962), the imbalance within the group of manufactures rose to 19 percent (in 1972), and then decreased to a slightly balanced situation in 1975 and 1976. Data for 1977 indicate a reverse trend along the former lines, but it seems to be too early to draw general conclusions. At least the development within the machinery sector continued to be symmetrical. Even when one looks deeper into the subgroups of the SITC classification scheme, this means that it is impossible to explain a large share of trade between the EC and the U.S. only by means of the traditional division of labor argument; one must also take into account such new phenomena as product differentiation, far going specialization, etc.(15)

Terms of Trade

The terms of trade are a measure of the relative level of export prices as compared to import prices. They can also be interpreted as an indicator of a country's competition capability vis a vis the rest of the world.(16) Also called "barter terms of trade," they are calculated as the ratio of the export price index to the import price index. The terms of trade index, therefore, shows changes over time in the relative level of export prices as a percentage of import prices.

The estimates show that the overall terms of trade of the EC (in its trade with the rest of the world, column 1 of table 9.10) increased continuously until 1971/72; since then – intensified by the oil price raise and by unfavorable short-term fluctuations – they dropped, and in 1977 reverted to the initial levels. On the contrary, the terms of trade of the U.S. underwent a remarkable deterioration during the time period considered; between 1975 and 1977 they declined by one-third.

A comparison of both developments (table 9.10, column 3) leads to the conclusion that the terms of trade have developed much more in favor of the EC than of the U.S. Even in 1972, the asymmetry coefficient was 1.65 in favor of the EC. It dropped to 1.23 in 1974 and reached its maximum so far in 1977, with an estimate of 1.68.

In the bilateral relationship, the EC's terms of trade also increased (1977: 147) whereas, at the same time, the data for the U.S. indicate a deterioration. However, since 1972 (when the asymmetry was extremely high), there has been an improvement, caused by dollar devaluations and

Table 9.10. Terms of Trade of the EC and the U.S. for Their Total and Bilateral Trade, 1962-1977 (1962 = 100); Asymmetries in the Development of the ECs and the U.S. Terms of Total and Bilateral Trade

Year	EC Terms of Trade	U.S. Terms of Trade	Asymmetry (1 : 2)	Terms of Trade EC - U.S.	Terms of Trade U.S. - EC	Asymmetry (4 : 5)
	1	2	3	4	5	6
1962	100	100	1.00	100	100	1.00
1965	102	97	1.05	115	87	1.32
1969	105	81	1.30	143	70	2.04
1970	106	83	1.28	133	75	1.77
1971	113	72	1.57	159	53	3.00
1972	112	68	1.65	175	57	3.07
1973	106	77	1.38	156	64	2.44
1974	91	74	1.23	142	70	2.03
1975	109	87	1.25	118	85	1.39
1976	96	74	1.30	118	85	1.39
1977	106	63	1.68	147	68	2.16

Sources: Tables 9.2 - 9.5.

198

other economic policy measures by the U.S. This led to an improvement of the competition capability of the U.S. in its trade with the EC. This trend (table 9.10, columns 4 to 6) was reversed again in 1975/76, leading to an asymmetry coefficient of 2.16 in favor of the EC in 1977.

The terms of trade of the EC have developed much more favorably vis a vis the United States than the rest of the world. In contrast, the deterioration of the U.S. terms of trade in its trade with the EC has not been as extensive as that toward its other trading partners as a whole. This means that, for both regions considered, trade with each other remains more advantageous than trade with the (aggregated) rest of the world.

SUMMARY AND CONCLUSIONS

The results of this study can be summarized as follows:

1. During the time period 1962 to 1977, the significance of foreign trade related to GDP has grown for both regions, for the United States even more than for the EC. Nevertheless, foreign trade is still more important for the EC (even without intratrade) than for the United States. The EC's export dependency appears nearly twice as high as it is for the United States (11.9 percent vs. 6.3 percent; data for 1977), its import dependency nearly one and a half times as high (11.3 percent vs. 7.6 percent).
2. The significance of bilateral trade for both regions has increased as well, although its growth rates have been lower than those for total trade. On the basis of GDP figures, in 1977 bilateral exports were nearly as important for the United States as for the EC (1.48 percent vs. 1.39 percent), whereas the bilateral imports were of greater relevance to the EC than to the United States, even though the asymmetry diminished remarkably after 1962. From the point of view of GDP, not only do these differences seem negligible, these figures also seem to be so small that even grievous disturbances affecting bilateral trade are unlikely to seriously impair the economies as a whole.
3. To a certain extent, this picture changes when one relates bilateral trade to the total trade of the EC and the United States, and when one takes into account certain commodity groups which are of considerable importance for both. As a general conclusion, one finds that during the time period under study bilateral exports remained nearly twice as important for the United States as for the EC (12.5 apercent vs. 21.9 percent), whereas in the import sector the data for 1977 indicate a nearly symmetrical situation when one compares the dependencies of the EC and the United States (14.6 percent vs. 16.5 percent).
4. The foreign trade intensity between the EC and the United States (bilateral trade volume as a share of either the exports or the imports of both) also decreased continuously from 1962 to 1977.

The shares of bilateral deliveries as compared with total exports and imports (16 percent and 15 percent; figures for 1977), although still remarkable, were not as high as they were in 1962. Changes in the regional composition of the EC's and the United States' foreign trade are, therefore, apparent.

5. The structure of the U.S. trade balance underwent fundamental alterations. The United States has had to accept deficits in several years since 1972; indeed, in 1977 this deficit amounted to $24 billion (9.2 percent of its trade volume). In its dealings with the EC, however, the United States has been continuously able (except in 1972) to realize a trade surplus. In 1977 it amounted to about 5 percent of the bilateral trade volume, i.e., nearly the surplus in the bilateral trade regarding food and some raw materials.

6. The EC's terms of trade with the United States developed more favorably than with the rest of the world. In contrast, the United States' terms of trade with the EC have not deteriorated as badly as they have with its other trading partners as a whole. This means that for both the EC and the U.S., trade with each other provides greater advantages than trade with the rest of the world. From the asymmetry of their terms of trade developments (1977: 2.16 in favor of the EC), we can draw the conclusion that the EC was able to manage its trade relations with the U.S. more advantageously than the U.S. managed its relations with the EC. The gains from bilateral trade have been higher for the EC than for the United States.

From all the different methods which were used to analyze the trade relationship between the EC and the United States, we can draw two general conclusions:

• This relationship has changed in favor of the EC. The asymmetry analysis shows that many of the advantages the United States was able to enjoy in its trade relations with the EC (largely as a result of its relatively low dependency on foreign trade) have disappeared. In 1977, transatlantic trade relations were more symmetrical than they were 15 years before, and since then there have been no indications that this trend will change in the near future.

• The second conclusion refers to the trend according to which the interaction intensity – as far as foreign trade between the EC and the U.S. is concerned – has decreased. Compared to 1962, bilateral trade in 1977 had lost some of its importance for both regions; mutual dependencies on bilateral trade declined. The EC and the U.S. obviously have found other regions which are better able to absorb their additional demands and deliveries.

Both conclusions signify that the trade relationship between the European Community and the United States has become more symmetrical and less intensive at the same time. With reference to the introductory remarks, this result can be reformulated as: The "talent for independence" of the EC vis a vis the U.S. has increased within the considered time period – at least as far as the trade sector is concerned.

West European-American economic relations have lost some of their tremendous importance to the world economy which they had in the postwar period. This importance was due only partially to the fact that, in the context of the world political and economic polarization between East and West, Western Europe and the United States formed a bloc in opposition to the Soviet Union and the other Eastern bloc states, which brought about a strong international cohesion. Above and beyond this, there existed (in the economic field) comparable political structural bases and similarly vested interests, which, under the wing of the economic and political dominance of the United States, led to a comparatively high level of prosperity for Western Europe.   But political and economic changes were already becoming evident in the 1960s: new actors appeared, the international distribution of economic and political power changed, and the effectiveness of the traditional system of international economic relations was undermined.   These developments seemed to indicate a freer hand for the European Community as regards dealings with third countries (COMECON, OPEC, etc.) and also with the United States. The American announcement on August 15, 1971 of a "new economic policy," aimed at an improvement of its economic competitiveness by protectionistic measures, had at least two effects: it preserved the foreign economic primacy of the U.S. for a few more years; and, at the same time, intensified the efforts of most European countries in diversifying their foreign economic relations and in finding new markets and other sources of deliveries.

The results of this study indicate that, to a certain extent, these efforts have been successful. Within the framework of the Yaoundé and Lomé Treaties, for instance, the EC members have been able to develop specific economic ties to certain less developed countries.   As these relations include more favorable conditions for the LDCs than other international agreements do, the EC has been able to broaden its export base and to further develop its position in the international division of labor. Due to the process of detente in Europe, the economic relations between East and West have improved steadily, too. In 1977, the Federal Republic of Germany was exporting more to the Eastern bloc (including the GDR) than to the U.S. The natural fit between both parts of Europe which contributed to extensive trade relations in Europe for many centuries is still existing, and provides one of the potential sources for West European trade expansion.(17)

Even when we have to state a diminishing asymmetry and a decreasing intensity in transatlantic trade relations, it would be by far exaggerated to characterize the trade position of the United States vis a vis the European Community as weak and defensive. But it seems clear that the general position of the U.S. in the transatlantic web of political and economic ties has been affected.

The U.S. cannot ignore its changing role in the international environment and has, therefore, to take into account the growing economic power of the EC. There are several sources of conflict which could arise from heightened economic competition in third markets in

less developed countries and in the Eastern Bloc. Within the Euro-
American System there are sources of conflict, too. The diminishing
dominance of the U.S. could lead to even more protectionism, increasing competition, and more measures to preserve U.S. economic primacy. Without respective adjustments, nobody can exclude that this would
contribute to misunderstandings, irritations, and even diverting policies
on both sides of the Atlantic.

NOTES

(1) See, for example, Marina V.N. Whitman, "International Interdependence and the U.S. Economy," in Contemporary Economic Problems,
edited by W. Fellner (Washington: AEI, 1976), pp. 183-223; Lawrence B.
Krause and W.S. Salant, editors, Worldwide Inflation (Washington: The
Brookings Institution, 1977); Norbert Walter, "Koordinierung der Kon-
junkturpolitik der westlichen Industrieländer – Notwendigkeit oder
Gefahr?" Europa Archiv 32, no. 8 (1977): 227-33; A. Lindbeck, "Economic Dependence and Interdependence in the Industrialized World," in
From Marshall Plan to Global Interdependence (Paris: OECD, 1978), pp.
59-68.

(2) There is an extensive literature about this subject. See, for example,
most of the contributions to W. Hanrieder, editor, The United States
and Western Europa (Cambridge, Mass.: Winthrop, 1974); J. Chace and
E.C. Ravenal, editors, Atlantis Lost: United States-European Relations
After the Cold War (New York: New York University Press for the
Council on Foreign Relations, 1976); Ernst-Otto Czempiel and Dank-
wart Rustow, editors, The Euro-American System (Frankfurt and New
York: Campus, 1976); Karl Kaiser and Hans-Peter Schwarz, editors,
America and Western Europe (New York: Praeger, 1978); and David
Landes, editor, Western Europe - The Trial of Partnership (Lexington
and Toronto: Heath, 1977).

(3) See for example, Richard N. Cooper, The Economics of Interdependence (New York: Council on Foreign Relations, 1968); Kenneth N.
Waltz, "The Myth of International Interdependence," in The International Corporation, edited by Charles P. Kindleberger (Cambridge,
Mass.: MIT Press, 1970), pp. 205-23; R. Rosecrance and A. Stein,
"Interdependence – Myth or Reality?" World Politics 26, no. 1 (October
1973): 1-27; R.D. Tollison and T.D. Willett, "International Integration
and the Interdependence of Economic Variables," International Organi-
zation 27, no. 2 (Spring 1973): 255-71; C. Fred Bergsten, Robert O.
Keohane, and Joseph S. Nye, "International Economics and International
Politics – A Framework for Analysis," International Organization 29,
no. 1 (Winter 1976): 3-36; and C.F. Bergsten and W.R. Cline, "Increasing
International Economic Interdependence," American Economic Review,
Papers and Proceedings 66, no. 2 (May 1976).

(4) The approach of comparing the power of nations by "power base" indicators was used by R.S. Cline, World Power Assessment: A Calculus of Strategic Drift (Boulder, Colo.: Westview Press, 1975), p. 11.

(5) These considerations are mainly based upon Albert O. Hirschman's pioneering analysis, A National Power and the Structure of Foreign Trade (Berkeley and Los Angeles: University of California Press, 1945).

(6) See Robert O. Keohane and Joseph S. Nye, Power and Interdependence (Boston: Little, Brown, 1977), p. 11; and Stanley Hoffman, Primacy and World Order (New York: McGraw-Hill, 1978), pp. 114-32.

(7) For a broader analysis see Hanns-D. Jacobsen, Asymmetrien in den Internationalen Wirtschaftsbeziehungen. Methoden und Indikatoren zur Strukturanalyse Internationaler Abhangigkeiten und Interdependenzen [Assymmetries in International Economic Relations. Methods and Indicators for the Structural Analysis of International Dependencies and Interdependencies] (Berlin: Wissenschaftszentrum Berlin, 1979).

(8) For some material concerning the preceding period, see Alfred Nydegger, Die Westeuropäische Aussenwirtschaft in Gegenwart und Zukunft [The West-European Foreign Economic Relations Today and in the Future] (Tubingen: Siebeck, 1962); Randall Hinshaw, The European Community and American Trade (New York: Praeger for the Council on Foreign Relations, 1964); Jürgen Rohwedder, Die Entwicklung des Aussenhandels Zwischen den Vereinigten Staaten und der Europaischen Wirtschaftsgemeinschaft von 1955 bis 1963 und ihre Bestimmungsgründe [The Development of Foreign Trade Between the U.S. and the E.E.C., 1955 to 1963] (Tübingen: Siebeck, 1967); and Lawrence B. Krause, European Economic Integration and the United States (Washington: The Brookings Institution, 1968).

(9) These data are available from IMF, International Financial Statistics (monthly).

(10) The International Comparison Project of the United Nations even developed a new comprehensive measure in order to go behind the simple exchange-rate converted dollar comparison, the "international dollar," the purchasing power of which is determined by the structure of international prices. See I.B. Kravis, A. Heston, and R. Summers, International Comparisons of Real Product and Purchasing Power (Baltimore and London: Johns Hopkins University Press for the World Bank, 1978), pp. 3-7. Comparing the figures of 1970 and 1973, the basis of the authors' conclusion is the assumption that in 1970 the exchange rate conversions understated the real GDP for all the other countries relative to that of the United States. Between 1970 and 1973, the devaluation of the U.S. dollar relative to the currencies of some industrialized countries (e.g., Japan and the FRG) sharply reduced these differences. See ibid., pp. 7-8.

(11) The evidence of these figures might be questioned to a certain extent when taking into account the results of the "International Comparison Project" (ICP) of the UN. In both years (1970 and 1973), the GDP of the United States in terms of "international dollars" was higher than the aggregate GDP of the EC; their aggregate was 79 percent of the U.S. aggregate in 1970 and only 78 percent in 1973. Contrasted to this, the figures were 61 percent for 1970 and 77 percent for 1973 using exchange-rate-converted comparisons (ibid., p. 9). These differences, however, disappear when one compares trade dependencies (exports and imports as a share of GDP), since both the GDP and the foreign trade figures have been converted with the same exchange rate and correspond to the ratios as expressed in national currency units.

(12) In particular, the figures of the EC might be a little exaggerated, especially some smaller states (e.g. Belgium and the Netherlands) are characterized by high export and import shares. But much over half of their foreign trade involves intermediate goods (e.g., imported inputs for exports) which do not contribute to the national income directly. See R. Blackhurst, N. Marian, and J. Tumlier, Trade Liberalization, Protectionism and Interdependence (Geneva: GATT Studies in International Trade No. 5, November 1977), p. 17.

(13) This broad analysis should be supplemented by evaluations on import vulnerabilities which could be estimated by comparing domestic consumption with imports and domestic production in various commodity groups. Some evaluations exist for the United States but not for the EC. See Council on International Economic Policy, Special Report on "Critical Imported Materials" (Washington: CIE, 1974); and S.B. Watkins and J.R. Karlik, Anticipating Disruptive Imports. A study prepared for use of the Joint Economic Committee, U.S. Congress (Washington: GPO, September 14, 1978).

(14) See M.G. Grubel and P.J. Lloyd, "The Empirical Measurement of Intra-Industry Trade," Economic Record 47 (1971): 494-517.

(15) See, for example, S.B. Linder, An Essay on Trade and Transformation (Stockholm-Göterborg-Uppsala, 1961); H. Hesse, "Die Bedeutung der reinen Theorie des Internationalen Handels für die Erklärung des Aussenhandels in der Nachkriegszeit", Zeitschrift für die Gesamte Staatswissenschaft 122, no. 2 (1966); and M.G. Grubel and P.J. Lloyd, Intra-Industry Trade (Basingstroke, 1975).

(16) The terms of trade concept has been used as a measure for unequal exchange as well. See Wolfgang Bartschi and Hanns-D. Jacobsen, Kritische Einfuhrung in Die Aussenhandelstheorie (Reinbek bei Hamburg: Rowohlt, 1976), pp. 48-53; and Wolfgang Bartschi, Ausbeutung und Einkommensumverteilung in den Internationalalen Wirtschaftsbeziehungen (Berlin: Duncker und Humbolt, 1976).

(17) These problems are broadly discussed in Max Baumer and Hanns-D. Jacobsen, "Changing Role of International Institutional Actors in East-West and North-South Relations," in Partners in East-West Economic Relations: The Determinants of Choice, edited by Z. Fallenbuchl and C. McMillan (Elmsford, NY: Pergamon Press, forthcoming).

10 External Implications of the European Monetary System*
Robert W. Russell

The European Monetary System (EMS) was inaugurated on March 13, 1979, accompanied by considerable rhetorical fanfare and supported by personal political commitments from Helmut Schmidt, Chancellor of the Federal Republic of Germany, and Valery Giscard d'Estaing, President of France. The rapidity with which EMS was designed and launched (the idea was first suggested by Roy Jenkins, Chairman of the Commission of the European Communities, on October 27, 1977), together with the active involvement of Europe's political leaders, have imparted drama and significance to the undertaking. But EMS is, in fact, only the latest step in a long, continuing effort to move toward European monetary and political union. There is little to suggest that EMS will be any more successful or consequential than earlier schemes.

The first plan for European monetary integration was drawn up in 1968 by Raymond Barre (then Vice Commissioner of the European Economic Community and later Prime Minister of France) and issued by the Commission in a memorandum of February 12, 1969. The Council of Ministers of the EC was unable to reach agreement on implementation of the Barre Plan, and instead appointed a special group, chaired by Pierre Werner, Prime Minister of Luxembourg, to study the subject. The Werner Group issued two successive reports in 1970 suggesting phased implementation of measures leading to full economic and monetary union by 1980. The Council moved slowly toward adoption of the proposals made by the Werner Group, but international financial developments soon disrupted the effort.

The progressive collapse during 1971 and 1973 of the fixed exchange rate system drastically altered the environment in which European monetary integration was being attempted. Instead of increasing the

---

*The views expressed are the author's personal views. The author is indebted to Joseph DiProspero for research assistance and to Beth Gill for typing the manuscript.

fixity of intra-European exchange rates within a world system of fixed, but adjustable, exchange rates, the European Community faced the far tougher challenge of fixing exchange rates in which many currencies, including the key currency – the United States dollar – were left free to float on market trends.

Nonetheless, the Community launched on April 24, 1972, an attempt to narrow the margins of fluctuation of their bilateral exchange rates. The Smithsonian Agreement of December 1971 had widened the permissible range of fluctuation for currencies of member countries of the International Monetary Fund to 2.25 percent above or below the currency's officially established parity with the U.S. dollar from the .75 percent margin previously allowed. The EC decided to try to keep variations between member currencies to 2.25 percent above or below their bilateral parity rates, instead of permitting the wider fluctuation which could occur if each currency were permitted to move the full range against the dollar. For example, if the German mark were at its upper limit of permissible fluctuation against the dollar under Smithsonian rules (2.5 percent above the mark's fixed parity with the dollar), and the French franc were at its lower limit of permissible fluctuation against the dollar (2.5 percent below the franc's fixed parity with the dollar), and the two reversed position over time (the mark reaching its ceiling against the dollar and the franc reaching its lower limit against the dollar), the two currencies would have moved 9 percent against each other, while each had moved only 4.5 percent against the dollar.

This attempt to reduce the fluctuations between European currencies while observing the permissible band against the dollar was quickly dubbed the "snake in the tunnel." The tunnel floor and ceiling consisted of the limits of fluctuation permitted against the dollar, while the width of the snake was set by the permissible fluctuations of one EC currency against another. The snake wiggled inside the tunnel as the EC currencies as a group moved nearer or farther away from their upper and lower limits against the dollar.

The snake initially included all six original EC members plus the four candidate members at that time: Britain, Ireland, Denmark, and Norway. Market pressures soon forced Britain, Ireland, and Denmark to drop out of the snake arrangement and allow their currencies to fluctuate more widely – in all three cases to depreciate against the remaining EC currencies. When the U.S. dollar was permitted to float in March 1973, after coming under heavy speculative attack, the "tunnel" no longer existed. The "snake" continued, however, in the form of a "joint float," as the remaining members, with the exception of Italy, sought to confine the fluctuations of their currencies against one another. France also had great difficulty staying within the snake and dropped out twice, remaining outside after March 1976. The snake continued on until formation of EMS, but as a "mini-snake" or "mark zone" composed of the German mark, Dutch guilder, Belgian and Luxembourg francs, and (from time to time) the Danish krone.

Efforts to reduce currency fluctuations in the Community were complemented from the beginning by development of a system of credits member countries could use in market intervention to support their exchange rates. The ability to borrow reserves is of interest, of course, only to countries with currencies which may tend to weaken against stronger Community currencies (in practice, the German mark in nearly every case). Countries whose currencies are strong and tend to appreciate can sell their own currency to hold down the exchange rate; countries whose currencies are weak and tend to depreciate must use strong currencies to buy the excess supply of their own currencies. Over time, only convergence of economic conditions, especially inflation, can prevent divergence of exchange rates; but, while measures to achieve economic convergence are taking effect, countries may wish to use their currency reserves and borrow additional foreign currency reserves in order to keep rates stable through market intervention.

The original Barre memorandum included an outline of credit facilities to assist members facing downward exchange rate pressure, in order that members could hold their exchange rates in place through intervention while taking appropriate corrective economic policy actions. The first limited credit facility to provide short-term assistance for renewable, three-month periods was agreed upon in February 1970, before the snake experiment began. A medium-term facility with credit available for two- to five-year periods was approved by the Council in February 1971. These facilities were enlarged periodically during the life of the snake. By the end of 1975, medium- and short-term facilities were each equivalent to nearly $3 billion.

The European Economic Community had established a common unit of account shortly after it was formed, based on the prevailing fixed exchange rates. Intra-Community payments for EEC programs were based on the unit of account, although the largest program involving transfer payments (the Common Agricultural Policy) relied upon a slightly different unit of account. After March 1973, when the U.S. dollar and several other major currencies began floating, the European unit of account (EUA) took on greater importance and the Community tried to reconcile the agricultural unit of account with a new and redefined EUA. The EUA remained, however, an accounting concept based on a basket of Community currencies combined in fixed proportions, not a functioning common currency.

Apart from and above the mechanisms of exchange market intervention, short- and medium-term credit, and units of account, the Community recognized the dependence of monetary integration upon economic integration. The goal of European monetary union cannot be achieved without harmonization of economic policies by all members of the European Community. Consultations with other Community members before adopting major economic policy decisions were obligatory by the Council's decision of March 21, 1971. Prior consultation on exchange rate adjustments had been obligatory since 1964. In practice, however, despite a host of consultative committees, national governments have continued to decide upon their economic policies first and inform the Community later.

The pressures of OPEC oil price increases and differing domestic social and political considerations would have made it nearly impossible, in any case, to keep Europe's economies sufficiently in line to maintain fixed parities among currencies. With the added disruptive impact of wide shifts in the value of the world's major currency (the dollar) and reluctance of European governments to sacrifice their economic sovereignty to Community needs, the plan to achieve economic and monetary union by 1980 was doomed. All that remained by 1977 was the mini-snake or Deutschemark zone composed of currencies dependent upon Germany, the credit arrangements, and a little-used European unit of account – that, and an idea which refused to disappear.

Roy Jenkins, President of the Commission of the European Community and former British Chancellor of the Exchequer, chose the occasion of the first Jean Monnet Lecture in Florence on October 27, 1977, to suggest a new initiative toward European monetary stability. To the surprise of most observers, the Jenkins proposals were taken up by Schmidt and Giscard d'Estaing at the European Community summit meeting in Copenhagen in April 1978 and, after further agreements at Bremen in July and in Brussels in December, the European Monetary System was put into operation March 13, 1979, less than 17 months after Jenkins' speech. By contrast, it took four years from the initial Barre Plan in 1968 to the adoption of the snake in April 1972. Such rapid acceptance and implementation of the basic features of EMS would not have been possible if it had not been essentially a warmed-over version of earlier plans, utilizing similar mechanisms and reflecting the same objectives.(1)

EMS OBJECTIVES

One of the principal stated objectives of the European Monetary System is to establish a zone of "monetary stability" in Europe. The effort reflects unhappiness with floating exchange rates; an unhappiness pervasive in European circles, except in Britain. The British seem not to have recovered from the painful experience of trying to defend an overvalued pound sterling in the 1960s.(2) Most Europeans, by contrast, have never become reconciled to the floating rate system which emerged after March 1973. From a purely national standpoint, European governments are accustomed to taking a view as to what the appropriate exchange rate for their currency is at any given time. The government's preferred rate might be higher or lower than the rate preferred by the market, depending upon the economic interests of the country as perceived by its political and financial leaders. The goal of most members of the European Community, therefore, is not merely to increase exchange rate stability by increasing the amount of official intervention in exchange rate markets, but to establish and preserve exchange rates which correspond to national economic policy objectives despite divergent market pressure.

A second objective of the European Monetary System is to structure international economic transactions so as to provide "discipline" for the domestic economy in order to reduce inflation. The view that the balance of payments should exert discipline upon the national economy is, like resistance to a freely-floating exchange rate system, a basic tenet of most European central bankers, economists, and politicians. It is an objective shared by countries with high as well as low inflation rates. Both Italy and Germany prefer that the balance of payments act as a restraint on domestic monetary expansion and, thereby, help to hold back inflation rates. The French, under Giscard d'Estaing and Raymond Barre, may have been especially interested in EMS as a justification for austere economic policies which would keep the franc linked to the mark, meanwhile holding down French inflation.

The rhetorical expression of the disciplinary objective is "monetary independence." When Europeans speak of independence from United States monetary policy, they mean principally independence from imported inflation. Only in rare circumstances since the early 1950s have the Europeans criticized the United States for not providing enough dollars to fuel Europe's economy. By contrast, there have been repeated strong denunciations of excessive U.S. monetary creation because it constitutes exporting inflation to Europe. Whether economically well-founded or not, the viewpoint has become firmly entrenched in Europe that an effective European Monetary System can function as a check on inflation rather than a factor contributing to inflation.

A third goal, and one highly touted in official statements, is the goal of advancing European unity. The idea of monetary union has been pressed tenaciously by "good Europeans." The formation of economic and monetary union was selected as the next step for advancing the cause of a united Europe, once the Common Agricultural Policy and the Common External Tariff were in place. European monetary union has proven to be most elusive; but, in a sense, while Europe has made little progress toward monetary union, it has also lost little ground. Monetary integration, depending upon how one chooses to look at it, is either as near fruition or as far removed as it has been for the past fifteen years.

Another objective of the founders of EMS is to acquire greater bargaining strength and influence in international monetary discussions and international political affairs, through the development of a common currency and a greater degree of unity. This is another manifestation of the desire for monetary independence from the United States and the dollar, but so far the Community has shown no unanimity in responding to U.S. initiatives on the IMF substitution account and reserve requirements for Eurocurrencies – proposals which could truly advance European monetary independence – and have offered nothing new for their part. One is left with the inescapable impression that the drive for EMS results from a conjunction of short-range national interests in combatting inflation and perennial Communitarian impulses toward integration.

EMS MECHANISMS

The European Monetary System, like its predecessors, is based upon exchange rate understandings which involve rules for market interven-tion when exchange rates diverge from agreed bands. In the EMS, the agreed range of permissible fluctuation is 2.25 percent on either side of the central bilateral exchange rates fixed between each pair of participating currencies. Participating countries may elect to observe a wider band initially, as Italy has decided to do (6 percent). Britain has elected not to participate in the exchange rate system at all. Interven-tion by both countries is required when two currencies reach the limit of the band. A second method of calculation based upon a new composite unit of account, the European Currency Unit ("ECU") is used to warn countries when their currencies are getting out of line with the Community as a whole. No one but a specialist need delve into the complexities of the "divergence indicator."(3) The point to grasp is that EMS rules require corrective action whenever a country's exchange rate diverges by 75 percent of its maximum permissible divergence from other EMS currency rates established in ECU. Intervention is one of several corrective actions which countries may take to deal with exchange rate divergence; other permissible measures are: adjustments in domestic monetary policy, changes in central rates, or other econom-ic policy measures. Should intervention be ultimately unsuccessful or should countries decide that divergence in underlying economic condi-tions is so great that central rates must be altered, a member country can adjust its rate, subject, however, to the consent of all the participants in the EMS.

The second central feature of the European Monetary System is a system of reserves and credit to enable countries to intervene to reduce or prevent divergence of central exchange rates. As the first step upon joining the EMS, countries have exchanged 20 percent of their gold and foreign currency holdings for accounts denominated in the new currency unit, ECU. Unlimited amounts may be drawn for daily intervention purposes, but balances must be settled within 45 days after the end of the month in which the intervention occurs. Countries may auto-matically defer payment for an additional 8 months, however, up to the maximum amount of short-term credit to which they are entitled. The total amount of short-term credit available under the new European Monetary System is 11 billion ECUs, compared to 4.5 billion ECUs under the old snake arrangement.

Medium-term credit (for periods from two to five years) is also available: a total combined facility of 14 billion ECUs compared to 5.5 billion under the old snake. Medium-term credit is available only upon agreement by the borrowing country to economic policy conditions laid down by the Community. The conditionality of medium-term credit is analogous to the conditionality applied to drawings from the Inter-national Monetary Fund. The European Currency Unit is used for credit settlement purposes as well as to denominate other Community trans-actions.

Finally, agreements to strive for better convergence of economic policies have been restated, and there is recognition that the economies of the European countries must converge if the necessity for frequent changes in central exchange rates is to be avoided. The documents and statements of all of the participants are refreshingly clear on this point, in contrast to statements accompanying some of the earlier attempts at European monetary integration.

EMS PROSPECTS

Most Americans have expressed considerable pessimism about the possibilities for the European Monetary System to survive for more than a few months. Predictions that the European Monetary System will fail are understandable, based on the Community's past experience with economic and monetary integration. Should EMS fail, the implications for other nations will depend considerably on the context of the failure as well as its exact nature.

Failure of EMS in one sense would be frequent adjustment of exchange rates. Economists wed to a floating rate system are inclined to argue that a European Monetary System which includes adjustable central rates will necessarily become a speculator's paradise. Opportunities for speculation without risk need not arise, however, if changes are made promptly and do not follow a predictable pattern.

The German Bundesbank has recognized the need for prompt rate adjustment when economic conditions no longer support existing central parities:

Necessary changes in central rates must be made in good time and without impediments . . . Judging from past experience, an attempt to defend exchange rates that have ceased to be credible leads to a rapid increase in interventions and, thus, to a reduction in the monetary autonomy of the countries with more stable currencies. Such risks must be kept as small as possible.(4)

Central exchange rates were adjusted on September 24, 1979, barely six months after inauguration of EMS. The German mark was revalued by 5 percent against the Danish Krone and 2 percent against other EMS currencies. The rate adjustment was not taken in an atmosphere of crisis, as was often the case when the "snake" rates were changed. The Danish Krone was devalued again on November 30, 1979, by 5 percent. These realignments augur well for the ability of EMS to recognize necessary adjustments and respond appropriately. Thus, one possible outcome is that the European Monetary System will fail to arrive at a common currency or a truly fixed-rate system, but an adjustable system analogous to the Bretton Woods system as it operated from 1958 to 1973 will emerge.

Other possible outcomes would be less benign. A sudden collapse of the EMS exchange rate and intervention system could lead to destabilizing shifts in international monetary reserve holdings. Uncoordinated official intervention in dollars could increase if the European Monetary System finds itself unable to coordinate intervention successfully in European currencies. Turmoil in currency markets could be severe if the United States were intervening in one direction while European central banks were intervening in another. A breakdown of the European Monetary System could create a crisis of confidence in all of the participating currencies leading to a sudden shift toward dollars, resulting in exchange rate swings not justifiable in terms of fundamental economic conditions. Furthermore, a collapse of the European Monetary System would be viewed as a discouraging sign by other countries hoping to achieve a gradual transition to a multiple reserve currency system, or attempting to establish their own regional zones of monetary stability.

A number of Americans have adopted the view that the European Monetary System is equally dangerous for the United States whether it succeeds or fails. Much of the discussion tends to confirm the European impression that Americans have difficulty accepting any arrangement not conceived in Washington.(5) The range of concerns which arise if the European Monetary System proves relatively successful are considerable. If the European Currency Unit (ECU) is made available to foreign central banks outside the European Community, it could become an attractive alternative reserve asset to the dollar and to Special Drawing Rights in the International Monetary Fund. There would be increased opportunity for central banks to diversify their reserve asset holdings away from dollars and Special Drawing Rights. While such diversification is not necessarily undesirable for the United States or the IMF in the longer run, the risk is that ECU assets could expand or contract precipitously, adding to international monetary instability.(6)

A strong European currency derived from the European Monetary System could, on the other hand, be the basis for greater stability in relations between OPEC and other primary product countries and the European Community. The ECU could become an attractive asset for OPEC to hold, or at least in which to denominate the sale of oil to Europe.

The attractiveness of either ECU reserves or ECU-denominated exchanges depends not only on the stability of the ECU in relation to the dollar and other currencies, but also on inflation rates in Europe and the availability of ECUs for transactions. OPEC reliance upon the dollar has not been so much a matter of preference for the dollar as the absence of alternatives. Unless ECUs are available for use without serious restrictions and with an attractive interest rate, there is little reason to think that OPEC nations would find it an attractive reserve asset. Nonetheless, if EMS succeeds, ECUs can become reserve assets attractive to foreign official holders.

Many economists also see one result of a successful EMS to be the loss by the United States of its "exorbitant privilege" to run balance of payments deficits in any amount without consideration of the effects on the domestic economy. The United States may have less monetary policy independence as a result of a strong EMS; in fact, that is one of the objectives of the Europeans. Increasing their monetary independence necessarily implies reduced monetary independence for the United States.

The EMS may well have significant implications for world trade. A successful EMS would be an additional incentive for intra-Community trade, displacing external trade to some degree. It seems more likely that the effort to keep exchange rates in line when economic conditions diverge will tempt European governments to resort to export subsidies, import protection, and exchange controls instead of adjusting exchange rates or taking fundamental economic policy adjustments. Given the strains already evident in world trade, the struggle to maintain fixed exchange rates in the European Community may well tilt the balance toward trade restriction and distortion. On the other hand, one could argue that the Europeans are already engaged in a worldwide struggle with the U.S. and Japan to win export markets and resist manufactured imports from developing countries. EMS could give the Europeans the self-confidence needed to resist the protectionist temptation, or, at the minimum, leave the balance unchanged.

The success of the European Monetary System could encourage other regions to emulate the EMS, leading to currency zones based upon such currencies as the Japanese yen, the Saudi rial, perhaps even the Brazilian cruzeiro. The result would be fragmentation of the international monetary system into a series of loosely-linked regional currency zones. The effect on the International Monetary Fund and global monetary cooperation would depend upon the ability to reach understandings concerning transactions between regions. The possibilities for successfully linking the European Monetary System to the rest of the world will depend very much upon the evolution of relations between the United States and the European countries.

The EMS has particular significance for Greece and the two candidate members of the European Community: Spain and Portugal. All three find themselves in economic situations analogous to Italy and Ireland; that is, each has an economy at a lower stage of development than the principal EMS states of Germany and France. The weaker economies risk being forced to pursue too stringent monetary and fiscal economic policies in an effort to keep their currencies close to the German mark and other strong EMS currencies.

Both Ireland and Italy negotiated significant economic "side deals" involving increased resource transfers from the wealthier participants. Greece, Spain, and Portugal could hardly be expected to settle for less, but in their cases the effect is to increase the price (and risks) of entry. EMS makes the Community less attractive to new low-income entrants, and such new entrants less attractive to the prime movers in EMS – Germany and France.

EMS within an expanding European Community has implications as well for the Nordic and East European states. The implications for Iceland, Norway, Sweden, and Finland are much the same as for Greece, Spain, and Portugal: EMS increases the difficulty of linking up with the

Community. The East European states, by contrast, may find EMS, as a growing fixed currency system, far more attractive than the loose and fluctuating monetary system it seeks to replace. The nonmarket economies find fixed rates a great aid in state planning. EMS will probably increase the pull of Western Europe on the economies of Eastern Europe, to the dismay of the Russians.(7)

CONCLUSION

The European Monetary System seems already to have spurred the United States to address more seriously its own inflation problems. Benjamin Cohen says the United States should resolve not to be "a source of instability in the future." He suggests that the United States should not "weaken its commitment to intervene more actively in the exchange markets to counter disorderly conditions," and should deal aggressively with its energy and inflation problems. In short, Cohen feels that the U.S. should "get its own economic house in order" in response to the European Monetary System.(8)

The predominant view is, therefore, that the European Monetary System is a form of discipline, upon the United States to the extent that ECUs successfully develop as an alternative to the dollar and reduce the need for world liquidity. The result could be to reduce the so-called "exorbitant privilege" of the United States, which consists of financing its balance of payments deficits without fear or pain. However, much depends upon what one thinks the appropriate discipline upon any economy should be. One line of argument is that if a country runs an excessive payments deficit its currency will depreciate – the exchange market will see to that – resulting in adjustments in trade and investment flows, which will restore payments balance. The floating rate response to the notion that discipline is either possible or necessary, therefore, is to reject both.(9)

The viewpoint persists, nonetheless, that the principal contribution of the European Monetary System is discipline upon the United States. A report issues by the First Chicago Bank states:

> [The EMS] . . . would reduce the international demand for dollars, and unless fewer dollars were offered, the dollar would tend to depreciate against the joint EC float. This implies a certain external discipline for the dollar in a form and with a force not felt since the de facto collapse of the gold standard in August 1914.(10)

The EMS signifies a basic difference in U.S. and European economic interests. As a large notion with a small trading sector, the United States will naturally continue to refuse to let external considerations set economic policy. The European nations have large trading sectors and find it difficult to refrain from trying to influence the exchange rates which affect their trade so powerfully. In addition, the objective of the European Community is to establish uniform policies, not merely to promote freedom of transactions between states. Floating exchange rates are fundamentally incompatible with economic and monetary union. Thus, Europe cannot tolerate floating rates from either a national or European perspective. But the repeated efforts to fix exchange rates will be costly so long as economic policies are not coordinated. The prospect is for a long, costly effort to achieve monetary union, an effort which appears generally unfavorable to world trade and monetary stability.

NOTES

(1) For a more extensive review of the early attempts to achieve European economic and monetary union, see Robert W. Russell, "Snakes and Sheiks: Managing Europe's Money," in Policy-Making in the European Communities, edited by H. Wallace, W. Wallace, and C. Webb (London: John Wiley & Sons, 1977), pp. 69-89.

(2) For a view reflecting the British preoccupation, see Samuel Brittan, "EMS: A Compromise that Could Be Worse than Either Extreme," World Economy (London), Vol. 2 (January 1979), pp. 1-30.

(3) For a thorough discussion, see The European Monetary System: Problems and Prospects, pp. 65-98, a study published by the U.S. Government Printing Office in Washington, D.C., in November 1979, for the use of the Joint Economic Committee and the Committee on Banking, Finance and Urban Affairs.

(4) Bundesbank Monthly Report, March 1979, p. 18.

(5) See Robert Triffin's spirited defense of the European side in his contribution to the Brookings Institution seminar on the European Monetary System, April 18-19, 1979.

(6) For discussion of the risks EMS poses for the United States, see Benjamin J. Cohen, testimony before the International Finance Subcommittee of the Committee on Banking, Housing and Urban Affairs, U.S. Senate, at hearings on International Financial Conditions, December 12 and 14, 1979.

(7) For an intriguing discussion of the possibilities from the Communist side, see Janos Fekete, "Monetary and Financial Problems in East and West," in Money and Finance in East and West, edited by C.T. Saunders (New York: Springer-Verlag, 1978), pp. 15-29.

(8) Benjamin J. Cohen, "Europe's Money, America's Problem," Foreign Policy, no. 35 (Summer 1979), pp. 31-47.

(9) See pp. 136-150 of The European Monetary System for an elaboration of this position.

(10) World Report (First National Bank of Chicago, November-December, 1979), p. 12.

11 European-American Crisis Management Cooperation
Reinhardt Rummel

THE EUROPEAN COMMUNITY AS A FOREIGN POLICY ACTOR: THE CASE OF SECURITY MATTERS

Although this chapter tries to tackle the comprehensive question of West European-American consultation, it concentrates on some aspects of mutual concertation in crises which are, on the one hand, outside or at the fringe of NATO competences, but, on the other hand, not central to the European Community's preoccupations. From both perspectives, these crisis events seem to be located in peripheral areas, although – in terms of their repercussion on the two institutions – they can be of more than marginal importance. There is no precise definition of the term "crisis" given here; it will be used for a wide range of "destabilizing" events which might occur in third countries and which are perceived as threatening Western interests. Although dangers to the West often arise without Soviet involvement, Moscow's growing military strength and worldwide presence signals additional threats without necessarily giving rise to NATO contingencies. Peripheral crises, which are very heterogeneous in nature, occur more frequently in practice than classical East-West conflicts at the center of the military alliances. In recent years, peripheral crises have increased not so much in number as in scope and degree of danger. Moscow and its proxies have been massively involved in some of these conflicts (i.e., the October War in the Middle East, Horn of Africa problems, Angola, Lebanon, Afghanistan, South Yemen, Vietnam). Another crisis series was interpreted as a possible threat by Western observers in terms of increasing Soviet influence and geopolitical advantages (i.e., Portugal, Cyprus, Zaire, Namibia, Turkey). In a third group of peripheral crises, Moscow has not been mentioned so far (i.e., Chad, West-Sahara, Canary Islands, and perhaps Iran).

The involvement of the West in the above-mentioned conflicts was motivated by that of the East as well as by some interests of its own.

218

This phenomenon has not yet been subjected to comprehensive and systematic analysis. This chapter, too, is restricted to raising some issues with respect to the foreign policy nature of the EC. The security aspect may reveal additional insights as to the state of a West European actor in international relations. By the same token, it is emphasized that the development and the implementation of European foreign policy continues to be contingent upon the Western superpower.(1) On this premise, it might be useful to determine the state of foreign policy cohesion between Western Europe and the United States and to examine whether significant trends are occurring in the area of non-NATO contingencies regarding a division of labor, either between the two sides or within the Community.

International crisis management might be an area in which to measure the readiness of the Community to pass from a passive "Europe of consequences" to an active "Europe of power." Is there any evidence for the assumption that the EC is likely to accept a role as a coactor in global crisis management? Is the EC in this context a coherent foreign policy actor, especially from the perspective of a sector-by-sector assessment?(2) It seems to be difficult as well as delicate to single out which kind of crisis deserves what sort of response. How can one determine the reasons for a worldwide crisis engagement? One explanation would be the demonstrated reluctance of Washington to continue its overall policeman function, another the "waking up" of the West European states in the aftermath of the 1973/74 Middle East crisis.

A different approach might address a more theoretical interest: crisis theory and its response or integration theory. What would be more appropriate: an "externalization" posture, a concept of "extension," or yet another analytical approach?(3) European participation in worldwide crisis management will lead to some changes in the institutional fabric of the Community. Will the existing decision-making systems be sufficient to fulfill the new functions or is there another one evolving?(4) So far, the EC could do more or less without the political consensus of a European public in terms of its selective foreign policy actions. But how much will the Community's effectiveness in crisis engagement be affected by its main structural weakness, i.e., living, for the time being, without a broad liaison with the grass roots consensus?(5)

It is obvious that one cannot follow up all of these assumptions in this chapter. The following considerations will have to forego detailed analysis. In particular, it is impossible to deal at length with the crisis case studies. Therefore, the following remarks should be viewed under the aspect of engendering useful hypotheses for further investigation rather than under the aspect of presenting the results of such research.

TESTING EUROPEAN CRISIS MANAGEMENT CAPACITY:
PROBLEMS OF COMPATIBILITY WITH WASHINGTON

The "declaration of identity," given by the Community Heads of Government in Copenhagen in 1973, is without any doubt, although only verbal, a call for more European commitment and participation in the international scene.(6) This includes aspects of security policy on the basis of an individual West European assessment. Collective security considerations of the EC presupposed a consultation process within Europe. Neither the transatlantic NATO nor the West European Common Market offered the procedural and political framework for such concertation. The European Political Cooperation (PC) and the European Council were suitable methods to be adapted to new functions in the crisis management field. Adaptation had to include also the link between the intra-European consultation process and the transatlantic consultation talks.

Concerning the concertation of Western crisis diplomacy, the experiences in the course of the Conference on Security and Cooperation in Europe (CSCE) were atypical. On these issues, there had been general agreement between the major West European states on the one hand and Washington and other NATO member states on the other. CSCE became a testing ground for EC, PC, and the European Council in terms of its responsibilities as well as its procedures. The latter included regular meetings of the nine Foreign Ministers prepared by the Political Committee and the groups of experts; establishment of an ad hoc group for CSCE issues; and direct coordination of diplomatic representatives of the member states at the conference location. More instructive than CSCE for the concerting of West European and U.S. diplomacy were the experiences in the aftermath of the Yom Kippur War. On November 6, 1973, the EC published a Middle East statement which satisfied the new self-confidence of the raw material producing countries and is still the basis of Western Europe's position in the Arab-Israel conflict.(7) When, in December 1973, spokesmen for the Arab League submitted their proposal for a dialogue to the European Council, they found that the latter had just formally passed a "Document on European Identity" which says: "The Community will implement its undertaking towards the Mediterranean and African countries in order to reinforce its long-standing links with these countries. The Nine intend to preserve their historical links with the countries of the Middle East and to co-operate over the establishment and maintenance of peace, stability and progress in the region."(8)

When Europeans went further and discussed specific plans for a European-Arab dialogue, Henry Kissinger (then U.S. Secretary of State) decided that the limits of Europe's margin of action had been exceeded. He expressed fear that this process might create a hostile attitude toward the U.S., jeopardizing his Middle East mediation efforts. The situation culminated in Washington's demand that the Community desist from making decisions touching upon U.S. interests without prior consultation.(9) Kissinger spoke of plans to institute a European PC-type mechanism for political cooperation among NATO members. It was the period when the Europeans – although Washington wanted to conceive a new Atlantic Charter with them – took more pride in working out an identity paper of their own. Only after the Gymnich Agreement did Kissinger relent following a talk with German Foreign Minister Hans-Deitrich Genscher, chairman of the Community at the time. A detailed definition of the Gymnich Agreement was provided by Genscher following the ministerial meeting on June 11, 1974, when he stated,

> The Ministers agreed that in the preparation of common foreign policy positions of the Nine the question of consultations of allied or friendly states arises. Such consultations are a self-evident part of any modern foreign policy. Ministers agreed on a pragmatic case-to-case approach. Consultations are conducted by the presidency on behalf of the Nine which follows corresponding instructions by its eight partners. In practical terms, this means that if one of the partners raises the question of information and consultations of an allied or friendly state, the Nine will discuss it and after having reached agreement will instruct the presidency to proceed on this basis.

> The Ministers trust that this informal gentleman's agreement will in practice lead to smooth and pragmatic consultations with the U.S. taking the interests of both sides into due regard.(10)

One month before the outbreak of the next crisis, the Cyprus conflict, a modus vivendi had thus been found for the relationship between West European and U.S. diplomacies. The Europeans had doubtless gained determination, endurance, and self-confidence from the U.S. fears. The U.S. administration had ended the many uncertainties and, more importantly, the unaccustomed and unpopular art of "lobbying" in Brussels and the other capitals could be dispensed with in the future.

Europeans had also learned an individual lesson from the Middle East conflict; the EC followed President Pompidou's recommendation of Autumn 1973 to be prepared for future crises. Beyond the different groups of experts for international issues which had analyzed crisis situations since 1971, the PC had been extended by adopting a procedure for urgent action. The official decision of the EC on crisis consultation was made at the Copenhagen summit on December 14 and 15, 1973. The communique read,

> They agreed to meet whenever the international situation so requires. It was agreed that the Foreign Ministers of the member states should, at their next meeting, decide on the means of crisis. The development of political cooperation will also enable them to make joint assessments of crisis situations, with the aim of foreseeing them and of defining common positions to meet them.(11)

Concrete proposals for the modalities of a crisis management were discussed by the Foreign Ministers on March 4, 1974, during a PC meeting. The outcome was a mechanism for a "consultation d'urgence" which provides – if necessary – for continuing consultations among the member states at the crisis location as well as in the capital of the nation holding the Presidency or in Brussels. It was made to guarantee a rapid working out of a common line in terms of crisis and was backed up by a special communications network among the foreign ministries of the member states in effect since 1974. In this context, not only the PC's relationship with the EC administration but also coordination within the national bureaucracies had been reshaped. Some capitals held that the working contacts between PC and NATO, not existing at that time, should be made up for by national bridges. Thus, by mid-1974, the EC had created the preconditions for future crisis management and established good communications with other Western states, especially the United States.

Within the Atlantic Alliance, agreement on the question of crisis consultations had been reached through the "Declaration of Ottawa." It was adopted by the foreign ministers of the member states of the North Atlantic Alliance in June 1974, signed by the government chiefs of these states in Brussels, and reads in part:

> The Allies are convinced that the achievement of their common goals requires the maintenance of close consultation, cooperation and mutual confidence and that this will promote the conditions necessary for defense and favorable for detente which complement each other. In the spirit of friendship, equality and solidarity which characterizes their relations they are strongly determined to always inform each other comprehensively and to strengthen the habits of frank and timely consultations by all suitable means on matters concerning their common interests as members of the Alliance bearing in mind that these interests may be affected by events in other areas of the world.(12)

The declaration regarding the necessity for consultation in crises outside the geographic NATO area has so far not resulted in any visible shift in Alliance tasks. There is no ready way within the NATO structure to discuss divergent views on peripheral crises and to co-ordinate operational steps.(13) Conflict involvements by individual states, such as France's commitments in Zaire, West Sahara, or Chad, are merely acknowledged by NATO. On issues such as the Greek-Turkish conflict or the possible dangers by communist government involvement in major member states, the Alliance displays helplessness and confusion. Altogether, the NATO system proved relatively more rigid than the European framework, which displayed adaptability, flexibility, and dynamic concern for new international challenges and contingencies.

WEST-EUROPEAN REGIONALISM: THE LINES
OF A REAPPRAISAL

While West Europeans resented the regional interest formula which Kissinger had presented in his Year-of-Europe speech in 1973, their behavior during the Yom Kippur War provided painful evidence. Against this background, West Europeans became aware of both their persistent regionalism (at least to the extent that it was perceived from outside Europe) and their increased dependence on the consequences of world-wide crisis. What used to be claimed as global interest on the part of France and Great Britain had more or less lost its strategic dimension of the 1950s and 1960s. Preoccupations of Paris and London had developed in terms of regions rather than in terms of a single global security theater. The FRG was still stuck in a Berlin-centered security definition. The orientations of EC policies reflected these lines of regionalism. The Europeans were "spoiled" in this respect by the ubiquitous American unilateralism. Washington often referred to the common perceptions of Western interests, but in practice "American action emerges out of an almost entirely American process of research, intelligence, discussion and policymaking."(14) Kissinger summarized the U.S. role more or less in fatalistic terms when he stressed,

> It is left to the United States because fate has put us in a position where we are the only non-Communist country that is strong enough and domestically cohesive enough to play a world role. Therefore, if certain things are not done by us, they will not be done by anyone. And while it may be fairer if somebody else took some of the responsibility, the fact is that a catastrophe is no less real for having been brought about by attempts to shift responsibilities to others."(15)

Since the 1973-74 period, it seems that a new phase has been unfolding on both sides of the Atlantic, though the implications for a collective global crisis management are still modest. Unlike earlier phases, peripheral crises can increasingly be described in terms of vital security interests of all members of the Alliance. With Western Europe extricated from colonial entanglement and the United States following a policy of selective involvements, peripheral crises were both more imminent and more genuinely a matter of common concern. By the same token, there was more evidence for the need of a European management. The energy crisis and the Marxist victory in the Angolan civil war helped to crystallize a new thinking on the European as well as on the national level. "Security" was spelled out in a wider range of international problems than previously. The December 1973 summit meeting was an unequivocal start in a direction which the EC partly followed deliberately and into which they were partly pushed from outside (the Arabs in this case). Since the events of Autumn 1973, complaints – coming mainly from the French – of an "absence Européenne" in remote crises has often been repeated. Other member states of the Community – including the FRG – voiced their readiness for contributions designed to stabilize conflict area situations.

These declarations must, of course, be confronted with the questions of what the Europeans are, in fact, capable of offering to the management of peripheral crises and how to concert with Washington in those cases. It was primarily with respect to crises in the European neighborhood that the EC member states tried to coordinate their instruments and to implement collective foreign policy decisions. In the Portugal political crisis, there were some positive outcomes from a coordination of PC diplomacy and EC means with an additional intensification of interparty-level relations.(16) The fundamentals of a Western-type democracy were stressed in connection with the beginning of the second enlargement round the Community. In the course of the Cyprus crisis, however, the Europeans embarked on some missions of reconciliation, partly in accordance with Washington, but without major success. Both played parts that tacitly or by outright agreement supplemented or substituted each other. A mood of mutual impediment – as in the case of the Middle East crisis management – did not crop up in the Cyprus case. Instead, there was a feeling of powerlessness even in joint efforts. Both have tolerated a weakening of NATO's southern flank which seems to be of a permanent nature.(17)

In the ups and downs of the Middle East conflict, the Europeans have, nevertheless, engendered a complex and subtle system consisting of common declarations, the Euro-Arab dialogue, and a multitude of bilateral arrangements which permit at least a strategy of damage limitation.(18) It is in the build-up of a common defense position that consensus among West Europeans is reached most easily. This category also includes selective contributions to crisis diplomacy, e.g., the Community recommendation of a "code of conduct" for European business plants in the Republic of South Africa, or the participation in the Namibia mediation endeavors.

Cases where Europeans could initiate a preventive stabilization as a means of best defense have yet to occur. Turkey could become such an example. At any rate, so far the Europeans have failed to effectively establish spheres of political influence. Moreover, it is doubtful whether this is the objective.

On the other hand, at least the major members of the EC have made it clear that they intend to rely less in the future on the regulating and leading force of the U.S. as a trouble shooter. They are looking for new ways of consultation and cooperation on the basis of a new sharing of responsibility. Even in the rare case where a European nation seems to be going it alone, it has to realize that American support remains indispensable for durable exercise of influence. This refers primarily to France's Africa policy.(19) Up to now, the other Europeans as well as Washington have largely been able to hide behind Paris' back. Giscard d'Estaing, not without a feeling of self-confidence, offered guarantees to francophone African states, although he realizes that for an efficient crisis policy a multilateralization is as necessary as it remains impossible.(20) London has not given any comparable reassurance to its former colonies, but tries to take its commitments as seriously as possible. In the Cyprus case, Britain has acted on its own account but rather unwillingly. In the Rhodesia/Zimbabwe case, it joined an Anglo-American initiative after having tried several approaches on its own although later it resorted to an initiative of its own again. Part of these unilateral or bilateral attempts are accompanied in many ways by the official platform of the EC. There are numerous declarations passed by the European Council or the foreign ministers which forego at least a line of common reference for member states or even imply a supportive function for unilateral crisis involvement. The FRG, too, shows more readiness to share worldwide responsibility compared to the period of Ostpolitik and before. In this respect, the German collaboration within the U.N. Security Council is a clearer sign than all the exaggerated extrapolations of the Mogadishou adventure.(21) Of course the more Bonn were to try to translate its conventional military and economic strength into political and security leverage on the international plane, the greater would be the historical-psychological barriers on the part of third countries as well as partner states. Yet, West Germany does not shy away from treating peripheral crisis areas as such. Thus, the FRG took an active part in the initiative of the "Five" (The United Kingdom, United States, FRG, France and Canada) on Namibia as well as in the case of the most recent action of stabilization in Turkey's favor in early 1979.

On balance, it appears as though the West European states are more willing to take on security tasks within a multilateral framework (including the U.S.) than within existing institutions. The regional fixation experienced at times in the past seems to have been relaxed.

THE STRUCTURE OF WESTERN CONSULTATIONS: A MULTITUDE OF MULTILATERAL PROCESSES

Although, other than NATO, there exists no Western institution to deal primarily with peripheral crises and threats, a number of consultation and action bodies have been established in the recent past which are used inter alia for Western crisis diplomacy purposes. The establishment of the International Energy Agency (IEA), for example, is an interesting example of European-American understanding in the important field of energy supply. The IEA covers, or tries to cover, specific components which might come out of political crises in nonmember-state areas. The mixed procedure of state influence and transgovernmental relations inside the Agency has not been put to a serious test so far.(22) Another Western forum of that type, although more on an ad hoc basis, is the Economic Summit of governmental leaders of the major industrialist countries of the West which has gained major importance in recent years for streamlining economic policies of these countries. In the context of this chapter, it is, however, more relevant to stress the fact that these summits have gone beyond handling economic questions while giving leaders an opportunity to discuss delicate aspects of contemporary international politics.

Closely related to these summits are the four-power meetings (the United States, Great Britain, France, and West Germany) which have meanwhile extended the scope of their discussions originally restricted to the Berlin question. This is the only forum in the Western Alliance where there is a certain readiness to deal with the whole range of international conflicts. The four get together on almost any occasion that offers itself (mostly on the occasion of other multilateral conferences, with the exception of the January 1979 Guadeloupe meeting). A somewhat firmer position in Western consultation is now being taken also by the group of Western U.N. Security Council members. Its work in terms of the Namibia contact group can be considered exemplary. In addition, it seems to be possible to convene ad hoc groups on an informal basis, such as the meeting in Paris on the Shaba conflict(23) or the American-British mediation in the Rhodesia/Zimbabwe case. The noninstitutionalized character of these forms of cooperation enables Western governments to assess jointly international crises and even to launch collective action. Although these activities cannot yield adequate action in serious crisis conditions, they have a general consensus-generating importance. Compared to the early 1970s, the cooperative potential has grown in East-West relations. Europeans have developed two limited but useful foreign policy tools, i.e., the EC and PC.(24) When used, they help to moderate extreme positions within the member states. Externally, the coordinated use of both instruments is as yet little employed; but it is no longer a taboo. Moreover, the European Council, the periodic meetings of the chiefs of government of the EC member states, increasingly coordinates their various policies, and also establishes a link with the higher Western Economic Summit.

Although interorganizational links (EC/PC-NATO) have not been seriously discussed so far, regular contacts have been established between the member states and the capitals of the other Alliance members (especially Washington). In the Cyprus case, for instance, the coordinated Western "lobbying" at Athens and Ankara was indispensable, though not sufficient. With some tasks of crisis diplomacy, such as the management of the U.N. resolutions, the West could not cope; NATO simply would not be able to face up to such a task.(25)

Away from the public, a foreign-policy "communauté de vue" has emerged among the member states during the past few years. Together with the rotating presidency system in the Council, it forms a concrete point of departure for a Western Europe "actor" in international relations at least from case to case.(26) To the extent that Western Europeans display self-confidence on foreign policy matters, they perceive cooperation with U.S. diplomacy less disturbing to their identity than was the case in the mid-1970s under French Foreign Minister Jobert's domineering influence. The relaxation in European-American relations which we are experiencing today is evidenced, for example, by former French Foreign Minister Guiringaud defending Washington's logistic aid in the latest Zaire operation and by stating that France would not be able to conduct such enterprises on its own.(27)

Indeed, Europeans do not have the potential or the radius of action that Washington can take in the technical-military sphere. This points up limitations of a purely European crisis diplomacy. An adequate military potential remains a prerequisite for almost all cases of crisis diplomacy. The special, mostly historically based, relations of some West European states with countries of the Mediterranean, Middle East and Africa have made their involvement in the recent local crises seem almost inescapable. On the other hand, European diplomacy cannot expect a bonus from these relations. In the Middle East conflict, the good relationship with the Arab states did not provide West Europeans with a head start over the United States. On the contrary, Washington's somewhat greater independence of Middle East oil than Western Europe's more than made up for any such perceived European advantages.

Europeans become especially aware of their vulnerability and dependence when possibilities for action are compared. Even Paris does not yet exercise much freedom of action, although it has filled in as "policeman" with great self-confidence and prudence in some recent African conflicts. Washington, which has become more selective, leaves areas of responsibility open which the Europeans are endeavoring to fill. The fact that this is, indeed, happening, at least to some extent (Cyprus) and that Europeans are again intervening in peripheral crises (Shaba) creates a new field of understanding with Washington. But this hardly simplifies the political consensus within the Community.

Thus, Paris probably has less difficulty with Washington than it does from old prestige needs within the EC. France still faces two major political-psychological barriers in dealing with the European bodies. One is its reluctance to communicate with all of the other partners; the other concerns genuine cooperative action with Washington. Some of the smaller partners often display a certain lightness in dealing with these sensitivities. When Belgium held the presidency in the EC during which the European Declaration on Sadat's visit to Israel in November 1977 was issued, it naively passed on Washington's communication that the U.S. government was willing to issue a joint assessment of the visit with the Europeans provided that they could come up with a text within a few hours. A telex forwarded to the European capitals on this obviously led to considerable psychological difficulties, in particular in Paris. Turkey offers a second example. In the Fall of 1977, Ankara cabled its willingness to Washington to show greater flexibility in the Cyprus conflict; but Washington passed this cable on to the Europeans as though this were an American success. Belgium – again without any explanatory text – circulated the information within the Community. As a consequence, the communication took on an unfavorable American overtone. Such inner-European sensitivities constitute a limitation for cooperation with the United States. France as well as other European states have an interest in living in "grey areas" as far as communication and consultation with Washington are concerned. Actual relations remain concealed for, at times, good reasons.(28)

Europeans today are less concerned that the United States will weaken its commitment toward Western Europe through involvement in peripheral crises than they are about its failure to take appropriate measures in these crises. Ever since the Middle East crisis of 1973/74, Europeans have become increasingly aware of their worldwide dependence. They have developed additional readiness in order to defend vital interests on their own to a larger extent than before. Altogether, however, dependence on Washington has hardly diminished.

On the American side, management of international diplomacy is no longer considered exclusively as a private domain of the U.S. Secretary of State. Diversifying the burdens resulting from commitments is one reason, but so is the recognition that even the United States has dependencies (oil supply) and that the trend is not toward a new peak in "imperial presidency."(29) On both sides of the Atlantic and for several reasons the road seems thus paved for non-NATO crises to be dealt with as a joint responsibility.

Yet there are also countervailing trends: increased dependence, growing political heterogeneity, more bilateralism. Also – as the Cyprus case, inter alia, suggests – the utility of concerted Western crisis diplomacy should not be viewed in too absolute terms. The prospect can hardly be general coordination. But, just as the West was able to find areas of cooperation in relations with the Soviet Union, Western Europe needs selective cooperation with Washington in crisis diplomacy. For some events, crises need to be managed through transatlantic cooperative means, for others, the Community, through its selective instruments and policies, seems to dispose of capabilities to achieve this end.

THE EUROPEAN COMMUNITY – AN EMERGING COACTOR IN THE SECURITY FIELD

Compared to the Community's activities in the economic field, where it seems to be "an important actor for both the industrial and the nonindustrial countries,"(30) Western Europe's influence in the security field seems to be of minor importance so far. The more the antagonism of the superpowers comes to the fore in a crisis and the greater the military intervention, the less would be Western Europe's role. Yet, the latter has developed into a coactor in conflicts open to management by diplomatic and economic software. However, closer study of such cases would be required before this trend could be confirmed or even extrapolated. Such analysis would also have to examine the use of the "externalization" argument according to which a growing dependence of the EC on third countries would imply a growing responsibility to take on stabilization efforts in the security field.(31)

The division of labor between Western Europe and the U.S., like that among West European nations, follows a very pragmatic line. It also seems to be more far-reaching than is externally visible. There is a preference for working within informal groups where the different national interests are fully exposed. Academically, that would support the theory of an "extension" approach. At least dual European-American cooperation or even competition is rarer here than it is, for example, in the commercial sector. To the extent that transatlantic management cooperation is affected by peripheral crises, it displays grave inadequacies: lack of background sharing, great differences in crisis awareness and in national readiness to take risks, lack of attempts at comprehensive crisis definition, breakdown into individual assessments based on individual results, lack of overview of the various management frameworks, deficient coordination of existing instruments, and security as to the crisis potential actually available. The degree of necessary and achievable European-American cooperation depends on the circumstances prevailing as well as on the nature of an individual crisis.

Perhaps it is the institutional field which lends itself most readily to conclusions. There is no transatlantic institution to deal with issues that lie in neither the economic area (EC, OECD, IMF, etc.) nor in the area of military security (NATO). Instead, there is "a multi-faceted system of close consultation at all levels."(32) This informal infrastructure overlaps with the different decisional systems of the member states. Some members of the EC (the major countries, the presidency) act as relay stations linking the intra-European with the intra-Atlantic process of consensus-building. Perhaps the assumption is correct that the West Europeans, in spite of their growing political weight, open their decision-making system to the U.S. to the extent that security issues crop up in European foreign policy. Hence, the policy of the Community has to be perceived as a mixture of multilateral, Community, and national elements. This mixture may well be the standard structure of the foreign policy actor, Western Europe, at least for the time being.

NOTES

(1) The same approach is followed by Charles C. Pentland, "L'evolution de la politique étrangère de la Communauté Européenne: Le contexte transatlantique," Etudes Internationales (March 1978), pp. 106-25.

(2) Michael B. Dolan and James A. Caporaso suggest that it might be misleading to ask whether the member states are a coherent foreign policy actor in general terms: "The External Relations of the European Community," in Annals of the American Academy of Political and Social Science 440, (Nov. 1978): 142. (Hereinafter referred to as Annals.)

(3) According to Pentland, externalization provides the more simple formulation. It means that once the members of a regional economic community have succeeded in realizing their basic agreements regarding the management of their mutual relations, they are compelled to adopt common policies toward Third countries regardless of their initial intentions. Extension, on the other hand, postulates that the most important member states of a community utilize this organization to recover, maintain, or reinforce their position as world powers (p. 118).

(See also the linkage model: C.C. Pentland, "Linkage Politics: Canada's external relations," International Journal 32, no. 2 (1977): 206-31.

(4) See the four decisional systems (Rome System, Concert System, Summitry, Political Cooperation) exposed by Glenda G. Rosenthal and Donald J. Puchala, "Decisional Systems Adaptiveness, and European Decisionmaking," in Annals, pp. 54-65.

(5) The weak linkages between Community activities and grassroots and elite politics at the national level is emphasized by Stuart A. Scheingold, "The Community in Perspective: Public Policy and Political Structure," in Annals, pp. 156-67.

(6) The "Document on the European Identity" published by the Nine Foreign Ministers in Copenhagen Dec. 14, 1973, is reprinted in: Press and Information Office of the Federal Government, European Political Cooperation (EPC), Bonn, 1978, p. 69-76.

(7) Ibid., pp. 67, 68.

(8) Ibid., pp. 73, 74. In the same document, the Community is seen as an organization that intends to exert a positive influence on world economic relations with a view to the greater well-being of all. "The Nine, one of whose essential aims is to maintain peace, will never succeed in doing so if they neglect their own security. Those of them who are members of the Atlantic Alliance consider that in present circumstances there is no alternative to the security provided by the nuclear weapons of the United States and by the presence of North American forces in Europe; and they agree that in the light of the relative military vulnerability of Europe, the Europeans should, if they wish to preserve their independence, hold to their commitments and make constant efforts to ensure that they have adequate means of defence at their disposal," p. 72.

(9) Europe's role in the "structure of peace" had not been defined yet. See William C. Cromwell, "Europe and the Structure of Peace," Orbis (Spring 1978), pp. 11 ff.

(10) "Document on the European Identity," pp. 85, 86.

(11) Ibid., p. 78.

(12) Europa-Archiv, Dokumente 29 (1974): D341.

(13) Paris does not take part in the work of the Defense Planning Committee, which, next to the Political Committee, is the only body of NATO dealing with crises outside the Alliance's range. France's occasional information about French crisis actions in other NATO offices is, therefore, though helpful, not very important.

(14) Alastair Buchan, Crisis Management: The New Diplomacy (Paris: The Atlantic Institute, 1966), pp. 57 ff.

(15) Interview in U.S. News and World Report, June 23, 1975, p. 27.

(16) Garret Fitzgerald, "Political Cooperation: Toward a Common European Community Foreign Policy," The Atlantic Community 16, no. 4 (1978): 452-56.

(17) John C. Campbell, "The Mediterranean Crisis," Foreign Affairs 53, no. 4 (1975): 605-24.

(18) David Allen, "The Euro-Arab Dialogue," Journal of Common Market Studies 16, no. 4 (June 1978): 323-42.

(19) Julian Crandall Hollick, "French Intervention in Africa in 1978," The World Today (Feb. 1979), pp. 71-80.

(20) Dominique Moisi and Pierre Lellouche, "Frankreichs Afrika Politik unter Giscard d'Estaing: Kampf auf Verlorenem Posten," Europa-Archiv 34, no. 2 (1979): 29-42.

(21) Roger Morgan, West Germany's Foreign Policy Agenda, The Washington Papers, No. 54, 1978.

(22) Robert O. Keohane, "The International Energy Agency: State Influence and Transgovernmental Politics," International Organization 32 (Autumn 1978), pp. 929-51.

(23) Upon France's invitation the representatives of five Western countries (U.S.A., France, UK, FRG, Belgium) met for a stock-taking of the political and military situation in connection with the Shaba conflict in Paris on 5 June 1978. Decisions were not made. The economic aspects were discussed shortly after that on 14 June 1978 in Brussels with ten countries (Belgium, FRG, Canada, Japan, Iran, Italy, France, UK, Netherlands, Zaire) as well as the World Bank, the IMF and the EC Commission attending.

(24) The PC's efficiency is analyzed more closely by H. Kramer and R. Rummel, Gemeinschaftsbildung Westeuropas in der Aussenpolitik: Zur Tragfähigkeit der Europäischen Politischen Zusammenarbeit (Bonn: Europa Union Verlag, 1978), pp. 221-62.

(25) Beate Lindemann, "Die Generalversammlung der VN: Testfeld für die globale Neuner-Diplomatie," in Die Europäische Politische Zusammenarbeit, edited by R. Rummel and W. Wessels (Bonn 1978), pp. 221-67.

(26) Geofrey Edwards and Helen Wallace, The Council of Ministers of the European Community and the President-in-Office, (London: Federal Trust for Education and Research, 1977).

(27) While Guiringaud stated in connection with the second Shaba conflict (1978) that France and the U.S. agreed to assist African states in the defense of disturbing forces (Suddeutsche Zeitung, May 31, 1978), the French President had said during the first Shaba crisis (1977) that France had acted without U.S. consent. There were situations, he continued, where Europe had to manifest itself, and in this case Europe had manifested itself through France (Suddeutsche Zeitung, April 14, 1977).

(28) If Washington's influence becomes too transparent, however, the danger of a "fuse blowing" may easily arise. In late January 1977, the EC planned a PC statement on the Middle East situation (i.e., the Palestinians' right to a homeland), publication of which displeased the U.S. Indeed, the PC withheld the statement, but only one day after this incident had become public, the wording of the declaration appears in El Ahram. Occasional reluctance on the part of Europeans to reveal their cooperation with the U.S. is based on national and always on European motivations. At times it also turns out to be counterproductive from the international point of view. Europe then appears as Washington's extended arm.

(29) Arthur M. Schlesinger, Jr., The Imperial Presidency (Boston: Houghton, Mifflin Co., 1973).

(30) Dolan and Caporaso, "The External Relations of the European Community," p. 135.

(31) In this connection, three basic questions arise: Where did a military-economic-political division of labor take place in the past? (Spain, Portugal, Turkey, Zaire?) What was its success? and Where would European states by themselves intervene militarily, in cases where Washington is either unwilling or unable to act?

(32) Deane R. Hinton, U.S.-EC Relations: Taking Stock, USA Documents No. 11 (Public Affairs Office, United States Mission to the European Communities), January 24, 1979, p. 3.

12 NATO-Europe and the United States: The "Two-Way Street" Concept

Eugene J. Mesaros

The term "two-way street" is a familiar one in NATO circles and is becoming increasingly known in the United States. The term is descriptive of the concept of increased cooperation between the United States and Western Europe in defense procurement matters pertaining to the Atlantic Alliance (NATO). Implicit in and a prerequisite to transatlantic cooperation is a United States' understanding that European nations will cooperate on a unified and collective basis. While there are many problems to be faced in creating a more balanced transatlantic arms-traffic flow than the current average estimate of 10:1 in favor of the United States, the most pressing is the formation of an organizational focal point among the European allies which can speak with collective interest and authority for the twelve European members.(1)

The two-way street concept embodies far more than the matter of joint arms procurement and the distribution of economic burdens and profits incident to defense economics. The concept transcends the issue of joint arms procurement policy to the more fundamental issues of the defense of Europe, freedom of the West, and the defense of that freedom without resorting to a nuclear option because of Alliance conventional force deficiencies. Yet, a strong conventional deterrent in NATO is paramount lest the conventional deficiencies evoke the use of the tactical nuclear option which, in turn, begets a strategic nuclear exchange. Apart from political, military, and economic considerations, the concept engenders the question of national security and survival.

Notwithstanding the defense/security factors which support the two-way street philosophy, the idealism of a harmonious union of nations dedicated to averting nuclear conflict by creating a superior conventional deterrent is overshadowed by the pragmatic realities of economic survival, political perspectives, and parochial national interests. In effect, it is these factors which are responsible for Europe's

---

*The contents of this paper reflect my own personal views and are not necessarily endorsed by the Department of the Navy.

233

inability to develop an organizational entity capable of negotiating with the United States on a unified basis. Conversely, the United States, unhampered by the problem of having to think and act with a multi-national mind, has been unwilling to cooperate primarily because economic necessity has not, in the past, demanded such cooperation.

In 1979, a reappraisal of Alliance mind-sets in light of contemporaneous events is in order. Starting with the basic respective sanctions – the Culver/Nunn Amendment to the Fiscal Year 1976 Defense Appropriations Act and the European Parliament's endorsement of the Klepsch Report – a state of inertia has been overcome and slight movement along the two-way street is noticeable.

THE ECONOMICS OF ALLIANCE

A CIA study comparing the cost of Soviet and United States defense activities from 1967 through 1977 indicates that while real U.S. defense spending has declined during this period, Soviet defense costs have grown at 4 to 5 percent per year. In 1977, estimated Soviet defense costs exceeded corresponding U.S. defense costs by 25 to 40 percent. In investment terms, Soviet expenditures were estimated to be about 75 percent greater.(2) It is clear that the Soviet production lines are producing weapons at a rate higher than the United States and, assuming that the present trend continues, the numerical imbalance will evolve to Soviet superiority soon. What options are available to counter Soviet military gains? An estimate given by William J. Perry, U.S. Deputy Undersecretary of Defense for Research and Engineering, is that U.S. defense expenditures would have to be increased by 40 percent annually to match Soviet defense expenditures.(3) The mere suggestion of such an increase is politically infeasible. Moreover, when assessed in terms of the Atlantic Alliance, a unilateral assumption of the burden to achieve equilibrium by the United States may be totally unnecessary.

The key to countering Soviet gains may be in improved efficiency, that is, to allocate defense expenditures efficiently on an Alliance-wide basis. With European members spending about $69 billion on defense in 1978, about 55 percent of what the United States spent, combined U.S. and European expenditures easily match the Soviets.(4)

It is clear that the total economic potential of the Alliance provides sufficient economic resources to counter Soviet military gains – if employed in a coordinated long-range procurement plan. The challenge, therefore, is to coordinate the national defense interests and appropriations of 15 member nations into a unified Alliance defense procurement plan. This challenge has eluded and been ignored by the member nations for their more than 30 years of "joint cooperation." Perhaps the most glaring testimony of the inability to achieve basic defense harmony is the failure to attain standardization and interoperability in NATO weapons. As an example, within the NATO arsenal there are presently:

Table 12.1. Defense Expenditures of NATO Countries
(Current prices in Local Currency – Millions)

Country	1974	1975	1976*	1977*	1978* (estimated)
Belgium	57,395	69,936	81,055	89,480	99,008
Canada	2,862	3,127	3,589	4,124	4,597
Denmark	4,439	5,281	5,680	6,343	7,135
France	48,153	55,955	63,899	73,530	83,414
West Germany	35,644	37,589	38,922	40,184	42,588
Greece	24,126	53,917	....	....	....
Italy (billion lira)	2,852	3,104	3,608	4,533	5,223
Luxembourg	710	836	983	1,029	1,160
Netherlands	6,423	7,246	7,817	9,260	9,367
Norway	3,938	4,771	5,333	5,934	6,756
Portugal	25,108	19,898	18,845	22,082	26,111
Turkey	15,831	....	....	....	....
United Kingdom	4,207	5,165	6,162	6,822	7,492
United States	85,906	90,948	91,008	100,928	105,135
AREA TOTALS (US $)					
Europe	46,261	51,951	51,914	58,363	68,951
North America	88,832	94,023	94,968	104,806	109,238
NATO	135,093	145,974	146,882	163,169	178,189

*Totals exclude Greece and Turkey

Figures in the table annotating total defense expenditures by NATO countries represent payments made, or to be made during the course of calendar year 1978, as compared with previous calendar years. The figures are based on NATO definitions and may diverge from those granted by national authorities or given in national budgets. Figures relating to the United States and Canada include expenditures for military aid programs. Figures shown for European NATO countries do not include the value of end items received under military aid programs from the US and Canada.

Source: <u>NATO Review</u>, February 1979.

- 23 different families of combat aircraft;
- 7 different families of main battle tanks;
- 8 different families of armored personnel carriers;
- 22 different families of anti-tank weapons;
- 36 different fire control radars;
- 8 different surface-to-air missiles;
- 6 different anti-ship missiles; and
- 20 or more different calibers of weapons 30 mm or larger.(5)

NATO GENERAL PURPOSE FORCES – THE ARSENAL OF BABEL

In a protracted conventional conflict where the interaction of attrition rates and resupply capability weigh the decision in favor of the contestant with the most effective supply channels, it is generally agreed that NATO general purpose forces are at a distinct disadvantage vis a vis the Warsaw Pact forces. In varying degrees, neither the land, nor the sea, nor the air forces of NATO can operate effectively together for any significant period of time. With different weapons and equipment, requiring different ammunition and spares, each allied country must look to its own (rather than a NATO) logistic support system for resupply. The often-discussed but never resolved problem of the failure to attain progress in the area of weapons/equipment standardization/interoperability evokes the query of how to continue the battle after the supply lines are exhausted. In such an eventuality, does the tactical nuclear option retain the status of an option, or does it become the only action available before a win/lose decision terminates the contest?

The foregoing stark example is, perhaps, an extreme, albeit very real, consequence of the failure of a coalition to wage war in concert. From a Warsaw Pact perspective, NATO is a military structure whose organization is preprogrammed in accord with the historic military axiom of "divide and conquer." The procurers of weapons for the "Arsenal of Babel" may do well to review the fate of their biblical namesake and consider the consequences likely to befall a coalition whose members cannot see beyond their national boundaries. Accordingly, in viewing the matter of joint arms development/procurement solely in light of a win/lose military decision and the increased risk of a nuclear encounter, the concept of the two-way street becomes the only prudent path of travel.

THE TWO-WAY STREET: STANDARDIZATION AND INTEROPERABILITY
BY ANOTHER NAME

The benefits to be derived from a joint U.S./Western European arms development and procurement program are synonomous with the virtues of standardization and interoperability. Generally, the same factors which have been perenially offered by the proponents of standardization/interoperability are those offered in support of the two-way street concept. If the foregoing is true and the two entities are, in fact, the same concept with merely a jargonistic term used to connote the more contemporary version, why then has the concept finally been sanctioned? Certainly, the same benefits to be gained by this imperative are still as valid as they were when espoused by their proponents a decade ago. The economic realities of burden/profit sharing, benefits of economies of scale, and reduction in the wasteful cost duplication of uncoordinated research and development efforts remain valid factors; the increased defense capacity and capabilities incident to common weapons systems still offer enhanced military effectiveness and efficiency; and, a high spirit of nationalism and varied national interests remain operative. Why, as we approach the 1980s, are standardization and interoperability reintroduced as the two-way street and suddenly the subject of generally popular acceptance? I believe the matter to be attributable to two factors: an increase in the relative intensity of economic and security-related pressures and a growing spirit of policy coordination among the Western European states.

COST/RISK ASSESSMENT

On the matter of increased intensity in economic and security-related matters, it is quite simply a realization that the tremendous economic burden of procuring and maintaining a national arsenal of expensive, unique weapons systems to counter a quantitatively and possibly qualitatively superior opponent have reached critical cost/risk decision points. National options involve either the appropriation of large defense expenditures in order to achieve an acceptable level of risk, or the acceptance of a high level of risk by either curtailing or maintaining the current level of individual national defense expenditures. The internal options afforded the nation alone are, at best, unattractive forms of suboptimization. The intensity factor is attributable to the growing superiority of the Warsaw Pact forces and the widening gap between Pact and NATO forces. This factor affects European and North American NATO states both individually and collectively. In a present-day cost/risk assessment of NATO general purpose forces, individual national costs may be considered acceptable but the collective risk is high. An efficient joint U.S./European arms development and procurement program could achieve an acceptable cost and lower risk relationship for Alliance members.

The linkage between the foregoing factor and what I perceive to be a mounting spirit of union among Western European states is causal insofar as the increased intensity of economic and security factors on national decision processes is antecedent to and the driving impetus toward more effective coalition actions. I submit that the factors existing at the present time are bringing previously divergent national interests into closer harmony. For the most part, the common exigencies of the economic environment and the increased threat to coalition/national security are the driving factors.

A PRUDENT PATH

In summary, from an Alliance-wide viewpoint, the two-way street is a prudent path of travel. In an environment of increasing defense costs, a joint coalition arms development/procurement program would provide individual members of means to counter the rising cost of national defense; reduce the redundancy of research and development efforts; enjoy the economies of scale incident to long production runs; and enable national industries to join in the collaborative efforts, thereby increasing domestic employment, participating in profits, and so forth. In addition to the economic benefits, gains would be made toward achieving the ever-elusive NATO objectives of standardization and interoperability with their inherent attribute of increased military effectiveness. In gaining a more effective military force, increased security is implicit. In view of the growing capability of the Warsaw Pact forces, this latter factor alone is more than sufficient to justify the construction and maintenance of a two-way street in U.S./Western European arms development and procurement.

In light of the foregoing, why then is there so little traffic on the two-way street? An examination of the respective United States and Western European perspectives and initiatives follows.

WEST EUROPEAN PERSPECTIVES AND INITIATIVES

Europeanization of Defense Procurement

The "Europeanization" of Western European defense within NATO is not a new concept; the idea can be traced back to efforts in NATO's formative years to construct a European Defense Community (EDC). In the 1960s, the concept reemerged in the form of notions of a continental defense industry composed of European countries serving European defense markets. Both the EDC and a European defense industry, however, were defeated by a number of factors, most notably, abiding strains of nationalism in defense affairs, disparate perceptions of security roles and requirements, a perceived dependence on the United States for strategic and conventional defense, and the exigencies of economics. More recently, Europeanization of defense procurement has, for the most part, taken the form of collaboration, i.e., the bilateral or multilateral development and production of specific weapons systems.

Generally, an Alliance-wide approach to a unified armaments procurement policy is alien to European experience. When a temporary ad hoc union was formed to cooperate on an individual item of defense equipment, the motivations for cooperation were primarily political and economic with little regard to Alliance strategic considerations. Quite simply, throughout the history of NATO, there has been no coherent European armaments scheme. The prospects of taking the total annual defense appropriations of the European allies – some $69 billion – and utilizing these assets toward a European arms procurement plan versus

12 separate national plans may be beyond the micro-economic mentality of some member states. As stated earlier, the realities of the challenges afforded by the 1980s demand the abandonment of the national, ad hoc, short-term, micro approach to defense matters. Alliance members must face up to the magnitude of the political and economic cooperation required to establish an Alliance-cooperative structure, macro-economic in scale, that is able to sustain the long-term military effectiveness of the alliance.

The Challenge

It is the sense of the Congress that standardization of weapons and equipment within the North Atlantic Alliance on the basis of a "two-way street" concept of cooperation in defense procurement between Europe and North America could only work in the realistic sense if the <u>European nations operated on a unified and collective basis</u>. Accordingly, the Congress encourages the governments of Europe to accelerate their present efforts to achieve European armaments collaboration among all European members of the Alliance.

Section 803 (c) 1976 Defense Appropriations Act

More than three years have passed since Congress approved legislation which provided the U.S. sanction and groundwork for the two-way street concept.(6) As a prerequisite to the flow of two-way arms traffic, Congress envisioned the necessity for the Europeans to coordinate their efforts through a single, unified, European agency. Accordingly, the greatest impediment to a joint U.S./European arms collaboration scheme resides in the inability of the Europeans to speak as one. Although a number of Western European organizations concerned with arms matters exist – either in the European NATO infrastructure, or in orbit around its peripheries – no single organization is properly structured to speak with the collective authority of Europe's 12 defense ministers. Although much discussion has taken place in European political circles, the most progressive, albeit less than conclusive, effort that has been taken to date has been the European Parliament's (less France) endorsement of the Klepsch Report. This report, essentially a feasibility study of the organizational options available to coordinate and achieve a transatlantic two-way street in arms procurement, provides a definite plan for structuring a "European Arms Procurement Agency." The proposal calls for the creation of this agency within the existing system and is presently under review.

Who Shall Speak for the Europeans?

Existing European Agencies Concerned with Armament Matters

A number of European agencies possessing a military aspect are operative, some more so than others, which represent segments and varieties of European Alliance members. The primary ones – the Western European Union (WEU), FINABEL, EUROGROUP, and the Independent European Program Group (IEPG) – have been responsible for generating a number of joint arms efforts and ventures. However, the question of whether any of the existing organizations is capable of, or the appropriate vehicle for, organizing European armaments production for a transatlantic scheme is doubtful in the minds of most concerned parties.

Western European Union (WEU)

Member include Britain, France, Belgium, the Netherlands, Luxembourg, the Federal Republic of Germany, and Italy. The primary value of this group is in its utility for a cohesive Western European defense. Members are bound to a 50-year treaty that is not renounceable. Functionally, the WEU Assembly is useful as a forum for Western parliamentarians who discuss possible collaborative projects in the armaments field. Although apart from NATO, it maintains close liaison with the NATO agency for standardization. The performance of WEU's Standing Armaments Committee in developing criteria for the development of new weapons has been disappointing.

FINABEL

Members include France, Italy, Netherlands, Belgium, Luxembourg, (FINABEL) the Federal Republic of Germany, and the United Kingdom. The group is primarily concerned with land armaments matters. FINABEL has been relatively successful in joint definition of requirements, the exchange of information, conduct of joint tactical and logistical studies, and joint testing of land armaments. An extra-NATO group comprised of NATO members, FINABEL has exerted some influence on member governments with regard to collaborative land armament projects.

EUROGROUP

This is a group within the NATO framework which includes all European members of NATO less France and Iceland. Organizationally, it is comprised of a number of subgroups, each of which concerns itself with a specific subject (i.e., tactical communications, training, force structure, etc.). The most important subgroup within EUROGROUP is concerned with joint arms development/procurement matters (EURONAD) and consists of the National Armaments Directors of the member states. A moderately successful group, its members have coordinated such collaborative projects as the 155 mm howitzer, the multirole combat aircraft (MRCA) Tornado, the Lance missile, and the purchasing arrangements with the United States for the F-16 fighter. For the most part, the EURONAD subgroup of the EUROGROUP has been relegated to a semidormant state with the advent of the IEPG, since the latter group's membership is comprised of all European Alliance members except Iceland.

The Independent European Program Group (IEPG)

Independent of NATO, the IEPG includes all European members of NATO with the single exception of Iceland. The IEPG has three basic aims:

- harmonizing national equipment schedules and replacement dates,
- agreeing on joint projects, and
- eliminating duplication of development efforts.

The primary utility of the IEPG is that it includes the continent's two major arms manufacturers in its membership – France and Great Britain. If France can be induced by the other IEPG members to be a full participant in a unified European Alliance arms development/procurement program, the IEPG would serve as an excellent forum for the conduct of dialogue along the two-way street.

Of the four European arms-related organizations in existence, only EUROGROUP is a part of the NATO structure. Further, of the concerned organizations, only one – the IEPG – has the desired membership necessary to conduct a forum on European armaments production matters. Consequently, of the extant European agencies concerned with armament matters, the IEPG is the most desirable from an organizational perspective. The IEPG is an extra-NATO organization whose NATO members have had successful prior experience in conducting negotiations on a transatlantic scale, notably with regard to the F-16 project. In view of the desirable characteristics of the IEPG, could or should it serve as the organizational entity for orchestrating the European arms program?

At least two leading North American proponents of the two-way street concept, Congressman Jack Brooks and Thomas Callaghan, intimate that the IEPG should be the focal point for U.S./European arms negotiations.(7) Conversely, Julian Critchley does not consider the IEPG competent to devise a common policy for the procurement and manufacture of arms as a necessary part of the economy and industrial life of the nations concerned.(8) Realistically, while the IEPG may be an appropriate agency to discuss military requirements, the IEPG does not have the authority to speak with regard to industrial matters relative to arms procurement. It is Critchley's contention that the EC is the only European institution in a position to bring about the restructuring of the European arms industry.(9) In essence, Critchley's proposal envisions a "European Arms Procurement Agency" as a section of the EC or as an agency responsible to it. The agency would interface with the IEPG. Accordingly, there is no basic disagreement between Critchley's views of the military/industrial interface and organizational vehicles required to implement a European arms scheme and those contained in the Klepsch Report. Specifically, the proposal contained in the Klepsch Report concluded that a European armaments industry could be structured successfully within the Commission of the European Community (EC) and the ministerial body of the Independent European Program Group (IEPG).

Why the European Community?

Previous experiences with collaborative arms efforts orchestrated through European political and military institutions have indicated that, in order for a unified European arms collaboration program to succeed, such a program must be linked to Community industrial policy. The European Parliament's Committee on Economic and Monetary Affairs examined the economic and financial aspects of the European defense equipment market and in its report of March 21, 1978, it forecast the danger of a decline in European defense industries if the present uncoordinated efforts in arms procurement practices continued. In view of this danger, the Committee called for a common industrial policy to include defense matters.(10) Accordingly, in concert with the foregoing, the Klepsch Report also concludes that armament policy be linked directly with industrial policy. Apart from the statement of the defense requirements (weapons specifications), which is a military function to be accomplished via NATO on the Atlantic scale and via the IEPG with regard to European involvement, the matter of arms development/procurement is an industrial concern. Appropriately, such matters as ensuring and coordinating proper financing of research and development efforts between firms in several member states, monitoring for duplication of efforts, coordination of plans and programs, streamlining of management structures to facilitate extranational efforts, and buildup of common buffer stocks of strategic raw materials are more likely to receive better attention through the Common Market structure.

The EC and the Economic Hammer

National military priorities and strategies in a multinational environment offer the potential for a less-than-coherent coalition weapons acquisition program. NATO is an on-going case study of this problem. Whereas a long-range military procurement plan based on the Alliance's risk assessment of the perceived threat 8-10 years hence may satisfy the coalition defense requirements, adherence to that plan is often jeopardized by fluctuating, short-term military, economic, and political priorities to individual member nations. Generally, when national interests are at variance with extranational obligations, a nation will opt to satisfy the national interest. Within NATO, exercising the national option has frequently been to the detriment of Alliance military posture, particularly with regard to military effectiveness. One of the primary reasons for such actions in the past has been the perception that whatever shortfall might be created in the Alliance posture by an individual nation's actions, the United States would quickly bridge the deficiency gap. Much too frequently, member nations have rationalized their individual lack of coalition commitment as being inconsequential because of the awesome nuclear umbrella of the United States. After all, what difference could it possibly make if I develop my own weapons systems, contract to my own industries, and provide jobs for my people? What are 50 tanks compared to 16 Polaris missiles?

In a rapidly changing political environment with attendant economic fluctuations, the Alliance is virtually powerless to hold a new government to the agreements entered into by its predecessor. Since there are few legal sanctions to cover this contingency, the "hammer" is generally economic. The immediate thought in mind concerns Italy, a nation in continuing political turmoil. Notwithstanding the successes of the Italian armaments programs (Tornado), the question of the Italian government's reliability in and commitment to long-term joint defense ventures generates a certain amount of uneasiness among its partners. In order to protect international partners, contractual obligations entered into by one member state must be honored by succeeding governments within that state with provisions provided for default. To this end, an international (Western European) consortium regulatory commission capable of enforcing contracts and imposing (economic) penalties is a prudent requirement. This factor, as well as the plethora of financial matters pertaining to joint arms development/procurement projects in Western Europe, logically requires a supervisory organization empowered to speak for and act through the European Community. Consequently, the matter of whether the "European Arms Procurement Agency" should be within the NATO infrastructure, the Western European political structure, or in the Industrial/Economic sector tends to favor its incorporation in the latter. Primarily, the rationale for making arms procurement matters resident in an agency that can coordinate the Alliance's Western European industries and impose penalties for noncompliance calls for vesting it in the EC.

In the National Interest

While it is in the general and collective interests of Western European members to embark on a joint U.S./European armaments program, it may not be in the national interests of individual states to do so. Certain European members have attained a high degree of self-sufficiency in arms production and their respective industrial bases are geared for exploiting the economic gains to be achieved via foreign military sales (FMS). Primarily, the Federal Republic of Germany, Italy, the United Kingdom, and France are the key European arms merchants, with the latter state being one of the world leaders in FMS.

In the case of the British and French armaments industries, FMS are an essential part of the industries' structure. This is not a factor which operates in favor of a coherent European arms development/procurement policy. Any Alliance-imposed restrictions on sales of weapons produced for the Alliance to nonmember states could generate an adverse economic impact on a country whose production philosophy is predicated on an industrial base geared for conducting arms sales in a free market economy.

The inclusion of the primary NATO maverick, France, in a joint European arms production venture would certainly enhance the potential for success. However, the political and institutional approaches of France with regard to exercising its sovereignty in virtually all matters presents little likelihood that France will cooperate on the two-way street. France would seem to prefer the unbeaten and lonely path that starts and ends on native soil. The supernationalism of France and its high degree of success in forging an increasingly capable defense force – considered by most military observers to be the most capable in Western Europe – coupled with their continued and increasing success in obtaining new FMS markets offer little motivation for the French to become an active partner in Alliance arms projects. In all probability, France will continue to engage in multinational endeavors as it suits her needs; and continued cooperation with Italy, the United Kingdom, and West Germany is likely. A new joint development project is presently being explored by the four-power consortium as a vehicle to continue their successful joint projects.(11)

The European assessment of the requirement for the British and French to participate in an Alliance arms procurement program approaches criticality insofar as most Europeans view British and French participation as the key to success or failure. Specifically, the Klepsch Report states that "It is only if the French and British armaments industries are included within one cooperative system that European armaments cooperation can succeed."(12) Although it is assumed that the foregoing statement was flattering to the French ego, it failed to elicit French endorsement of the Klepsch Report – France was the only Western European member not to endorse the report.

To the Beat of a Different Drummer

Why are the French marching to the tune of a different drummer? What motivates their negative approach to Alliance overtures for participation, and what incentives can be offered to the French to entice their participation?

The French mind-set of maintaining its national sovereignty and independence naturally polarizes France from involvement in any international organization which possesses a supranational character.

Another factor in explaining French reluctance to cooperate in Alliance projects is the long-standing French policy on nonintegration with the superpower blocs. Insofar as France perceives the United States as exerting an indirect but strong influence over NATO affairs, fear of U.S. domination causes France to shun Alliance involvement. The foregoing tends to account for France's reluctance to join the EURO-GROUP and opting for the attraction of the all-European IEPG outside the NATO structure.

It is unlikely that any proposed forum for a European Defense Market/procurement agency will appeal to the French. The IEPG offered some appeal, but the framework suggested in the Klepsch Report – the EC – was alien to French thinking. France has been consistently opposed to using the Common Market as a basis for a common European defense industry; and the French government recently said "The proposal [Klepsch Report] aimed at giving the European Community competence in the manufacture of armaments is not acceptable."(13) In view of the prominent status of the French armaments industry and the advanced weapons technology and economies of scale benefits to be gained by French participation, it is clear that a European arms market without France would be severely weakened, if not doomed to failure. How then might the French be seduced, bribed, or coerced into cooperating?

If the advantages of participation/cooperation are not appropriate inducements to the French, perhaps the disadvantages of nonparticipation are. Specifically, as the cooperation of European allies advances in her absence, France clearly runs the risk of being excluded from potential arms markets in Europe – a not unimportant factor for a country that depends heavily on the export sale of weapons. Additionally, the denial to France of U.S. technology transfers to the European industrial base may arouse French interests. Consequently, although risky, it is incumbent upon Alliance members to proceed without France and to entice French participation through demonstrated successes – no mean task to be sure.

NATO – An Appropriate Forum?

In placing the matter of a European arms procurement program under the purview of the EC and the IEPG, both extra-NATO organizations, the implication can be drawn that NATO is no longer an appropriate forum for matters of import either in Alliance-wide matters or in Western European affairs. Such a conclusion would be premature and erroneous. Since NATO is an Atlantic Alliance (e.g., both European and North American members), it is an inappropriate forum for discussing matters pertaining strictly to European affairs. NATO's utility and worth as a forum for other matters of joint European/U.S. interest is still great, and has been recently attested to during the Helsinki meeting of the Conference on Security and Cooperation in Europe (CSCE) and the Belgrade followup meeting. In a report presented to the

U.S. House Committee on International Relations by the Chairman of
the Commission on Security and Cooperation in Europe, it was stated
that:

> ... from a U.S. point of view, the most important of these
> [caucuses] was the 15 member NATO caucus which met regu-
> larly and sometimes daily or more often. Here, common positions
> at all levels of conference work were generally agreed upon.
> The nine European Community countries also met regularly and
> sometimes produced common positions which were later intro-
> duced in the NATO caucuses.(14)

In matters of mutual interest to the Alliance members, NATO exists
as an effective forum for Alliance members to establish joint positions
for presentation in a larger international context. While NATO's track
record in recent times has been more impressive in solidifying Alliance
political positions than security/defense-related issues, nevertheless, it
provides an effective platform for the exchange of dialogue. In light of
the effectiveness exhibited at Helsinki and Belgrade, Alliance members
should exploit the successes achieved in the realm of political and
economic detente and link these gains with efforts in the military area.
Specifically, a continuation of the CSCE process should be tied explicitly to criteria of parallel progress in mutual and balanced force
reductions (MBFR).

Proceeding?

As matters stand today, the model for the "European Arms Procurement Agency," as presented in the Klepsch Report and endorsed by the
European Parliament, links arms procurement with Community industrial policy. The IEPG, at the ministerial level, would define the
military requirements concerning the weapons to be developed or
purchased, and the EC would orchestrate European industrial endeavors
accordingly.   The European action program for the development and
production of conventional arms within the framework of the common
industrial policy as called for by the European Parliament on June 14,
1978, is still under development. Recent information indicates little
progress has been made with regard to the execution of Dr. Klepsch's
proposals. Matters are still under review.
    In the interim, in early April 1979, the IEPG met to discuss the
status of four collaborative projects currently in progress. The matters
addressed were:

- a comparative study of U.S. and U.K. 105 MM tank ammunition,
- a joint West German, United Kingdom, Italian, and French program
  to develop a tactical combat aircraft,
- selection of either a West German or a British short-range anti-tank
  weapon, and
- a collaborative minehunter project developed by France, Belgium,
  and Holland.(15)

Notwithstanding the initial enthusiasm over the Klepsch Report and the verbal commitment to unify European arms development/procurement matters at the Western European level, member nations continue with business practices as per usual.

AMERICAN PERSPECTIVES AND INITIATIVES

Stalled on the Two-Way Street

On the North American side of the two-way street, the initial flurry of enthusiasm which accompanied the passage of the Culver/Nunn Amendment has subsided. The Amendment, which established the framework and legal requirement within the United States to attain NATO standardization and interoperability, has not been supported by follow-on legislative initiatives required to attain these objectives. During the past two years, U.S. promotion of the two-way street concept has been verbal, with little being accomplished in the areas of legislative and institutional reforms.

In Senator Jack Brooks' address to the North Atlantic Assembly Plenary Session in September 1977, he cited five areas of study being explored by Charles Duncan, then Deputy Secretary of Defense, which were intended to facilitate transatlantic arms cooperation.(16) Those areas included:

1. a policy whereby the United States will give considerable weight in the competitive process to equipment the Europeans would collectively agree on as their standard;
2. procedures to expedite United States government approval for cooperative development and production programs;
3. revised policies on industrial teaming to better utilize allied capabilities, technologies, and designs for U.S. systems;
4. disapproving programs when the weapons system is primarily for NATO use if we see that NATO standardization and interoperability requirements are not met by the program; and
5. strengthening procedures to insure that U.S. decisions are based on complete and valid data in foreign candidate systems.

These policy and procedural initiatives have yet to be resolved in full and, presumably, are still under review. Of Secretary Duncan's five points of concern, only points 3 and 5 are being pursued to any degree.

Legislative Obstacles

A report prepared by the Congressional Research Service of the Library of Congress concerning defense procurement statutes that have adverse impacts on U.S./NATO standardization efforts lists the following legislative impediments:(17)

- Buy America Act
- Department of Defense Balance of Payments Policy
- U.S. restrictions on foreign procurement to protect the U.S. economy and industrial base
- U.S. restrictions of foreign research and development contracts
- Examination of contractor records
- Submission of cost and pricing data requirements
- U.S. cost accounting standards

While it is well-recognized that statutory authority is required to move ahead on codevelopment schemes with the European allies, and some minor initiatives have been taken in this regard, little real progress has been achieved. Specifically, the Department of Defense-sponsored HR 12837 was introduced in the 95th Congress and intended to ease certain procurement laws that present an impediment to transatlantic cooperation. The bill encountered a stone wall in Congress. The House Armed Services Committee's special subcommittee on NATO standardization and interoperability held one hearing on the matter in 1978.(18) In calendar year 1979, a key issue – the transfer of military equipment and technology to a third country – generated significant controversy in the Legislative branch and remains to be resolved. This issue has divided Congress between those whose primary interest is in arms transfer restraint and those whose primary interest is in NATO standardization and interoperability. The issue, therefore, of third country FMS for European/U.S. codeveloped weapons systems presents a key impediment to continued progress along the two-way street. It is considered likely that those congressional members in support of arms transfer restraint will predominate in this matter.

Concerns of U.S. Industry

A paramount concern of American industry focuses on the transfer of technology issue and the adverse consequences likely to befall U.S. industry (in both domestic and FMS) incident to that transfer. Primarily, U.S. industrialists fear that Europe will compete with them using their technology. These concerns are genuine and well-founded, and the arguments offered in rebuttal do little more than mitigate and rationalize rather than dispel the concerned anxieties. The counterpoint thrust is three-fold: (1) the U.S. will receive as well as give technology; (2) the U.S. will be compensated for transferred technology, either in money or in kind; and (3) the U.S. will be assisting the allies to whom we are formally committed. Accordingly, transfer of technology is an essential and sensitive area concern that must be satisfied if the two-way street concept is to function in the manner for which its architects designed it. Without a transfer of technology, future research and development projects would continue in the same manner as today – redundant and wasteful. Coproduction efforts would be extremely limited in scope and confined to "grenade and mortar" projects. In any case, transfer of technology opponents – primarily U.S. industrialists – have rallied their forces and are using their well-established lobbies to convert congressional leaders to their cause. Gains are being made.

Negative forecasts by key administration officials, such as Deputy Secretary of State Warren Christopher, who predicts adverse effects on some U.S. companies as a result of increased transatlantic cooperation, do little to promote administration goals and even less to pacify the industrialists.(19) The area of greatest impact, of course, is FMS and, in particular, FMS in aerospace systems. Several U.S. firms are substantially dependent on FMS. Bell Helicopter derives 42 percent of its revenue from FMS; Northrop, 34 percent; Grumman, 26 percent.(20) United States industrialists' focal concern over the transfer of technology issue – which is generally acknowledged as being the key factor in United States' predominance over other world arms manufacturers – is augmented by other concerns. These concerns involve the increased pressure being placed on U.S. industry by the Europeans and include such factors as:

- Political and financial backing by European governments of aerospace hardware developments, and a willingness to experience early financial losses to stay in the market.
- Constraints imposed against some third country sales of equipment containing U.S. subsystems and components. This has become a factor in forcing European industry to sometimes accept subsystems with lesser technology and capability, but with no restrictions.
- Ability of European industry to compress development and production lead times to provide military hardware ahead of U.S. competitors.
- Rise in European consortiums, particularly the teaming of French and German companies using technology from both nations, with financing derived from German and French marketing skills.
- Favorable European government financing of equipment at interest rates not possible elsewhere in the West.
- Aggressive sales campaigns for military hardware with conventions where buyers are invited and government forces demonstrate hardware fire power.(21)

At best, there is a skepticism among U.S. defense industrialists and a growing concern that the U.S. government is not protecting their interests with regard to two-way street initiatives. An example of their concern is a perception that William Perry, Under Secretary of Defense for Research and Engineering, is forcing U.S. industry to participate in competition and to let European industry into weapons system research and development programs, but that NATO countries are not letting U.S. companies bid on Alliance weapons developments.(22)

Legislatively and in theory, the United States has opened the door for the Europeans in a free competition with U.S. arms manufacturers. The European Parliament, in principle, has sanctioned its members to join in the competition for arms contracts and, presumably, is structuring an organization through which its members can collectively compete. On the North American side of the two-way street, it will be incumbent upon U.S. companies to seek their own protection, either through the consortium approach or through the "back door" to Congress. U.S. industrialists perceive the two-way street as a road that takes the U.S. arms industry from a position of preeminence in the Alliance to a role of mandatory partner/developer. They perceive the two-way street as a means of providing the Europeans an increased opportunity to assume a position of increased import over their present role – to be accomplished at their expense. There is little question that U.S. industrialists will do everything in their power to combat what they perceive to be a prostitution of their role in the world armaments scheme.

The Traffic Directors

Key U.S. proponents of the two-way street concept include both congressional and administration leaders. Senators Nunn and Bartlett and Congressmen Brooks and Daniel are the most vocal – and published – congressional proponents. Within the administration, Deputy Secretary of State Warren Christopher and Under Secretary of Defense for Research and Engineering Dr. William J. Perry constitute the key players, with the latter official being a true crusader for the advance of transatlantic arms cooperation. It is Dr. Perry who has been the Department of Defense architect for a proposed framework for improved armaments cooperation. This framework consists of a triad of cooperative actions along with a supporting management structure.

Triad of Cooperative Actions

The proposed Department of Defense triad of cooperative actions includes: general memorandums of understanding (MOUs) in reciprocal purchasing; dual production in NATO countries; and the family of weapons concept.(23)

The purpose of the general memorandums of understanding is to open up the defense market of each country to fair competition by NATO's defense industry. These memorandums waive various "buy national" restrictions on a reciprocal basis. MOUs have thus far been negotiated between the United States and Canada, United Kingdom, Germany, Norway, the Netherlands, and Italy. Initial results have been encouraging, and NATO allies who have not yet entered into a MOU with the United States have been extended an invitation to do so.

Dual production is the second leg of the cooperative triad. This concept proposes that once a nation has developed a system that is useful to the alliance, that nation should make its system available for production by other countries or consortiums of countries. The objective is the elimination of unnecessary duplication of research and development efforts and the avoidance of trade and labor imbalances that would result from exclusive sales by the developing nation. The United States is engaged in dual production arrangements on the French/German-developed ROLAND, and has offered the United States-developed AIM-9L air-to-air missile, the Copperhead laser-guided artillery projectile, and the Stinger surface-to-air missile to European consortiums. If cooperation continues and expands, NATO forces could enjoy the latest technology at the lowest cost.

The family of weapons concept is the third leg of the cooperative triad. The objective again is to further reduce needless duplication in research and development programs. In essence, this initiative calls for a joint review of proposed weapons development plans and the combination of similar-type projects. The United States is now discussing application of this concept for four families: antiarmor weapons, naval mines, antiship missiles, and air-to-ground weapons. Contractors, both U.S. and European, would be selected on a competitive basis that uses as its yardstick best technology at least cost.

The Comptroller General's Report

In the Comptroller General's report to Congress of March 21, 1979, entitled "Transatlantic Cooperation in Developing Weapons Systems for NATO – A European Perspective" a generally pessimistic view is presented with regard to U.S. involvement in the two-way street concept. The report, based on the views of numerous government and industrial representatives of the major industrialized countries of Western Europe, cites the major impediments to transatlantic arms cooperation as perceived by the Europeans. The report then lists what actions are necessary to be accomplished by the United States in order to overcome the perceived impediments. For the most part, the major European concerns (e.g., U.S. domination, equal partnership concerns, third country sales options, transfer of technology, etc.) have been addressed elsewhere in this chapter. The concomitant changes – policy and legislative – that are required have also been addressed, largely relative to the inaction toward those changes. The Comptroller General states in his conclusions and recommendations that ". . . the changes that may be required are too far reaching to be made without further assessing the implications they hold for major foreign and domestic programs and goals."(24) Further, the Comptroller General states that, "There is little prospect that the United States would buy more than a very few European weapons to meet its needs."(25) The Departments of State and Defense registered strong objections to the foregoing statements. There is no question that the Report has done little to promote progress along the two-way street and, in all probability, has injected a set-back to the administration's program in achieving stated objectives. However, the report does put into writing the many reasons why policy and legislative support for a transatlantic program regarding armaments has been stifled – the matter is of such complexity that it must progress to a position of compromise on military, political, and economic issues involving the 15 individual nations of NATO. In the bureaucratic vernacular, the issue would receive a categorization of being "too hard."

CONCLUSIONS

After more than four years of philosophizing over the two-way street concept, it is obvious that neither the United States nor the Western European NATO allies are rushing en masse down their respective lanes in a race toward a common transatlantic defense market. In a way, the two-way street is like the Yellow Brick Road leading to Oz; it is based on common aspirations that are desired by most, but unfortunately have little foundation in the real world. On a large scale, a two-way street in transatlantic arms development/procurement is unrealistic in view of the tenacity with which each country clings to and protects its domestic armaments industry. In a word, nationalism is the foremost impediment to success. Notwithstanding the tremendous cost of weaponry, the rising threat of the Warsaw Pact forces, and the benefits to be realized in a coordinated armaments development/procurement program, the prisms of nationalism filter out logic and common sense.

Regardless of the outcome of transatlantic cooperation, Europeans seem to be committed to multinational codevelopment for the future. Their experiences over the past years have demonstrated that they can cooperatively build sophisticated systems in many high technology areas. Although European codevelopment has been mostly in the field of aircraft and missiles, it is moving to other weapons systems. But in spite of a sound structural approach to coordinating their arms efforts (as presented in the Klepsch Report), the absence of French participation and the political friction inherent in such ventures provide little forward momentum in the quixotic quest for a "European Arms Procurement Agency."

On the North American side, United States legislative barriers and the powerful industrial lobbies tend to slow traffic on the two-way street. In spite of legislatively defined and mandated objectives, realities of international life and transactions dictate procurement policy. In actuality, the United States' initiatives toward the two-way street have been less than required to ensure a successful program. Like the Europeans, the United States continues with a system-by-system, nation-by-nation approach with regard to weapons procurement and development efforts. This course is likely to remain constant in the foreseeable future.

Generally, it is considered that the two-way street will bear increased traffic in the future, however not to the degree that Culver, Nunn, and Klepsch so idealistically forecast. The increased traffic will primarily be in the form of transatlantic collaborative projects considered to be in the mutual interest of the participating countries. The structure will be two-tiered, with American preponderance in the major weapons platforms and increasing European collaboration in tactical missiles, tanks, and other armaments.(26) A factor operating in favor of increased collaboration/cooperation attempts is that the time is propitious for such actions. Insofar as armed forces continually update their inventories of arms and equipment, there are program decision points which dictate major replacement actions. We are entering one of those periods now – the 1980s. Basic decisions (e.g., F-16 procurement) regarding what weapons will be deployed and who will produce them are about to establish patterns of production and procurement for the next decade.

If any factors are to provide impetus for increased traffic on the two-way street, they will, in all probability, be based on economic exploitation of the Alliance's forthcoming military requirements and a changing perception of an increased danger to European, ergo, United States security as a result of gains to the Warsaw Pact forces.

NOTES

(1) LTCOL Michael D. Eiland, USA. "The Two-Way Street in NATO Procurement," Strategic Review (Summer 1977), p. 60. See Egon Klepsch, Two-Way Street - USA-Europe Arms Procurement (London: Brassey's, 1979).

(2) "Modernization to Hike NATO Budgets." Aviation Week and Space Technology, June 11, 1979, p. 109.

(3) Ibid.

(4) Julian Critchley, "A Community Policy for Armaments," NATO Review (February 1979), p. 30.

(5) Patrick Wall, "NATO Must Standardize," The Atlantic Community Quarterly (Spring 1977), p. 50.

(6) Public Law 94-361, Sec. 802(a)(1).

(7) Thomas Callaghan, "No Two-Way Traffic Without a Two-Way Street," NATO Review (October 1977), p. 25.

(8) Critchley, "A Community Policy for Armaments," p. 13.

(9) Ibid.

(10) "High Hopes and Expectations," NATO's Fifteen Nations (February-March 1979), p. 37.

(11) David A. Brown, "European Cooperative Trend Continues," Aviation Week and Space Technology, March 12, 1979, p. 59.

(12) Klepsch, Two-Way Street, p. 25.

(13) Eugene Kozicharow, "European Defense Unity Pushed," Aviation Week and Space Technology (March 5, 1979), p. 12.

(14) U.S. Congress, House. Committee on International Relations, Subcommittee on Commission on Security and Cooperation in Europe. The Belgrade Followup Meeting to the Conference on Security and Cooperation in Europe: A Report and Appraisal. May 17, 1978. U.S. Govt. Printing Office, 1978, p. 15.

(15) Eugene Kozicharow, "Modernization to Hike NATO Budgets," Aviation Week and Space Technology, (June 11, 1979), p. 110.

(16) Dewey F. Bartlett, "Standardizing Military Excellence – The Key to NATO's Survival," AEI Defense Review, no. 6 (1978), p. 12.

(17) General Accounting Office, Report to the Congress, Transatlantic Cooperation in Developing Weapons Systems for NATO - A European Perspective, March 21, 1979 (Washington DC), pp. 33-34.

(18) Katherine Johnson, "NATO Standardization Efforts Increase," Aviation Week and Space Technology (October 30, 1978), p. 64.

(19) Ibid.

(20) Anne Hessing Cahn, Joseph J. Kruzel, Peter M. Dawkins, and Jacques Huntzinger, Controlling Future Arms Trade (New York: McGraw-Hill, 1977), p. 68.

(21) Clarence A. Robinson, Jr., "Europeans Challenge U.S. Role," Aviation Week and Space Technology (June 18, 1979), p. 16.

(22) William Perry, "NATO Two-Way Street Called Essential," Aviation Week and Space Technology (February 12, 1979), p. 49.

(23) Ibid.

(24) General Accounting Office, Transatlantic Cooperation, p. v.

(25) Ibid., p. 37.

(26) Cahn, Kruzel, Dawkins, Huntzinger, Controlling Future Arms Trade, p. 75.

Index

About the Contributors

WERNER J. FELD is a Professor of Political Science at the University of New Orleans. He is the author of numerous publications, including Transnational Business Collaboration Among Common Market Countries (1970), Nongovernmental Forces and World Politics (1972), The European Community in World Affairs (1976), Domestic Political Realities and European Unification (with John K. Wildgen) (1976), and International Relations: A Transnational Approach (1979). In addition, Dr. Feld is the author of more than 50 articles in various journals. He received a law degree (Referendar) after attending the University of Berlin and a Ph.D. in political science from Tulane University.

STEVEN J. BAKER is Assistant Professor in the Department of Government, University of Texas, Austin. He is presently on leave with the professional staff of the Senate Democratic Policy Committee in Washington where he is the Foreign Policy Advisor to the Senate Majority Leader. His major teaching interests are international relations, American foreign policy, and comparative politics with emphasis on Western Europe. He has many publications; among them "Nuclear Proliferation: Monopoly or Carter?" in Foreign Policy, Summer, 1976; and "The Great Powers Nonproliferation Policies towards the Third World with Particular Reference to the Middle East and Persian Gulf," in Milton Leitenberg and Gabriel Shjeffer, eds., Great Power Intervention in the Middle East.

MAX BAUMER is a Research Fellow at the Research Institute of the Stiftung Wissenschaft und Politik (Ebenhausen near Munich). He received his M.A. from the University of Indiana where he was the recipient of a Fulbright Fellowship. He is author of Zur Multilateralisierung des Aubenhandels der RGW-Mitgliedstaaten, (1975) and has co-authored several articles and contributions to readers on COMECON integration and East-West economic relations.

GAVIN BOYD is a Professor in the Political Science Department of Saint Mary's University, Halifax, Nova Scotia, Canada. He was the editor, with Charles Pentland, of Issues in Global Politics (1980), with James N. Rosenau and Kenneth W. Thompson of World Politics (1976), with Wayne Wilcox and Leo Rose, of Asia and the International System (1972), and author of Communist China's Foreign Policy (1962).

ROBERT M. CUTLER is completing his Ph.D. dissertation on the formulation of Soviet foreign policy in the 1970s, at the University of Michigan. He is translator-editor of a forthcoming anthology of M.A. Bakunin's speeches and writings, and his manuscript on "Soviet Dissent under Khrushchev: An Analytical Study" is scheduled to appear in Comparative Politics. During 1979-80 he was Albert Gallatin Fellow in International Affairs at the Graduate Institute of International Studies, Geneva, Switzerland.

CHRISTIAN DEUBNER has a doctorate in political economy and is Research Fellow at the Research Institute of the Stiftung Wissenschaft und Politik in Ebenhausen, West Germany. He has lectured political science and political economy at German and American universities and college institutions in Berlin-West, Constance and Bremen. His publications concentrate on economic and sociopolitical processes in international relations, for instance: "The Expansion of West German Capital and the Founding of Euratom," International Organization, Spring 1979, and Die Internationalisierung des Kapitals, Frankfurt/M., 1979 (co-editor).

MICHAEL B. DOLAN is an Assistant Professor of Political Science at Carleton University and he is associated with the Norman Paterson School of International Affairs at Carleton. His principal interests are international integration and asymmetrical relations between countries, specifically European external relations with Africa, and Canada-U.S. relations. Professor Dolan's research in these areas is published in International Organization, International Studies Quarterly, The Annals of the American Academy of Political Science, Papers of the Peace Science Society, the Journal of European Integration, and several collected works on European and Canadian affairs. He received his Ph.D. in International Studies from American University, Washington, D.C.

HANNS-DIETER JACOBSEN has a doctorate in political economy and is a Research Fellow at the Stiftung Wissenschaft und Politik. He is author of Die Wirtschaftlichen Beziehungen Zwischen West und Ost and co-author of Kritische Einfuhrung in die Aubenhandelstheorie. He has been a J.F. Kennedy Memorial Fellow at Harvard University and has published many articles on international economic interdependence, COMECON integration, East-West and transatlantic relations.

EUGENE J. MESAROS is a Commander in the U.S. Navy and is currently assigned as the Mobilization Plans Officer on the staff of the Chief of Naval Reserve. CDR Mesaros is a graduate of the University of Miami (Florida), the United States Naval War College, and is currently enrolled in the Masters program in Political Science at the University of New Orleans.

REINHARDT RUMMEL is Research Fellow at the Research Institute of the Stiftung Wissenschaft und Politik, Ebenhausen (Fed. Rep. of Germany), and Lecturer for International Politics at the University of Munich. He is co-editor of Die Europaische Politische Zusammenarbeit, Europa-Union-Verlag, Bonn 1978, and co-author of Gemeinschaftsbildung Westeuropas in der Aubenpolitik, Nomos Verlagsgesellschaft, Baden-Baden 1978.

ROBERT W. RUSSELL is Counsel to the Subcommittee on International Finance of the Committee on Banking, Housing, and Urban Affairs of the United States Senate. Prior to joining the Subcommittee Russell was a tenured associate professor of political science at Northern Illinois University in Decalb, Illinois. Russell received his Ph.D. from the Fletcher School of Law and Diplomacy in 1967. Among his recent publications are: "Three Windows on Debt: LDCs, the Banks, and the U.S. National Interest," in Lawrence G. Franko and Marilyn J. Seibert, eds., Developing Country Debt (1979); "International Monetary Reform: Don't Just Do Something, Stand There," International Organization (Winter 1977); and "Monetary Policy: European Monetary Cooperation under Floating Exchange Rates," in Helen Wallace, ed., Policymaking in the European Communities (1977).

WOLFGANG WESSELS is the Director of the Institute for European Politics in Bonn, West Germany, and Chief Editor of Integration, an academic quarterly on European Integration Affairs. He has been Secretary General of the Trans-European Policy Studies Association (TEPSA) from 1976 to 1978. He is the author of many publications including "Die EG: Versuch einer freiheitlich-demokratischen Integration souveraner Staaten?" in Konvergenz-Koexistenz oder Zusammenarbeit in Europa, Bonn (1973); co-editor, with Reinhardt Rummel, of Die EPZ - Leistungsvermogen und Strukturen der EPZ; and contributor to Die EPZ - ein neuer Ansatz europaischer AuBenpolitik. His Ph.D. is from the University of Colon.